THE END OF
THE BEGINNING

THE END OF
THE BEGINNING

Revelation 21-22 and the Old Testament

The Moore Theological
College Lectures 1983

William J. Dumbrell

LANCER BOOKS

Distributed in North America by
BAKER BOOK HOUSE
P.O. Box 6287
Grand Rapids, Michigan 49506
U.S.A.

Typeset by Colourscene, Sydney, Australia
Printed in Singapore by Singapore
National Printers (Pte) Ltd

© W.J. Dumbrell, 1985

LANCER BOOKS
3-5 Richmond Road
Homebush West NSW
Australia

ISBN 0 85892 269 X

Also by William J. Dumbrell
COVENANT AND CREATION:
An Old Testament Covenantal Theology

PREFACE

This study is dedicated to the many, many students in whose patient presence these ideas were formulated. My thanks are due to my family for their unfailing tolerance and not the least to the careful and very helpful work of Mark Strom, editor of Lancer Books, Sydney, Australia.

Bill Dumbrell
Vancouver, 1985.

CONTENTS

THE NEW JERUSALEM

THE NEW TEMPLE

THE NEW ISRAEL

THE NEW CREATION

The Presentation in Revelation 21-22

The Old Testament
  i.   Creation and Redemption: Exodus 15: 1-18
  ii.   Creation and Redemption: Genesis 1-11
     a. *Genesis 1:1-3*
     b. *Genesis 1:26-28*
     c. *Genesis 2*
     d. *Genesis 3*
     e. *Genesis 4-11*
  iii. Isaiah 40-66
  iv.   Apocalyptic Literature
  v.   Wisdom Literature
Summary

The New Testament
  i.   Paul
     a. *Colossions 1:15-20*
     b. *Other Pauline Statements*
  ii.   New Creation and the Gospel
  iii. Paul Again
  iv.   Revelation Reconsidered

ABBREVIATIONS

AB	Anchor Bible
AnBib	Analecta biblica
AusBR	*Australian Biblical Review*
AUSS	*Andrews University Seminary Studies*
Bib	*Biblica*
BibOr	Biblica et orientala
BSac	*Bibliotheca Sacra*
BT	*The Bible Translator*
BZAW	Beihefte zur Zeitschrift fur die alttestamentliche Wissenschaft
CBQ	*Catholic Biblical Quarterly*
ConBOT	Coniectanea biblica, Old Testament
EvQ	*Evangelical Quarterly*
HDR	Harvard Dissertations in Religion
HSM	Harvard Semitic Monographs
HTR	*Harvard Theological Review*
Int	Interpretation
JAAR	*Journal of the American Academy of Religion*
JBL	*Journal of Biblical Literature*
JETS	*Journal of the Evangelical Theological Society*
JJS	*Journal of Jewish Studies*
JSOT	*Journal for the Study of the Old Testament*
JSS	*Journal of Semetic Studies*
JTC	*Journal of Theology and Church*
JTS	*Journal of Theological Studies*
NCB	New Century Bible ⸲
NICNT	New International Commentary on the NT
NovT	*Novum Testamentum*
NovTSup	Novum Testamentum, Supplements
NTS	*New Testament Studies*
OTL	Old Testament Library
OTS	*Oudtestamentische Studien*
RTR	Reformed Theological Review
SBLDA	Society of Biblical Literature Dissertation Series
SEA	*Svensk exegetisk drsbok*
SNTSMS	Society for New Testament Studies Monograph Series
SOTSMS	Society of Old Testament Studies Monograph Series

TDNT	G. Kittel and G. Friedrich (eds.), *Theological Dictionary of the New Testament* (1964-74)
TDOT	G. J. Botterweck and H. Ringgren (eds.), *Theological Dictionary of the Old Testament* (1974-)
TynB	*Tyndale Bulletin*
USQR	*US Quarterly Review*
VT	*Vetus Testamentum*
VTSup	Vetus Testamentum, Supplements
WTJ	*Westminster Theological Journal*
ZAW	*Zeitschrift fur die alttestamentliche Wissenschaft*
ZTK	*Zeitschrift fur Theologie and Kirche*

INTRODUCTION

Each of the following five stories deals with a major idea found in Revelation 21-22 and seeks to answer the question, "Why is this such an appropriate way not only to finish the Book of Revelation but to conclude the story of the entire Bible?" This question, of course, leads to other questions such as, "Where did these ideas come from?" and "How have they changed or developed down through the Bible's story?"

It is these questions which are responsible for the approach taken in the five studies. We will begin with a brief examination of the particular idea or theme as it occurs in Revelation 21-22, then trace the birth and growth of the idea throughout the Old Testament, the Gospels, and the Epistles, and finally return to Revelation 21-22.

At first glance the approach of Revelation 21-22-Old Testament, Gospels, Epistles-Revelation 21-22 may appear somewhat awkward or even contrived. Upon further reflection, however, it becomes apparent this movement serves to answer one basic, yet crucial, question: "How did the seer of Revelation arrive at the content of his panoramic final vision?"

The approach implemented in the following pages is the method of biblical-theology. As a discipline biblical-theology often assumes a wide variety of expressions. Yet at the heart of each of these expressions is the overriding presupposition that the rich diversity of Scripture serves its profound unity. Further, this "diversity within unity" is most clearly seen through a consideration of the historical development of theological themes. And, this historical progression of ideas runs from one end of the Bible to the other. In other words, the entire Bible is moving, growing according to a common purpose and towards a common goal (thus we can say that the whole Bible is "eschatological").

So to discern the origins of Revelation 21-22, the very end of the Bible's story, we must go back beyond the important contributions of the traditions of the Gospels and Epistles all the way to the Old Testament.

We are not setting out merely to compile a list of favourite "proof-texts", nor to embark on a thorough discussion of only those texts directly alluded to or quoted in Revelation 21-22. What must be explored is the Old Testament origin of each of the major themes present in the heart of John's vision, Rev 21:1-5:

the New Jerusalem — v2
the New Temple — v3
the New Covenant — v3
the New Israel — v4
the New Creation — v1.

Once we are clear as to their origins, the subsequent development of these themes in the persons, events and institutions of Old Testament history must be examined. We can then move on to study the way the person and life-events of Jesus colour the theme in the Gospels and Epistles. From this vantage point we will be able to appreciate fully the actors and events of John's final scene.

In this way each of the five themes serves as a window on the entire structure of the Bible. Each works as a single perspective from which to view the whole. This is not to say that each perspective is of equal importance nor that each is equally capable of capturing the same breadth of biblical data. Nor indeed that these are the only possible themes for consideration when the question of biblical eschatology is taken up. Neither is it to say that each of the themes is independent of the others. For example, a discussion of the New Creation theme must obviously cover a broad area. Indeed it really absorbs each of the other four themes as sub-themes. Likewise, considerable overlap and interaction will be discerned between the New Covenant and New Israel. One could also easily envisage a study in its own right of a totally new perspective such as a New Exodus or Promised Land. Or even of discussions devoted exclusively to more narrow ideas like Holy War and Theophany (the occasions when God appears to his people).

Yet, for the sake of clarity of presentation, a chapter is devoted to each theme. The order of presentation of the themes is admittedly subjective. We begin with the New Jerusalem since this is given a major emphasis within Revelation 21-22. Correspondingly we conclude with the New Creation for this is the goal to which the Book of Revelation and the Bible itself has moved. The New Temple material follows that of the New Jerusalem. First, holy city and temple are related biblical themes and, secondly, it is the divine presence which makes Jerusalem the New Jerusalem. Biblically the concept of covenant precedes that of people. Thus the New Covenant precedes the New Israel. Any separation of themes such as we have indulged in is bound to be arbitrary, and this is indicated by overlapping use of some major sections of the OT. This, of course, is also shown from the fact that St John has fused all these details into his one great vision of the end.

On the other hand, however, the five themes are distinct and important themes which contribute to any picture which biblical eschatology seeks to construct. This much is also clear from their use within Revelation 21-22. John has majored on the presentation of the New Jerusalem, a city emphasis dictated by the purpose of his book. For him, however, the New Jerusalem has become virtually a synonym for the New Creation. If the covenant, temple and people of God do not receive quite the same emphasis in this final vision, the allusion by John to these concepts within the chapters nevertheless makes it clear that his presentation presumes their content.

There is, then, a peculiar rationale to the choice of our five subjects. They are, as we have noted, the themes most obviously alluded to in Revelation 21 and 22. Secondly, each has an immediate relevance to the Bible's wider concept of government, the Kingdom of God. Viewed in this way, the New Jerusalem is the symbol of government and those governed; the New Temple is the seat of government; the New Covenant is the instrument of government; the New Israel reveals those governed and their role; and the New Creation is a final comprehensive presentation of both the governed and the Governor.

In several places the discussion overlaps that found in my monograph *Covenant and Creation* (Lancer/Paternoster, 1984). The reader is encouraged to consult that work for more detailed argument in these instances.

There are also occasional instances where the argument required a more detailed exploration of either the structure of the text or of a peculiar linguistic phenomenon. It was decided that such interludes should remain optional reading so as not to exclude the non-technically trained reader. These sections are enclosed in smaller type and may be passed over without losing the sense of the discussion. To further assist the reader all Hebrew and Greek words and phrases are translated wherever necessary. All abbreviations are from "Instructions to Contributors", *Journal of Biblical Literature* 95 (1976) 331-46. Unless otherwise indicated all quotations are from the Revised Standard Version.

NEW JERUSALEM — SUMMARY

In one powerful symbol the final vision of the Revelation of John captures the concepts of governed, government, and world-centre. That image, of course, is the New Jerusalem coming down from heaven. And it is the arrival of this reality which inaugurates the new Creation in its full manifestation. The chief anticipator and theological catalyst for this development within the Old Testament was Isaiah. Yet even before the prophet, mainly through the influence of the Samuel-Saul-David narratives and the Psalms, Jerusalem-Zion has been identified as the world mountain, the source of paradisiacal waters and the destination of a future universal pilgrimage. At Zion Yahweh had defeated and would defeat all of Israel's enemies, whether mythical-chaotic, historical or eschatological!

Jerusalem dominates Isaiah's concerns as is demonstrated by a close examination of the book's structure. Oscillating between historical and eschatological horizons, the prophet alternates oracles of doom and hope to move us from the scene of Jerusalem decadent and suicidal to the everlasting Zion at the heart of the New Heavens and the New Earth. By the ministry of the Servant, the righteous retrace the "ancient" steps of a New Exodus to the glorious city with its consummation of all the Abrahamic promises and reversal of Babel's din. A similar note is sounded, albeit in different keys, in Lamentations and the exilic and post-exilic prophets. For these Jerusalem's fall and subsequent exile not only effect the curses of Deut 28 but invite a new expression of the unquenchable divine fidelity.

Of course, all of this is the death knell of political Jerusalem. In his oracles of woe and the crucifixion-resurrection, Jesus not only rejects Jerusalem forever, but replaces the city by assuming its traditional role as the light of the world. This repudiation is further emphasized by Jesus' shift from Jerusalem of the prophets to Galilee of the gentiles. Finally, in a remarkable telescoping of all subsequent history, Jesus declares the end of the age to have come with his passion and the destruction of the ancient city. And so it only remains for Paul to introduce the heavenly Jerusalem, the supreme symbol of divine rule and presence in the New Age, and for Hebrews to direct our gaze to Zion, the fast-approaching end of the believer's pilgrimage.

In the final vision Jerusalem from above is now the symbol and centre of the New Creation. It is the meeting point of heaven and earth. All enemies are now defeated. The nations have come within its gates. And the waters of paradise flow along its streets.

1

THE NEW JERUSALEM

The Presentation in Revelation 21-22

The term "New Jerusalem" only occurs biblically in Rev 3:12 and 21:2; the former look forward to the reality which the latter describes in detail. Having come down from heaven this New Jerusalem emphasizes continuity with the old order by its name, and the inbreaking of the New Creation by its descent. In fact the New Jerusalem is mentioned almost in the same breath as the New Creation. We pass from one image to the other as a matter of course. She comes down as a bride adorned for her husband; hence, an image which is frequently employed in the NT for the church (2 Cor 11:2; Eph 5:23-32) indicates that we are not merely dealing with a symbol of government (i.e., the city) but with the people of God symbolized in terms of the city.[1] It is important to note that "city" images dominate the presentation of the eschatological reality at the end of the Bible. This indicates the completely political direction which the Kingdom of God assumed. This heavy political emphasis will be sustained as we survey the origin and development of the Jerusalem symbolism in the Bible. The notion of the city indicates at once the forms of government by which the people of God will be regulated.

There is a fluid oscillation between these motifs of governed and government in Rev 21-22. The nuptial images in 21:2 also indicate the consummation of history is at hand. This descent of the city is thus the denouement, the end of all things, the ushering in of the new age. Clearly, we are operating within the domain of previously erected OT expectations. The exaltation of Jerusalem as both a symbol of divine government, and the world centre for the governed, is an idea to which the eschatology of the OT was particularly directed.

One must pause, however, and consider first the concept of "city" in the religious symbolism of the ancient world. The legendary foundation of the city was invariably understood to be a religious act. Even the site itself was determined by some divine intervention or theophany, i.e., the manifestation of some god to a mortal. The building of the city was then seen to proceed under divine prompting and was considered the intersection of divine and human interests. Such an ideal conception of the ancient city as a world centre may be readily transferred to OT Jerusalem: contemporary social notions informed the understanding of her choice and function. Thus the capture of Jerusalem in 2 Sam 5:6-10 is divinely endorsed by the entry of the ark of the covenant (chap. 6), while the site is delimited more precisely as sacred by David's purchase in 2 Sam 24:18-25 of space for the later temple. When finally in 2 Kgs 8 all the Exodus traditions are concentrated on the newly built Jerusalem temple (cf. vv 14-21), the conquest is now theologically complete. The blessings of "rest" in the promised land are now open to Israel at the height of its political power.

Thus, the book of the Psalms significantly underlines the importance of Jerusalem. It has been remarked[2] that the vision of the Psalms presents Jerusalem as containing something of the beauty of Athens as well as the strength and influence of Rome. Describing Jerusalem as "beautiful in elevation, the joy of the whole earth" Ps 48:2 echoes the often repeated NT statement Jerusalem was the city "of the great king" (Matt 5:35). To her the tribes of the Lord go up, for in Jerusalem thrones were set for judgement. (Ps 122:4-5 i.e., the law which brought light and life proceeded from Jerusalem cf. Isa. 2:2-3.) Thus, the elements of Israel's integrity and unity are associated with Jerusalem, the city where righteousness and peace dwell together (cf. Pss 72, 122).

Jerusalem is therefore the divine centre and fortress, untouched (as Pss 46 and 48 point out) by the process of disintegration to which the remainder of the world was exposed. Jerusalem's foes would be defeated in any assault at her gates (Ps 46). This interior tranquillity characterizing the city was due to the presence of Israel's God, and thus the ideal political constitution to which it points and represents is the Kingdom of God. For the Psalmist outside of this centre lay the nations; undifferentiated, chaotic, exposed and unclean, the prey of the demonic powers of the world.[3]

Thus the symbolic, which Rev 21-22 presents as actual, is summed up in the book of Psalms at various points. We will, however, need to trace the OT development by which Jerusalem has become for the

Christian, and we suspect for many others, the most compelling of all societary symbols, the *civitas dei*, "the city of God". How appropriate that this great biblical hope of fellowship in the presence of God should take the form of a city! Small enough to convey the notion of the narrow structure of intimate relationships by which believers will be bound together, and yet complex enough to deal with the distinctions in roles which will characterize the citizens of the end-time Kingdom of God. Before commencing our OT assessment which will place particular emphasis on the book of Isaiah however, we return to the NT and continue with the picture of fulfilment drawn in Rev 21-22.

When the description of the New Jerusalem resumes more fully in the "Jerusalem appendix" (Rev 21:9-22:5), the seer in Ezekiel-style fashion is taken to a very high mountain to witness the descent of the city, and to be informed of its description and details. The description is an elaboration of the city's endowment of the glory of God (21:11). First described as "radiant" (Gk. *phoster*, "light-giving", v 11) these concepts of light and glory, or light proceeding from glory, serve to remind us that the description alternates between people and place. It is the function of the people of God in the NT to shine as lights in a dark world, to let their light shine, to operate as a city which is set on a hill whose light cannot be hidden. At the same time it is the function of the world centre in the eschatology of the OT to manifest light from glory, and thus as the world beacon to draw nations and their kings to the brightness of her rising (cf. Isa 60:1-3 which forms the basis for the Rev 21-22 presentation).

The seer's attention is next drawn to the wall of the city as a secondary item, together with her gates. The detail reads somewhat strangely since the wall as a city feature was protective in its function. Yet metaphor and symbolism are not far away here for the OT expected the New Jerusalem's walls would be salvation and gates would be praise (Isa 60:18, cf. 26:1). Perhaps here the walls function as an image of steadfastness and fidelity and thereby confirm the OT notion that God himself would wall off the new city (Zech 2:5). J.M. Ford has demonstrated that the notion of God enveloping Jerusalem virtually brings us back to the bride image and thus to community symbolism.[4] Twelve gates give access to this four-square city, in four sets of three. Thereby perfect access is offered to the pilgrim who enters these gates with praise. Once again the oscillation between city and community continues for, as Ford argues,[5] gates may also be a community term as the point of reference moves from the gate as the ancient point of assembly to the citizenry of free men assembled there. Certainly Isa 54:12 which refers to gates of carbuncles was interpreted at Qumran in terms of Israel's leadership.[6] The foundations represent solidity but also point to leadership in Revelation 21 as they are engraved with the names of the twelve apostles of the lamb. On them the new community was to be erected (Eph 2:20).

The city is built four-square with equal length, breadth and height. It is thus a perfect cube, the symbol of divine perfection.[7] The extent of the city is too vast to be conceived, hence the figurative presentation of the perfect number twelve multiplied 1000 times by the accepted measure of distance (the Greek stadion): a clear presentation of infinity.[8] Thus Jerusalem becomes virtually co-extensive with creation itself! The jewels which are set into the wall (Rev 21:19-20) are a patent reminder of the breastplate of the OT High Priest (Exod 28:13 LXX). Also through Ezek 28:1-14 the reader is reminded of the resplendence associated with the garden of God (Gen 2, cf. Ezek 28:13-14). Each gate contains a pearl, a note introduced lest any element of the OT expectation be overlooked (cf. Isa 54:12). The streets of the city are of pure gold, emphasizing the quality of life to be found within, a quality which comes from God dwelling with men.

In the new Jerusalem the binary oppositions of the old creation (day and night) disappear thus resulting in a fusion of the celestial with the terrestrial. God, the Lamb, nations, and kings enjoy uninhibited access to Jerusalem (Rev 21:22-27; except for the unclean). Waters of life proceed from the city (22:1-2) and the benefits of divine grace are accessible in the shape of the tree of life, the fruit of which never fails to satisfy. In this habitat makind will be perfectly obedient to God and thus will realize their destiny in service as priests and kings. What was realized particularly in the OT and NT is now experienced fully. God's face is seen, emphasizing the intimacy and reality of this new communion (v4). The inaccessibility of the OT vanishes, for His "glory" (21:11 Gk. *doksa*) shines, shedding divine radiance for all. Kings and people walk in Jerusalem's streets in democratic concord (v24).

We may note in passing the confluence of imagery which has occurred in Rev 21-22. New Covenant, New Creation, new people all flowing together into this grandiose depiction of the New Jerusalem in which people and place are combined. This endorsement of continuity with the OT projections encourages us to turn to the OT for the origins of the concepts. On the other hand the emphasis upon newness in Rev 21-22 requires us to recognize that the OT only inadequately prepares us for what is encountered in this vision of fulfilment. We turn now, however, to survey the OT evidence that initiated this massive

Jerusalem image, and to ask the question why the dominant eschatological presentation at the end of the Bible is understood in terms of a city.

The Old Testament

i. Isaiah

Isaiah is dominated by Jerusalem imagery. The book's structure is, as we will demonstrate, informed by Jerusalem orientated theology. Commencing (Isa 1) with a depiction of absolute corruption seizing the city (c740-690BC), the prophecy concludes (66:20-24) with the emergence of a New Jerusalem as God's holy mountain. Further, it is to this mountain the world will go in a pilgrimage of worship. It is clear from the final chapters of this great prophecy that the New Jerusalem and the New Creation are intimately linked. This link is sharpened in 65:17-18, where the New Jerusalem entails a New Creation. The New Jerusalem is thus a symbol of the New Creation and is finally presented as an obvious juxtaposition with the city initially described. There is thus good reason to see this book as a "tale of two cities" (a motif on which the book of Revelation is largely based). We will confirm this preliminary hypothesis by appeal to the particular units comprising the book of Isaiah.

An immediate question is raised: what accounts for the corruption denounced in Isa 1 and the transition to the New Jerusalem concluding the work? Before we enter into details we should note it is not merely the appearance of Jerusalem at the beginning and end of Isaiah which excites our interest in the developing theme. The first half of this major work ends with a threatened exile pronounced upon Hezekiah and his city Jerusalem (chap. 39). With chapter 40 the second half of the book begins with an announcement of a prospective return from exile in general terms ("Comfort Ye, Comfort Ye!"). But immediately the prophet translates this comfort extended to "my people" into the Jerusalem of verse 2 who is to be spoken to "comfortably". The prophet is to tell her that in quantitative terms she has suffered enough since she has not only reached the limit of her endurance, but the power of Babylon is now to be curtailed.

Presumably, though not certainly, Isa 40:1-11 is addressed to the exiles in Babylon, geographically some hundreds of miles away from the destination to which they are directed. A second Exodus lies before the people of God, a concept which is outlined in the most elevated terms in the following verses. But as is later disclosed, the entire focus of verses 1-11 is Jerusalem. In the overall development of chapters 40-55, once the general tenor of the return has been discussed in chapters 40-48, Jerusalem/Zion becomes the direct point of attention in 49-55. Jerusalem is invested with a community concept not seen in the earlier chapters of Isaiah. Calvin suggests as the rallying point for the ideal return the city became a figure for the church. While that may be going too far, certainly some amalgamation of the notions of people and place occurs within these chapters. In fact the parallelism of 40:1-2 makes this clear. Thus, the prominence given to Jerusalem at the outset and conclusion of both halves of Isaiah (chaps. 1-39, 40-66) points out the dominant note of the book is the historical fate of Jerusalem. Isaiah is concerned with the punishment and redemption which culminates in the presentation of Jerusalem at the end of the book in community terms. She is then both the bride of Yahweh and the city of God in the New Creation.

Since the movement within the book as a whole is from an apostate Jerusalem to a New Jerusalem, any analysis of the book must advance reasons for the conditions depicted in Isaiah 1 and for the change that gradually superintervenes and takes us to chapter 66. The series of interconnections within the individual sections of Isaiah which serve to keep the Jerusalem theme before us are now explored. However the broad movement of the total work is to be kept in mind.

a. Isaiah 1-12

Isa 1-39 moves from Jerusalem under judgement to the impending threat of exile directed against the city in chapter 39. We are now required to review chapters 1-12 in some detail to ascertain the underlying reasons offered by Isaiah for the demise of the southern kingdom. As P.R. Ackroyd[9] points out, the content of chapters 1-12 moves alternatively between the motifs of threat and promise. In this way the outline of 1-39 (threat) and 40-66 (promise) is foreshadowed by these introductory chapters.

Isa 1 is plainly a threat against Jerusalem. 2:1-4 outlines the prophetic hope of Zion which is expanded in chapters 60-62, whereas 2:5-22 is a threat directed against a society given over to pride and its converse, idolatry. The threat continues in chapter 3 and is directed at Jerusalem leadership and social upheavals occasioned by the reversal of roles in society. This alternation of motifs continues with the promise of a returning remnant to Zion (chap. 4) and the lament of the impending rejection of Judah and Jerusalem (in 5:1-7). A set of seven woes against prevailing social conditions is formed by 5:8-10:4 (interrupted by 6:1-9:7) while the remainder of chapter 10 is interwoven with oracles of divine punishment first to be visited by Assyria upon Judah and Jerusalem, and then upon Assyria itself. The complementary message of hope points to an ideal community established under messianic leadership, and is presented in Isa 11:1-9. Following this description is a picture of the transformed new age established by a new Exodus (vv10-16). A salvation hymn (chap. 12) completes this first section and concludes on a note of praise uttered by the inhabitants of Zion, in whose midst Yahweh dwells. This general outline of Isaiah needs further development.

Isa 1:1, an introduction, is followed by verses 2-3 which disclose Judah's breach of covenant. Because of the nation's longstanding refusal to be the people of God. corrupt foreign armies will ravage her territory: however, there will emerge an historical remnant (vv4-9). The centre of the chapter (vv10-20) is a prophetic attack on the perverted cult, and is a speech in two parts (vv10-17, 18-20). Sacrifices, festivals, and even prayers are rejected (vv10-17). Sin is now too ingrained to be forgiven.

Perhaps the language of Isa 1:18-20 is purposely ironic since Jerusalem's fate has been decided upon![10] The indictment against Jerusalem is continued in verses 21-23 while in verses 24-31 the consequences of punishment are detailed. Two groups emerge: a repentant righteous who will be delivered (v27), and the wicked who are to be destroyed (v28). A final image of destruction emerges (vv29-31) in which idolators are paid in kind. We are clearly moving from the narrow national plane of covenant to an elective picture in which the redeemed city will correspond to a redeemed community.

To account for the savagery of this prophetic assault one must turn to Isa 6:1-9:7, since it offers us an analysis of the factors underlying Jerusalem's political and social situation that led to her ruin. The insertion of these chapters into the sequence of threat and promise seems to be an intrusion of emphasis since chapter 6 contains the call of the prophet and directs us towards his vocation. In the light of threat and promise provided by the surrounding material we might expect to find the same sequence in 6:1-9:7. And indeed we do since 6:1-8:22 deals with judgement directed against the ruling Davidic dynasty and the resulting desolation of Jerusalem. Then, 9:1-7 presents a picture of ideal Davidic leadership brought about by divine intervention at some future period.

Isa 6 opens with a reference to the successful fifty-two year reign of king Uzziah. Uzziah restored and repaired the fortunes of the southern kingdom of Judah, and brought it to its former state of Davidic greatness. Irrespective of whether the call of Isaiah occurred before or after the death of the king, verse 1 is not merely a dating formula but the indication of the end of an era. The strong leadership of Uzziah left the resources of the southern kingdom in excellent shape. However, by the end of the chapter the prosperity is dissipated and the busy and prosperous land lies desolate and decimated (vv11-13). All that is left of the grandeur of Uzziah's period is a shoot from the truncated stump of the once vital national tree.

Clearly, Isa 6 is concerned with presenting a contrast of staggering proportions. Implicitly, what is raised in verse 1 is the means whereby the future kingdom of Judah and the city of Jerusalem will find their salvation. What will provide for the good ordering of the kingdom? Compliance with past methods? More of the influential political thinking and beneficial administration which had characterized the reign of Uzziah? Isaiah's vision introduces kingship of another order ("I saw the Lord"), and therefore thunders a reply in the negative. Uzziah's kingship contrasts starkly with Yahweh's leadership! Only the proper acknowledgement of that latter kingship will ensure future success. A series of brilliant images presents the heavenly setting of Yahweh's kingship. Surrounded by his heavenly attendants Yahweh is seated on a throne, an ominous note which betokens judgement at the outset.[11]

Within the heavenly scene our attention is riveted upon the seraphim; they are mentioned in five of the thirteen verses (Isa 6:3-5,6-7). Their role is obviously important despite the difficulty of determining their status. The winged uraeus or cobra was a symbol of kingship in Egypt, and mixed creatures of this character are well known in the ancient Near East as deity guardians.[12] Seraphim therefore appear to be temple ministrants, temple guardians in the heavenly palace/temple setting. They praise the kingship of Yahweh with a superlative of a superlative ("holy, holy, holy" v3). His power, i.e., his glory and unapproachability, is as extensive as the universe he fills with his presence. Perhaps the cry of the seraphim is a witness to the theophany taking place at the same time in the earthly temple (Heb. *bayit* v4) since its foundations rooted in creation (cf. Ps 78:69) and representing total stability are shaken. R. Knierim has plausibly suggested that the cry of the seraphim represents a doxology of judgement concluding the proceedings of the heavenly council, proceedings at which the prophet has been an auditor and in which judgement has been pronounced upon Jerusalem.[13]

The following confession of sin by Isaiah (Isa 6:5) is the key to the chapter since it too identifies what has been seen as a vision of judgement. "Woe is me," he cries, "for I am a man of unclean lips." Had the utterance stopped at that point it may have been no more than a typical prophetic reserve to a divine call. The prophet, however, proceeds at once to identify himself with his people and to involve himself in what has been their error and sin. Undoubtedly this vision caused him to put kingship into proper focus, for he remarks that eyes have seen *the* king (v5). Why, we may ask, is this emphasis placed upon the uncleanness of his and his people's lips? What caused this reaction? Since it is in response to the confession of the seraphim (v3) from whose lips he has heard the endorsement of divine kingship as an act of heavenly worship, it may well be that a clear disparity has been established. The disparity is between what he has just heard and the perfunctory acknowledgement of Yahweh's kingship by Jerusalem and perhaps himself in the Jerusalem cult. Since 6:1-9:7 deals with kingship under judgement to be followed by a restored Davidic kingship, it would seem, then, the sin which is acknowledged clearly involves Judah's replacement of trust in Yahweh's kingship with what could be achieved through political kingship and adept diplomatic manoeuvring.

Because the prophet's vision of the worshipping seraphim accounts for his concern, the tirade against official Jerusalem worship in Isaiah 1 becomes clear. Further, how this tirade relates to the temple vision, and why the book commences with the denunciation is thereby explained. It is not difficult to establish the connection given that official worship in Israel and Judah was pre-eminently an acknowledgement of divine kingship. The temple on which the Jerusalem cult was centred was also the divine "palace" and as such was the seat of Israel's final political authority. Israel's worship was intended to be a recognition of this fact. Perhaps Isaiah is acknowledging in chapter 6 that he also had uncritically accepted the prosperity of the age of Uzziah as a mark of divine favour. The disorders which had effected the central core of Israel's responses to Yahweh (cf. 1:10-20) represent ultimate rejection of Yahweh's rule, and thus an abrogation of the covenant. While the call of the prophet (chap. 6) directs his attention to this gross national abuse, chapter 1 expresses the condemnation which must inevitably ensue for the nation treading the path of covenantal rejection.

The voice of the Lord which follows the cleansing (Isa 6:8) commissions Isaiah to take this terrible message of judgement to Judah and Jerusalem. There can be no remission. Politically, state and city are doomed, yet from the catastrophe there will arise the faint hope of the emergence of a faith community (v13). A holy seed will sprout, the potential from which further life may spring. The seed will be holy because Yahweh himself brings it into being. Therefore throughout chapters 1-12 the vulnerability of Jerusalem is made plain (1:21; 10:27b-32; cf. 18:7; 24:10; 29:1-7; 32:13-14), while at the same time there is an emphasis that the Zion ideal would survive (7:1-9; cf. 14:28-32; 17:12-14; 29:1-8; 30:27-33; 31:1-9).

It is therefore not surprising that the eschatology of Isa 1-12 should be directed towards the re-establishment of Zion as the city of God and world centre after its condemnation in chapter 1. In its positioning as responsive promise to the threat of the first chapter, the prophecy of 2:1-4 is critical and its detail unfolds the eschatological direction in which the book will move. The seeds of the New Jerusalem are presented in this section, and thus the promise motif begun. This may explain what almost seems a new beginning to the book (cf. 1:1 and 2:1). We have argued elsewhere[14] that the Zion imagery of 2:2-4 received its impetus from Yahweh's choice of Jerusalem in 2 Sam 6, and that the particular form which the eschatology took, that of world pilgrimage to the city of God, was heavily influenced by the visit of the Queen of Sheba to Solomon's court. Her coming brought her world (1 Kgs 10:24-25) and was an indication of world recognition for the grandeur of the Solomonic court in which the physical promises given to Israel through Abraham had been realised (cf. 3:8). This argument cannot be taken up in detail here, though it is to be noted that OT eschatology invariably projects content drawn from the past history of salvation as the shape of future expectation.

As to its meaning, the thought of Isa 2:2-4 seems clear. The chosen city of Jerusalem will become the redemptive centre of the world by a final renewal of the city and the reversal of the judgement threatened in chapter 1. Zion, the tiny hillock, will become a towering world mountain. Nations which had assailed her would come as supplicants. The use of Heb. *nahar* "flow" (v2) in this connection is suggestive of the reversal of chaos combat myths which are present elsewhere in OT Zion theology (cf. Ps 46).[15] Nations come to Yahweh as judge (i.e., as world king) for *torah* "law" (Isa 2:3). Because *torah* is paralleled by the "word of the Lord" (v3), we are not dealing with a prescriptive code but with divine instruction understood in the broadest terms — divine regulation of the affairs of the world in the new age. What is affirmed in this passage is divine kingship. Nothing is stated or suggested regarding Davidic traditions. This eschatology of chapter 2 becomes basic in chapters 40-66.

b. Isaiah 13-23

These chapters largely contain oracles against foreign nations. The important fact which appears to link them together is the nations concerned are those who have suffered or will suffer at Assyrian hands and who will seek defence against Yahweh's instrument by searching for security in foreign alliances, a practice against which Jerusalem has been warned. Concurrent in these chapters is the expected theme that God alone will ransom Zion.[16]

In these chapters there is prophetic condemnation of Judaean attempts to establish diplomatic connections with Babylon (Isa 13-14); with Philistia (14:29-32, where we note that the alliance policy is rejected out of hand since Yahweh has founded Zion and he would protect it); and with Ethiopia (18:1-6). In the latter instance it is noted that Yahweh will intervene before the final harvest, i.e., before complete destruction by Assyria (v6 perhaps refers to the fate of Assyria and what appears to be a Zionistic note is introduced at v7). The undependability of Egypt is stressed in chapter 19.

As for the remaining material in these chapters, Isa 15-16 are directed against Moab and may refer to the abortive stand by that state against the Assyrian, Tiglath Pileser III in 734BC. The oracle suggests that Moab would pay the price for the non-recognition of Yahweh's historical purposes being accomplished through the Assyrian menace. The threat against Damascus, 17:1-11, would fall into the same time category. 21:1-10 links the names of Elam, Media and Babylon together and could point to a time c700BC when the fortunes of those three nations converged, and when they were dealt with by Assyria, who appears to be the devastator of verse 2. The message of verses 1-10 is clear. No hope is to be reposed by nations in the doomed Babylon. Verses 11-17 appear to be related to Assyrian campaigns of the period against the Arab peoples.

Erlandsson,[17] to whom our indebtedness in questions arising from Isa 13-23 is due, has suggested that chapter 22 refers to political measures taken when Jerusalem was threatened during the reign of Hezekiah and that the detail indicates an attack on Jerusalem society for its reliance upon defences and not upon Yahweh in her time of need. Finally, Tyre and Sidon (chap. 23) were involved in the western coalition against Assyria c734BC and had strong commercial links with Judah.

The recurring theme in Isa 13-23 is faith; confidence that Yahweh's purpose, and not foreign policies, will protect Jerusalem. Yahweh will crush Assyria, and is the guarantor of Zion's security (14:27-32). Perhaps 17:12-14 refers to an attack upon Zion, with the aggressors being described in the typical chaos imagery of "many waters". This offensive is thwarted by Yahweh at the last moment. Chapters 13-23 thus carry forward the dominant Jerusalem theme initiated in chapters 1-12.

c. Isaiah 24-27

J.J.M. Roberts has argued that these chapters are likewise held together by a heavy Zionistic emphasis, even if it remains difficult to identify precisely the two cities involved.[18] They may be Babylon and Zion or equally, and perhaps more likely, the wicked city of these chapters may be Jerusalem (cf. Isa 24:10; 25:2) in contrast to Zion, where God will reign (24:23). The appearance of Yahweh with his elders in this last reference is reminiscent of Exod 24. Yahweh as the replacement for the sun and the moon (Isa 24:23) heralds the introduction of the new age at the end of a chapter largely given over to the question of a cosmic catastrophe engulfing the city (perhaps Jerusalem, cf. the language of v5 and imagery of v13). A brief synopsis of Isa 24-27 is now offered.

Sifting judgement has been pronounced upon the earth with the centre of focus directed against some city (Isa 24:1-13,17-23). The righteous who wait lift up their voices in the interlude of praise at verses 14-16. Yahweh's victory (vv21-23) leads to a song of praise in 25:1-5 followed by a feast held upon the (world) mountain (vv6-8) with an appropriate response of praise by the faithful. The reference to Moab in these final verses is difficult but may depict the victory in terms of a new entry into the promised land, as W. Millar suggests.[19] Zion (26:1-6) offers a song of trustful confidence and verses 7-19 broadly deal with the life in the final age which Yahweh has brought about. Yahweh's control over death (v19) is now revealed. In the oscillation of motifs which these chapters contain, a short lament (vv20-21) follows, concluding (27:1) with the assurance that Yahweh will slay the dragon, thus removing any threats to the new age. 27:2-6 reverses the song of the vineyard in 5:1-7. In 27:7-11 we appear to return to the theme of punishment of Jerusalem, while verses 12-13 close the chapter with a picture of an eschatological return to the promised land by Israel's scattered people, all coming to worship on God's holy hill of Zion.

The Jerusalem emphasis of these chapters is undeniable despite the overall obscurity of their content.

d. Isaiah 28-33

These chapters are also difficult to date precisely, owing to the absence, at times, of specific detail. The uncertainty of their exact location in time is reflected by the very different positions taken by the commentators. However, there is nothing to suggest that they do not provide material dealing with Assyrian activity directed against Judah and Jerusalem in the later period of the reign of Hezekiah, with the exception of the reference to Samaria in Isa 28:1-4. That clearly presupposes a time prior to the fall of the city in 722BC. Editorially the chapters are unified by the introductory formula: Heb. *hoy* "woe" (cf.

28:1; 29:1,15; 30:1; 31:1; 33:1). The details of these chapters confirm their Zion emphasis and call upon the city and her people to rely upon the cornerstone, Zion, the temple in Jerusalem. The message to avoid foreign alliances and the certainty of the defence which Yahweh himself will afford Jerusalem is characteristic of these chapters.

Isa 28:1-4 offer judgement upon Samaria, verses 5-6 salvation for the remnant in Israel, verses 7-13 condemnation of Judaean indulgence, and verses 14-22 rejection of Jerusalem leadership which trusts in political agreements. Faith ought to have relied upon the cornerstone laid, which is Zion the temple in Jerusalem. W.H. Irwin[20] suggests that the cornerstone referred to is Zion herself (cf. v16). The community of faith is thus called to take their stand upon the doctrine of God's purposes as bound up with Jerusalem, while Yahweh conducts his strange work of sifting and punishing. Verses 23-29 offer to the faithful an assurance of God's perfect timing in the unfolding of events.

In the Ariel proclamation (Isa 29:1-8) Yahweh first occasions the siege of Jerusalem and then relieves it. Verses 9-12 trace the spiritual lethargy of the people of Jerusalem, a lethargy which is the result of a basic religious insecurity (vv13-14) and invokes punishment. Verses 15-24 threaten the perverse (vv15-16) but promise salvation to the meek (vv17-24). A golden age will then result.

Isa 30:1-5 condemns trust in Egypt. Verses 6-7 seem to belong to the same period and strike the same note but the details are in doubt. Perhaps ambassadors are en route to Egypt (v6). Egypt's help will be worthless (v7). Verses 8-18 call for the prophet to summarize his message (v8), then detail the rejection (vv9-11), its consequences and the salvation which has been spurned (vv12-18). For the community of salvation, however, who dwell in Jerusalem (vv19-26), blessings await in the shape of the defeat of the oppressor and the full transformation (v26) of the cosmic order. The consequences for the oppressors of history, with Assyria particularly in view, are then graphically outlined (vv27-33).

The contrast between the search for support (from Egypt) and the true source of Zion's protection continues in Isa 31:1-9. The hymn of chapter 32 appears to draw out the consequences of the new era of deliverance which is granted to Zion. Just government will prevail (vv1-2), sensitivity and understanding will be the property of all in the new age (vv3-5) and a contrast between the former and the latter leadership is provided (vv6-8). The reference to the 701BC siege of Jerusalem which has dominated these chapters seems continued in the excoriation of the women of Jerusalem 32:9-14), whose reversal of social roles has been characteristic of the social conduct which has brought Jerusalem down (cf. 3:16-26). Then follows in (32:15-20 a section which ushers in the ensuing age of salvation when all life will be regulated by the divine Spirit which is poured out.

As indicated the Zion emphasis seems clear in the closing hymn, Isa 33. The defeat of a powerful enemy risen up against Jerusalem and the ultimate glorification of Zion is the theme. Chapter 33 is heavily "Zion invested" and though difficult to date could well be ascribed to the period of Jerusalem deliverance by Yahweh in 701BC.

The argument of these chapters is at times difficult to unravel but they make it clear that Yahweh is the ultimate defender of Jerusalem. Nevertheless, that city must first pass through the fires of judgement.

e. Isaiah 34-35

A clear contrast between these chapters is provided by the Zion motif. Enmity idealized in the shape of Edom is ranged against Zion (Isa 34 cf. Ezek 35), but this will be destroyed allowing the redeemed of the Lord to return through a transformed wilderness to Zion (Isa 35). These two eschatological chapters are linked by many commentators with the material of chapters 40-55. The very general character of their projections, however, make their presence in the first half of the prophecy perfectly congruent. Conveying a comprehensive view of the future of the people of God, Zion once again functions as the world centre.

f. Isaiah 36-39

These chapters deal with the historical period of 701BC and with the question of the defence of Jerusalem against the attack by the Assyrian king Sennacherib. Strikingly, Isaiah 39 closes with a prophecy of exile, but primarily refers to the deportation of the Jerusalem leadership (cf. vv5-8).

g. Outline of the Structure of Isaiah

We are now in a position to discuss the material of Isa 40-66, having noted the consistent threat in chapters 1-39 of the impending destruction of Jerusalem and the equally consistent eschatological note of God's protective role to be exercised on behalf of Zion and the remnant who will populate it. How is this worked out in chapters 40-66? Chapters 40-55 represent almost pure eschatology, while 56-66 is a blend of history and eschatology. In terms of the overall structure of the book we thus have the following arrangement:

Isa 1-12 History and Eschatology
Isa 13-23 History
Isa 24-27 Eschatology
Isa 28-33 History
Isa 34-35 Eschatology
Isa 36-39 History
Isa 40-55 Eschatology
Isa 56-66 History and Eschatology.

h. Isaiah 40-55

In Isa 40-66 the theology of a renewed city of God is taken up in earnest. Following hard upon the promise of the exile and the threat to Jerusalem with which chapters 1-39 had concluded, 40:1-11 begins with an emphatic message of comfort extended to Jerusalem. The structure of verses 1-11 is important and must be carefully regarded.[21]

Material relating to Jerusalem is found in Isa 40:1-2 and 9-11 with both sets of verses bound internally by thematic considerations. Thus verse 2 contains the causal clauses (introduced by Heb. *ki* "that") which provide the ground for the statement of verse 1. There are two imperatives in verse 1 and two more in verse 2 and these would seem to unite the two verses since where a double imperative occurs in chapters 40-55 (as it does in 40:1) it is continued with further imperatives and linked by the same context (cf. 51:9;17; 57:14; 62:10). Not only is 40:9-11 linked by the Jerusalem theme to verses 1-2, but we also note that three "behold" (Heb. *hinneh*) clauses in verses 9-10 balance the three causal clauses of verse 2. Like verses 1-2, verses 9-11 begin with an imperative and continue with a double imperative (v9b). In turn, both passages encase material relating to a new Exodus. Verses 3-5 refer to the preparation of a divine way through the wilderness; and verses 6-8 make it clear these events will happen as a result of the proclamation of the divine word. It is to be noted these three themes of verses 1-11, consolation for Jerusalem, the new Exodus from Babylon, the power of the divine word which accounts for all transformations, also explain the context of 40:12-55:13. The message of 40:1-2,9-11 is developed by 49:1-52:12; 40:3-5 and the return to Jerusalem considered as a new Exodus is developed in 40:12-48:20. Finally 40:6-8 dealing with the power of the divine word to effect final change finds emphasis in the material of 52:13-55:13.[22]

Who are the speaker and audience in Isa 40:1? The plural imperatives rule out the prophet or Jerusalem as either speaker or addressee. We are probably in the well-known prophetic realm of the divine address to the heavenly council, and action is being outlined which must subsequently be taken by prophetic initiative. It is sometimes suggested that by "my people" (v1), language which is clearly covenantal and which has the renewal of the covenant in mind (cf. "says your God" in the same verse), a vocative address is intended and thus the comforted people of verse 1 are to be the consolers of Jerusalem in verse 2.

However, this is not likely as Isa 52:7 which deals with the fulfilment of the promise of the Jerusalem return suggests the royal herald as a messenger is to be distinguished from the people, who are watchers on Jerusalem's walls. Thus, in that context, not the people but the divinely commissioned herald brings the message of comfort anticipated in 40:1. As we have noted, covenant renewal is plainly in view by the old covenant mutuality language ("my people"/"your God," v1) and it therefore seems the following chapters are directed towards the

15

fulfilment of all Israel's covenant expectations. This means nothing less than the restoration of Jerusalem and her inhabitants. All roads will lead to the restored centre and there, as evidenced in the development of the prophecy, the New Creation as the full incidence of covenant expectation will find its location. The Jerusalem goal, set forth in 40:1-2,9-11, is to proceed by way of a new Exodus (vv3-5), and Jerusalem is now presented as the prophetic substitute for everything resulting from the Sinai covenant. Since we will argue in the New Israel chapter that the Sinai covenant was an extension in Israel's experience of the Abrahamic bond, concomitantly Jerusalem is presented in chapters 40-55 as the fulfilment of the Abrahamic promises (cf. chap. 54). In Jerusalem the twin Abrahamic notions of people and sacred place are fulfilled.

We should also note "comfort," in Isa 40:1, is not consolation in the midst of sorrow but the message that sorrow has been removed (cf. 2 Sam 12:24). In this context the phrase "speak to the heart" (Isa 40:2) bears the connotation "makes a significant change in the circumstances" (cf. Gen 34:3; Judg 19:3; 2 Sam 19:7; Hos 2:14) and foreshadows" an imminent development. "Double for all her sins" (Isa 40:2) does not appeal to a particular theory of atonement but simply indicates Jerusalem's sufferings have now gone beyond the point of endurance.

In Isa 40:9-11, although the text is ambiguous, the general context demands that Jerusalem is the evangelized and not the evangelist. Here we refer again to the distinction drawn between royal herald as messenger of good tidings and the city in 52:7. Otherwise as K. Kiesow notes,[23] we should have the grotesque picture in 40:9-11 of Jerusalem ascending a high mountain. The message is simple; God is coming as King! This is clearly stated in 52:7, while the shepherd imagery of 40:9-11 frequently used of divine kingship in the ancient Near East, implies the kingship of Yahweh as well. The arm of Yahweh (40:10; 52:10), the saving instrument of the Exodus, will achieve all this. In short, God, by engineering a new Exodus, re-establishes His covenant for His people who are to be gathered to the divine centre, Jerusalem.

Isaiah 40:12-31 begins, after the highly condensed outline delivered in verses 1-11, the unfolding of Israel's future. In response to Israel's complaint the course of history is running against her, a reversal of the historical process is imminent. Judgement through the advent of Cyrus the Persian king is about to be pronounced upon Babylon. The mood is set by a tightly reasoned argument running from 40:12-42:4.[24] Israel's complaint that her "way" (i.e., the present historical realities) is "hidden from Yahweh" is the issue 40:12-31 takes up (v27 links Heb.

derek "way" and *mispat* "justice" (RSV "right"); note also the use of *mispat* in v14).

The prophet argues Yahweh is able to withstand Israel's three enemies: the nations themselves (Isa 40:12-17); their rulers and princes (vv18-24); and the astral deities who back them (vv25-26). Further, Yahweh is not merely able, he is also willing (vv27-31). Yahweh is about to bring to pass "justice" (Heb. *mispat*). Chapter 41 is introduced and concluded by two trial narratives in which the nations are arraigned (vv1-4) and the deities of the nations are called to the bar (vv21-29). The chapter terminates with "behold they are all a delusion and their works are nothing" (v29). Chapter 42 which introduces the work of the servant opens with "Behold my servant, whom I uphold". In other words, the content of 42:1-4 is intended to provide for a reversal of what has preceded.

In sum, the redress of Israel's plight and thus the blueprint for her salvation, as delivered in Isa 40:1-11, is to be effected by the work of the servant. We cannot dwell upon this but we note its world-wide effect is signified in 42:4, in the remark that the isles (i.e., the world beyond Israel) will wait for his "law" (Heb. *torah*). Clearly, by the reference to *torah* and the eschatological expectations associated in Isaiah with that term (cf. 2:2-4), some note of international pilgrimage underlies the successful outcome of the ministry of the servant. Therefore, the intention of 42:1-4 is to point out the present course of history will be reversed for Israel through the ministry of the servant, and Israel's "right" will be properly established. Justice will be done by God for His people!

The following two servant songs (Isa 49:1-6; 50:4-9) are embodied in "Zion narratives", and are bound up with the larger argument commencing in 49:1 concerning Zion's future.

These "Zion songs" are introduced with reference to a further phase of the servant's work which results in (Isa 49:1-6) the response of kings who stand up to watch the return of Israel in processional Exodus to the promised land (49:7-13, cf. Exod 15:12-18). Yahweh has not forgotten Jerusalem (Isa 49:14-26). That she is engraven on his palms (v16), indicates the relationship is clearly unbreakable. The nations who have oppressed Israel will return her. It is indicated (Isa 50:1-3) that discipline and not divorce was intended by the exile. 50:4-9 thus offers an exhortation to the servant to persevere, and calls (in vv10-11) the exiles to respond to his message. 51:1-8 address a faithful Israel who will inherit the promises, while verses 9-11 spell out the return to Jerusalem in terms of a New Creation. Verses 12-16 offer consolation to Jerusalem for Yahweh stands behind her, and the covenant is thereby to be restored (v16). Jerusalem is then called upon to rouse herself (vv17-20); her cup of wrath is to be passed on to Babylon (vv21-23). Jerusalem is to put on garments appropriate to the new age (i.e., queenly robes, 52:1-6). 52:7-10 provides a climax to the expectation of 40:1-2, 9-11 and the return to Jerusalem (viewed prophetically as completed 52:11-12) is seen to parallel the Exodus from Egypt.

In Isa 52:13-53:12 the ministry of the servant, resulting in the restoration of Jerusalem and the advent of God as King, is appraised. The disfigured and rejected servant, the results of whose ministry were nonetheless so effective, is presented in 52:13-15. Then in 53:1-9 we are confronted with the confession of the gentile kings (of 52:15), who stand astonished at the new Exodus and restoration. A prophetic (53:10-11) and a divine (v12) assessment of the servant's ministry follows. What is obvious is that it is the servant's ministry which makes possible this great change of the return of God's people to his city. The confession of the kings bears eloquent testimony to the eschatology of 2:2-4.

As we will note in our discussion of the New Covenant there is a bewildering array of covenantal language in Isa 54 reviewing the details of what has been accomplished by the servant. Thus we move rapidly in the chapter from Abrahamic (vv1-3) to Sinaitic (vv7-10) to Davidic themes (vv11-17). The chapter climaxes in extravagant imagery of Zion's rebuilding and repopulation (vv11-17). From the newly restored city the waters of life flow (55:1-2) while all her people are now sharers in the promises of the Davidic covenant, and are thus kings and priests (vv3-5).

i. Isaiah 56-66

An international pilgrimage to a sacred mountain, presumably Jerusalem, begins the sequence (Isa 56:1-8), likewise the note of a similar pilgrimage concludes it (66:18-24). The promises of 2:2-4 bearing on Jerusalem's role are expanded in chapters 60-62 as follows:

Isa 60:1-9 resumes the themes of chapters 49-55 but with the expectation of the return to Zion presented as imminent. 60:10-22 describes the manner of the return. The wealth of nations and peoples led by their rulers will stream into the renewed Jerusalem, in fulfilment of the Abrahamic promises (vv21-22). In 61:1-3, a servant figure announces the victory. Verses 4-11 are concerned with the physical reconstruction of Zion which is to be populated by priest kings (v6). World homage is to be offered (v9) to the bride Zion (v10) with an attendant transformation of nature (v11).
The particular election of Zion to privilege is the subject of Isaiah 62. She is vindicated and restored (vv1-2a), a new name is given to her and (vv2b-4a) her future is referred to in the covenant imagery of marriage (vv4b-5). Zion's security is the tenor of verses 6-9, while the call to the people of God to enter Jerusalem as a sanctified people and to occupy that holy space completes the chapter (vv10-12).

P.D. Hanson[25] points to the dualism which pervades Isa 56-66. Only a small group within the community will be the recipients of the return promises. Thus in 65:19 we are dealing with concepts of "my people" as opposed to those who "forget my holy mountain" (cf. v11). In verses

17-25 the elect people of God (the remnant of chaps. 1-39) enjoy the blessing of the new age resulting from divine intervention. Yahweh revives the theme of the New Jerusalem as he "roars" from his heavenly temple (66:5-6). Judgement upon his enemies follows and the metaphor of Zion's miraculous birth of many children (vv7-9) points not only to Abrahamic covenant fulfilment, but to the suddenness of the transition to the new age. Again, such a consolation is available only to those "who rejoice with Jerusalem" (v10). Traditional imagery returns in the description of the new age (vv12-14), and Yahweh's judgement is described in the divine warrior motif (vv15-16). Beyond this judgement the end is heralded by the return of the chosen to Zion (vv18-24). The book concludes with a picture of uninterrupted temple worship by all which is, as C. Westermann notes,[26] the consummation of history.

Summary

The book of Isaiah moves from the perverse "worship" of physical Jerusalem under judgement (because of the neglect of Yahweh's kingship), to the worship of Yahweh in the New Jerusalem. Gradually in the course of this great book Jerusalem becomes a major biblical symbol uniting city and saved community; combining sacred space and sanctified people. Isaiah makes it clear there can be no thought of a restored Israel without the prior restoration of Zion. It is Yahweh's presence alone which makes Israel the people of God. Davidic king and temple receive little attention, for Isaiah is concerned with the ultimate end. His Zion is an ideal; the perfected community; the righteous people of God.

As a political concept, however, Isaiah's notion of Jerusalem reminds us that God's saving activity occurs within history. From the "Babylons" of this world, as from ancient Babylon, God saves his people. He will found a city for them. A city which is the image of a unified political community. The Babel concept of Gen 11 and its attendant divisive consequences have been reversed. Isaiah's concept of Jerusalem thus replaces the ill-conceived humanistic dream of Babel's tower builders. Prompted by a desire for a centre those men of Babel had also built a city looking for the governmental unity by which men might be perfectly regulated. Isaiah now sees this quest for unity as divinely supplied!

It is the function of the book of Isaiah to bring this "theology of the centre" before us. Through the pervasive biblical symbol of the city the notions of governed and government are combined. However, the historical setting in which this symbolism occurs alerts the reader to the fact that eschatology projects a definite historical fulfilment. Faith and history will fully meet, reality and symbol will finally coincide. The presentation of Isa 40-66 graphically anticipates the message of Rev 21-22 — the conclusion of history.

ii. *Prophetic References to Jerusalem until 587BC*

The emphasis upon Jerusalem, her punishment and hopes, continues in the pre-587BC writings and the writings which reflect the conditions of the period. In this survey we leave aside for later consideration the book of Ezekiel which spans the 587 period.

Contemporary with Isa 1-39, Micah abounds in Jerusalem emphases. Like Isa 1-12, Micah is structured around the alternation of the themes of doom and hope[27]. It is in the hope sections that the note of Zion's future is struck. Yahweh's leadership, with judgement pronounced upon present corrupt Jerusalem (Mic 1:8-9; 3:9-12) will restore the city and provide for Davidic leadership (2:12-13; 5:2-6). The seven oracles of Mic 4-5 (4:1-5,6-8,9-10,11-13; 5:1-6,7-9,10-15) all depict a hopeless situation from which Yahweh redeems Jerusalem. He will re-establish his temple and rule from Zion (4:6-8) and offer his people renewed covenant status (vv1-5). Punished, Jerusalem will be divinely rebuilt (7:1-10,11-13). The blessings of the first Exodus will be renewed (vv14-15), causing the world at large to be submissive and awed (vv16-17).

Having centered his message on the fortunes of Jerusalem, Micah ends his prophecy with an appropriate acknowledgement of Yahweh's incomparability. Salvation, however, is extended only to the remnant (Mic 7:18). All of this is in fulfilment of the Abrahamic promises (v20) implemented as a result of the comprehensive and complete forgiveness of sins, and presented in a manner which anticipates Jeremiah's doctrine of New Covenant forgiveness (v19).

The presentation of Jerusalem as culpable for her spiritual apostasy was common to the prophetic mood of the period and Jeremiah proves to be no exception in this regard. Thus Jer 4:11-14 promises punishment but then offers a return for the faithful. The prophet declares he is unable even after a thorough search to find an upright man in Jerusalem (5:1-3). The excessively proud (13:9-11) and idolatrous city (1:16-18; 2:28; 11:13), despite her earlier happier days in the Exodus period (2:2-3), is doomed. We cannot survey the extent of the Jerusalem references in this extensive prophetic work, but the tenor of the judgement oracles reflects Jeremiah's awareness that divine wrath had been poured out on the rebellious city (cf. 42:18). Of course there are messages of hope, especially the reconstitution of the covenant (31:31-34) an act in which Jerusalem is at least indirectly involved. Additionally, a return to the promised land after an interval of seventy years is promised (25:11). But the clear message for the immediate future is identical with Isa 1-39: Jerusalem must share in the general exile.

We note in passing that Zeph 1:12 also adheres to the general conviction that Yahweh will sift the guilty city and bring the sinner to account.

iii. *Jerusalem's Fall and the Future of Israel's Institutions: The Book of Kings*

The theme of the fall of the Davidic dynasty is the preoccupation of the books of Kings. Prospectively, it was perhaps to have been expected given the consistently ambivalent attitude to the kingship of Solomon, as disclosed in the narrative of 1 Kgs 1-11. Though the reforming kings (Asa, Jehoshaphat, Joash, Hezekiah and Josiah) attempted to arrest the drift, their activities never seemed to secure the support of the leadership or general populace. Thus, although Kings concludes with the release of Jehoiachin in 562BC (2 Kgs 25:27) hope is extinguished since he is now dead (an inference from v29). In any case, it is a very tenuous doctrine of Davidic continuity the conclusion of 2 Kings presents. The Davidic king, Jehoiachin, eats defiled food at a pagan king's table! Apart from the reference to his death, this in itself is an eloquent commentary upon the puppet status to which Davidic kingship had been reduced. This stands in stark contrast to the other significant (and perhaps royal) personage of the exile, Daniel. Refusing to defile himself with food from a pagan king's table, Daniel maintains himself and his faith throughout the exile. Thus, Daniel is presented as a survivor, having outlived the Babylonian empire.

Confirmation for the prophetic denouncement of the monarchy and the invoking of the curse traditions (cf. Deut 28) occurs with the fall of Jerusalem (587BC). The possibility of the change Jeremiah preached did not occur, therefore judgement, without pity, is Jerusalem's lot (Jer 15:5). Jerusalem had been visited with her "day" (Ps 137:7): people, cult, political institutions, kingship, even land, are destroyed, and the covenant appears irrevocably withdrawn. The second aspect of the prophetic preaching, particularly that of Isaiah, was Zion as the city of divine choice, the site of the Great King. From this perspective the temple was the centre of world government and to it all nations would eventually come in pilgrimage. Therefore, the OT notion of divine kingship centred upon Jerusalem demanded an eschatological restoration of this divine seat. This ideal, however, was distorted, resulting in the exile.

As to whether God's purposes for Jerusalem had come to an end in 587BC, however, a resounding prophetic "no!" had already been heard. Yahweh would establish his royal reign in Jerusalem (Isa 24:23; Obad 21; Mic 4:7; Zeph 3:15; cf. Pss 146:10; 149:2). Jeremiah knew this also (Jer 33:16) and thus concludes his New Covenant eschatology with the concept of a restored Jerusalem, linked to the motif of a New Creation (31:35-40). The redeemed would ask the way to Zion (50:5), recognizing the goal of the return is the establishing of a right relationship in the terms of the New Covenant. A firm expectation of victory in Jerusalem is pervasive in the prophets to the exile (Obad 21; Mic 7:10; cf. Joel 2:32).

iv. *Lamentations*

Lamentations, whose setting is that of the desolated Jerusalem of 587BC, is our major source of information, revealing community attitudes to the exile and the reflections of that same community on the destruction of Jerusalem. The mood of the book is established by the first few verses, depicting a lonely solitary widow. No longer a princess, she is become a servant. The five poems which comprise this book do not appear to establish any progression. Common to them all is the theme of a tragic reversal, expressed repetitively from the vantage point of differing speakers, themselves participants of the tragedy.

A great contrast is drawn between Zion's former glory and her present ignominy. The powerful personification of Zion as a degraded, rejected woman in the first chapter underscores the psychological indignity which presents the greatest feature of her suffering. In Lam 2 the fall of Jerusalem from heaven is presented in terms similar to the mythical language used in Isa 14:12-21 to depict the fall of Babylon. Zion had suffered an eclipse from her place in the heavenly vault: all her honoured institutions, even the sanctuary, had been spurned. As B. Albrektson has noted,[28] Lam 2:15c, in which Zion is described as the "joy of all the earth", is almost a direct quotation fom the Zion hymn, Ps 48:2. The hymn speaks of the elevated position of Zion as the mountain of the divine assembly, the city of the Great King. But the real issue of Lam 2 is that the unbelievable had happened to Zion. Verse 20 touches upon this sad truth: "Look, O Lord, and see. With whom have you dealt thus?"

Lam 3 provides the centre of the book in terms of position, metre and content. In this most detailed presentation of Jerusalem's sufferings the mood is intensely personal as the fate of the nation recedes into the background. Yet unlike Lam 1 and 2, chapter 3 calls for retribution on Jerusalem's foes (3:64-66). Though God has brought all this about, belief in His good providence has not been surrendered (vv37-39), thus there remains an undercurrent message of hope.

In the fourth chapter there is a vivid description of the siege of Jerusalem and its consequent suffering: the high born are brought low and even maternal cruelty towards children occurred. Neither Sodom or Gomorrah experienced such severe punishment (cf. Lam 4:6). Yet the familiar motif of Zion's impregnability is taken up again in 4:12. It is expressed in the strongest possible terms to provide a contrast with the astounding nature of the city's fall. Even the kings of the earth, the inhabitants of the world, did not believe an enemy could enter Jerusalem! The sacral traditions upon which this verse draws records that kings had once plotted against Jerusalem and attacked this divine stronghold only to be repulsed (Pss 46:6-7; 48:4-8; 76:4-6,12). As Albrektson has also noted[29] in Lam 4:20 Jerusalem royal court ideals surrounding kingship are couched in the strongest of terms. All life depends upon this royal figure who is the "breath of our nostrils" (cf. Gen 2:7 and Ps104:29 where all life stems from God's grace). That we are in the main stream of Jerusalem royal temple theology is clear from the second half of the verse's allusion to the king as the tree of life (cf. the supposition voiced: "under his shadow we live among the nations").

The last chapter is the only poem of the five which is not an acrostic. It does not function as a lament upon Jerusalem but as a penitential plea for all, arising out of present troubles (Lam 5:1-18). A cry for help bound with the hope of restoration, and a final lament taking account of the present reality (vv19-22) close the book.

Lamentations is a theological attempt to come to terms with the event of 587BC, its effect and rationale. It is too simplistic, as Albrektson sees,[30] merely to suggest a doctrine of retribution is being applied here. That does not account for the detailed and frequent appeals to the traditions of Zion's inviolability which are scattered throughout the book. There is tension here involving the reconciliation of history and faith. How is the election of David, the choice of Zion, to be handled in a situation of complete destruction? The temple is burnt and Jerusalem ravaged: the two pillars of Jerusalem orthodoxy are thereby destroyed. But mixed with the Zion appeals, and indeed preponderating is material from the curse traditions of Deuteronomy 28 (cf. Lam 1:3,5,9; 2:20; 3:45; 4:10,16; 5:12).

Two lines of tradition meet in this book. First, the eternal character of the Davidic covenant which endorsed both Jerusalem and the Davidic kingship it housed and around which the exalted theology of royal Zion had been constructed. Second, the notion from Deut 28 that election to high privilege carries enormous responsibility. Life as a covenant people demands continual response to a series of obligations. Jerusalem fails politically and ethically, and failure on these two counts is echoed in the two lines of OT traditions which converged at the fall of Jerusalem. Their new reconciliation was the daunting task facing post-exilic theology.

v. *Ezekiel*

Ezekiel is neatly divided into two balanced halves: chapters 1-24 deal with the condemnation of Jerusalem and Judah, and chapters 25-48 take up the question of their restoration. For Ezekiel, Jerusalem was a city bent upon self-destruction (12:1-11 and 21:25-27 indicate the manner in which this destruction will be carried out). The deep-rooted iniquity of this blood-guilty city (22:2-5; 24:6) is bound up with her pagan origins which despite redemption she never overcame (16:1-16). Clearly those origins contributed to her prevalent idolatry (chaps. 8-11) a fact to which the pre-exilic prophets had continually drawn attention. Therefore, Jerusalem as a temple city will cease. The city which David besieged will be captured, a pronouncement foreshadowed by the death of Ezekiel's wife at the beginning of the siege of Jerusalem (24:18).

Like Isa 40-66, however, Ezekiel viewed Jerusalem as the carrier of the Sinai traditions. The birth and selection of Jerusalem are described in terms which throw the initiative solely upon God's sovereign choice, in keeping with the similar rationale in the choice of Israel (Deut 7:7). The marriage imagery of the Sinai covenant by this time had been plainly applied to Jerusalem (Ezek 23).[31]

When judgement was completed with her capture, Ezekiel turns to the theme of restoration. Introduced as a new phase by the repetition of the "watchman" prophecy (Ezek 3) in 33:1-20, it is developed in a series of six messages bearing upon the restoration and apparently delivered in the same night.[32] They climax in the defeat of Gog by Magog (chaps. 38-39), which ushers in the vision of the end in the form of the temple city (chaps. 40-48).

Ezekiel's description of this city begins with a visionary sequence delivered to him on a high mountain (Ezek 40:1-2). In view of the final declaration of the book (48:35), the promise of Yahweh's presence, the temple city described in the following chapters must be Zion. The links, however, with Sinai in 40:1-2 seem clear[33] as they do throughout chapters 40-48. What is planned in this great vision must be construed as a new Exodus, even as the true goal of the Exodus. The prophetic affirmation of Jerusalem as the centre of the world (38:12), the fulcrum on which world government rests, is now to be implemented eschatologically. This identification of the end-time Zion as God's holy mountain embodies a series of identifications recalling, as J. Levenson has noted,[34] motifs associated with the initial Eden.

The "high mountain" of Ezek 40:2 resumes the notion of "my holy mountain" (20:40), the mountain height of Israel, the world centre. Eden links are established via 28:14; there the "holy mountain" and the "garden of God" (v13) are connected. The fabulous wealth of the garden, while directly referring to Gen 2:6-14, also reminds the reader of the extravagant descriptions of Zion in Isa 60-62. Healing streams flow from under the temple (47:1-12), a fact which makes Zion the joy of all the earth (Joel 3:17-18). No room is made for the pre-exilic sense of Davidic kingship in Ezek 40-48 (as we will note in more detail under the New Temple). The "prince" of these chapters, as part of the dyarchy of prince and priest which Ezekiel contemplates, is not overtly connected with the house of David. The name of the city "Yahweh is there" (48:35) may avoid a direct mention of Zion and Jerusalem because of the connotations still associated with the apostate and fallen city. Zion is not otherwise mentioned by Ezekiel, which may constitute an avoidance of Davidic eschatology as well. Further, the name Jerusalem occurs only once (36:38) in the restoration prophecies after the report of its destruction in 33:21. The political connotations ascribed by Ezekiel to the Jerusalem of his prophecy would not have made the transfer of his eschatological concepts to it an easy matter. Indeed, a "city of God" concept does not appear in the book until after the final defeat of the nations in chapters 38-39. It is thus a concept to be associated with the final indwelling of God and not with any prospect of an intermediate reign.

vi. *Zechariah*

The only other OT book to reflect at length upon the question of Jerusalem is the book of Zechariah. Zech 1-8 is also heavily temple orientated: emphasizing the rebuilding of the temple, Yahweh's return to Jerusalem (1:16) begins a process of restoration concluded at the end of the first section of the prophecy by Jerusalem becoming the world pilgrimage centre (8:20-23). Gentile reaction to this is noted in 8:23 in the oft repeated confession "God is with you". Reminiscent of Abimelech's perception of Abraham (Gen 21:22), it once more is employed to sum up the blessings extended to the world through the New Jerusalem.

Zech 9-14 presents roughly the same sequences as chapters 1-8 and thus appears to be both complementary and interpretative. The details of Zechariah 9 are bewildering, and it seems preferable to take the seemingly historical references as symbolic.[35] Thus, 9:1-7 deals with the conflict between Yahweh and the traditional enemies of Israel. Yahweh marches from the entrance to the old northern boundaries of the Davidic empire down to the temple and Jerusalem (v8); the entry of the divine king into Jerusalem is proclaimed (v9); the universality of his reign is manifested (v10); captives are released (vv11-13); there is a theophanic appearance of Yahweh as warrior (v14); typical sacrificial and banquet themes arise (v15); and there is an allusion to the fertility of the restored order (vv16-17). The intervening material to chapter 14 deals with the purification of Israel's leadership, the elimination of opposition to Israel, and the cleansing of the land—all dominant themes in chapters 1-8.

In Zech 14 the centrality of the place of Zion emerges again in the eschatology of the prophet. The nations gather against Jerusalem, manifesting the common theme of Zion's election (vv1-2). Victory is achieved through the intervention of Yahweh as warrior (v3), who himself prepares a processional way to Jerusalem by levelling natural obstacles (vv4-5, cf. Isa 40:1-11), and enters the city with his holy ones (the community of faith or a heavenly assembly? — perhaps the former). A harmony of orders within the New Creation appears, eradicating the binary oppositions denoting the old order, and emphasizing the thorough-going nature of the "newness" (Zech 14:6-8).

Jerusalem is the explicitly stated centre of life from which living waters continually flow, an expansion of Ezek 47:1-12. In Zech 14:9-10 the universal reign of Yahweh from the city of Jerusalem is declared (note the similarity of the city dimensions to those of Jer 31:38). Thus the surrounding territory is turned into an extensive plain throwing the elevated Jerusalem into clear prominence (cf. Isa 2:2-4). Jerusalem will thereafter dwell securely (Zech 14:11), but covenant curses (i.e., final judgement) is the lot of Yahweh's enemies (vv12-15). The survivors of the nations will proceed annually to Jerusalem for the feast of tabernacles (vv16-19); the kingship festival par excellence. This annual pilgrimage, an extension of Isa 2:2-4, indicates semi-national parameters still maintained. There is not yet the emergence of thorough-going universalistic apocalyptic. Zech 14:20-21 disclose the purity of the New Jerusalem: temple prescriptions now apply to the whole city. Temple and city have thus merged at the end of the OT period.[36]

Thus we conclude our OT survey. The rise of the Jerusalem concept of the OT is directly related to divine kingship. We have noted that the political promises given to Israel, especially those related to the Davidic dynasty, are gradually transformed by OT prophecy into eschatological hopes. Isa 40-66, in particular, located Zion as the divine centre of the New Creation. Because of Yahweh's presence, Zion is the focal point of worship in the new age. Privileges of citizenship and access to the New Jerusalem are included among the final rewards awaiting believers. In the OT Jerusalem is the scene of righteousness and peace because it is the divine seat. Concepts of creation and people of God are all part of the multiform series of identifications which make the notion of the New Jerusalem a major eschatological symbol.

The New Testament

i. *Gospels*

We have left out of our survey the intertestamental and apocryphal evidence simply noting that the series of expectations generated within the OT period are continued and expanded.[37] Our NT survey must necessarily be brief.

In Matt 5:14-16 the image of the city set upon the hill is transferred to the new community.[38] Though Jerusalem is called the "city of the Great King" (v35, cf. 27:53) it is not greatly emphasized in the gospels as a summarizing factor for the concentration of eschatological hopes. Jesus' transference shifts the eschatological hopes centred in Jerusalem to the new group he had gathered, and foreshadows the end of political Jerusalem. We will deal with the rejection of Jerusalem and the temple (Matt 21) in our discussion of the New Temple. In the gospels Jerusalem is pre-eminently the place where Jesus must die (16:21; cf. Mark 8:31; 10:32-34; Luke 9:22, 13:32; 17:11; 19:28). Since in the transfiguration narrative Jesus' exodus is to be conducted there (Luke 9:31) we may assume that it will be the city of the New Covenant.

The rejection of Jerusalem is even more pointed in John's gospel than in the synoptics. John 12 completes the Jerusalem centred discourses of Jesus. The quotation from Zech 9:9, associated with Jesus' entry into Jerusalem in the synoptics, is followed in John by the advent of the "Greeks" seeking Jesus (John 12:20). This in itself indicates that other ways must now be sought to refract the "light" looked for than via national Israel or political Jerusalem. The coming of the Greeks leads Jesus to proclaim that now the "hour has come for the Son of Man to be glorified" (i.e., lifted up in death). As Son of Man, the figure in whom the ministry of judgement upon the world is supremely compacted, Jesus inflicts this ultimate act of judgement upon Jerusalem by his death. It is therefore only as he is lifted up that Greeks and others may "see" him. Jesus makes this point clear by declaring that when he is lifted up (as Son of Man) he will draw all men to him. In other words, the cross will be the judgement bar at which all humanity will be assessed (vv29-33). As the light of the world (15-36) he thus supplants Jerusalem's traditional role.

We need not dwell upon the prophecies relating to the destruction of Jerusalem in the synoptic gospels. Their fulfilment in 70AD meant the end of an age. Jerusalem had failed to recognize the things which pertained to her peace (Luke 19:42), the time of her visitation (v44b), and her "house" had been left desolate (the city in that context). It is noteworthy in this connection that following the seven woes pronounced upon Israel (in the form of her leaders) in Matt 23 we end with a final woe pronounced upon Jerusalem (vv37-39). To the question of the disciples in Matt 24:2 concerning the destruction of the temple (and Jerusalem) and of the end of the age, Jesus answers that these two questions as in fact one. The destruction of Jerusalem is the end of the age, the finish of political Israel. In the discourse which follows, if Matt 24 may be taken as typical, Jesus therein emphasized the close relationship between the destruction of Jerusalem and the parousia. By eschatological telescoping, the one virtually follows the other.

It is a peculiarity of the gospels that there is a major emphasis upon a Galilean ministry. Jesus begins and ends in Galilee in both Matthew and Mark. The messianic light dawns there (cf. Matt 4:15, quoting Isa 8:23 Heb.). Further, in predominantly Gentile Galilee (in Matthew) the disciples are commissioned by the exalted Son of Man. It is interesting to note that the tenor of commissioning indicates an emphasis on the judgemental character of their ministry. In keeping with Matthew and Mark is the Galilean emphasis in John, for it begins in Galilee and in John 21 we are in Galilee again. Luke, however, maintains the Jerusalem emphasis. Early in Luke's gospel the expectations of the community of faith are communicated within a Jerusalem framework (Luke 2:25-35,36-38,41-52). The response to this expectation is given by Jesus in Nazareth (4:16-30) in terms of the background of Isaiah 61.

This general Galilean emphasis, particularly in the matter of the resurrection narratives, indicates that it is the Gentiles who are now sharers (by that resurrection) in the promises originally given to Israel. In Galilee the divine light dawned and through death became the light to lighten the gentiles: this is the supreme rejection of Jerusalem. Yet the enabling power for this ministry is given in Jerusalem. The gift of the

Spirit to the New "Israel" is given in the upper room (John 20:22), and the Spirit commissions their preaching ministry in Acts 2. But it is *from* Jerusalem, as Luke points out, that the church moves out finding its final centre within the Acts narrative in Rome for the time of the Gentiles has been conclusively ushered in.

ii. *Paul*

The command to the disciples in Luke 24:49 and Acts 1:4 to remain in Jerusalem excites the curiosity of the band. Is the fulfilment of the kingdom, and thus the restoration of all things (the New Creation), about to occur? Will Israel's role to the world then be brought into play? Jesus makes it clear however that Christian ministry must now be developed. In the remainder of the NT the nature of this ministry is best demonstrated in the Pauline writings. It is paradoxical that, as the apostle to the Gentiles, Paul's ministry is Jerusalem centred. For him the gospel begins in Jerusalem (cf. Rom 15:19) and in their collection for the poor Jerusalem saints Gentiles must recognize the spiritual centrality of Jerusalem. Paul organizes this collection as a major component of his ministry to provide by it a symbol of Jewish-Christian unity. The first fruits of Paul's Gentile ministry therefore must be brought in pilgrimage to Jerusalem (vv16-23).

Paul thus endorsed the older prophetic eschatology. Pauline theology of this character was Abrahamic in its bent as his epistles make clear (cf. Rom 4; Gal 3). It was a visit to Jerusalem on a mission of this nature which provoked his arrest. This in turn provided the occasion for the dismissal of the earthly Jerusalem by Luke (Acts 21:27-29) and its replacement by Rome as the final point of focus (chap. 28). Paul thereby preserved in his missionary experience the OT tensions between reality and eschatology as connected with Jerusalem. By his journey to Rome Paul parallels the journey of Jesus to Jerusalem which ended in his arrest and death (Luke 9:51-18:14). In both journeys the rejection of Israel and Jerusalem had been pronounced.

The unique phrase in Gal 4:26 "the Jerusalem which is above" needs discussion. Paul appears to be responding to the language of his opponents, though it must be said that the concept of a "heavenly Jerusalem" does not seem to be prominent in either intertestamental literature or late Judaism, even though the notion of a restored Jerusalem within the eschaton is frequent. His argument in Gal 3-4 is connected with Abrahamic spiritual descent. Chapter 3 is virtually an elaboration of verse 8 in which the Abrahamic promises of Gen 12:1-3 are repeated. Vital to Paul's argument in these two chapters is the denial of justification by the law, since justification depends solely upon fidelity to divine promises. As law was dependent upon prior promise, attention to the law kept Gentiles under suppression and prevented them from entering the kingdom. Thus to say the law "does not rest on faith" (Gal 3:12) means that God had never accepted anyone on the basis of legal obedience. The positive function of law within the OT had been to reflect a response to promise. By accepting the law as a condition of entrance to the kingdom (4:1-10) Gentiles were returning to idolatry since Judaism was a false religion for Paul.[39]

After making a personal appeal based upon his earlier relations with the Galatians (Gal 4:11-20), Paul reverts to the Abrahamic discussion in verses 21-31. The aim in what follows is to turn the issue of physical descent from Abraham against his opponents. He does this by reference to two Jerusalems, the earthly and the heavenly. Paul's concept of a heavenly Jerusalem has its biblical roots in such passages as Isa 54:1 (Gal 4:27), yet though echoed somewhat in Heb 12:18-24 the thought does not appear in Jewish literature until the second century AD.[40] It is to be noted, however, that there is no equation in Galatians 4 between the heavenly Jerusalem and the church since the "our" (v26) plainly indicates that believers are still on earth: "the heavenly Jerusalem is rather to be viewed as the new age depicted in spatial terms and the anticipation of the full life of this new age is now present in the church".[41]

iii. *Hebrews*

Heb 12:18-24 depicts the present transformed state of the believers in terms of OT eschatology. Their experience is contrasted with the congregation of Israel which stood before Sinai, since the present addressees come to "Mt. Zion, and to the city of the living God, the heavenly Jerusalem, and to the innumerable angels in festal gathering, and to the assembly of the first-born who are enrolled in heaven, and to a judge who is God of all, and to the spirits of just men made perfect" (vv22-23). The analogy drawn between Zion and Sinai is that of covenant conclusion. What is put before the recipients of the epistle in these verses is the prospect of final New Covenant inclusion. The eschatological paradox is that believers *have now come* to Zion (v22), the city towards which they *are yet still moving* (13:14). What is meant in 12:18-24 is that the readers are already members of the New

Covenant community, but with the fullness of covenant blessings still to be revealed. We may also notice in these verses that Zion is again conceived spatially separate from its inhabitants, but incomplete without them.[42]

iv. Revelation Reconsidered

Finally, the contrast between the two Jerusalems could not be clearer than that which is provided by the book of the Revelation. Identified with Sodom and Egypt (Rev 11:8), the earthly Jerusalem is rejected. However, with the descent of the New Jerusalem the boundaries between the two cities, indeed between heaven and earth are blurred (chaps. 21-22). We have pointed to all this at the commencement of this chapter and we content ourselves here merely with concluding remarks.

As the symbol of the New Creation, the arrival of the New Jerusalem means the advent of the new paradisiacal age. In the light of this we may return to the question raised earlier in this chapter: namely, why the symbol of the city should have been used to convey the major theme of biblical eschatology? The answer which the Revelation of John gives by its two city contrast (Babylon and Jerusalem) is that for biblical readers the city is pre-eminently a symbol of world government. Therefore, the New Jerusalem asserts the fact of final Kingdom of God rule, combining people, place and divine presence. With the advent of the New Jerusalem we have moved to the end. Unlike Ezek 40-48 (upon which Rev 21-22 is so much dependent), the new city does not rest upon a cosmic mountain (cf. Ezek 40:2), but "comes down" to earth and turns the whole earth into a paradise by its presence. Language in these final chapters runs beyond itself in an endeavour to describe the felicity of the end. Only paradox may speak here since binary opposites which characterized the old creation (i.e., sun and moon as we noted earlier) now disappear and world geography is fused by the relationship of all life within and without to the city. Life reigns supreme in this new city landscaped with trees of life stretching in a mighty boulevard of endless array (Rev 22:2). The metaphors of absolute triumph, fertility, and joy abound in the presentation as the fertilizing waters flow forth for the healing of all nations (vv1-5).

In short, the older Zion theology with all its implications is now realized:[43]

1. Jerusalem has become the meeting point between heaven and earth.
2. The river of paradise flows from the New Jerusalem.

3. All enemies, chaotic and therefore historical, have been defeated before Zion.
4. All nations will now come to Zion for "torah" and in their coming will discover that the promise of total redemption (cf. Gen 12:1-3) is fulfilled in this new age.
5. Babel is reversed and the humanistic tendencies which conceived it are gone. All things have become new!

We may best sum up the Christian expectation of this New Jerusalem by appropriating the words of the last stanza of *Jerusalem the Golden* by Bernard of Cluny:

> *O sweet and blessed country,*
> *The home of God's elect!*
> *O sweet and blessed country*
> *That eager hearts expect!*
> *Jesus, in mercy bring us*
> *To that dear land of rest;*
> *Who art, with God the Father*
> *And Spirit, ever blest.*

Notes

1. On the use of the bride metaphor in the OT as an image of the people of God, cf. G.R. Beasley-Murray, *The Book of Revelation* (NCB; London: Oliphants, 1974) 309-10.
2. By N.W. Porteous, "Jerusalem-Zion: The Growth of a Symbol", in *Living the Mystery: N.W. Porteous, Collected Essays* (Oxford: Blackwell, 1967) 93-111.
3. Cf. J. Dougherty, *The Fivesquare City* (Notre Dame: Notre Dame University, 1980) 6.
4. J.M. Ford, "The Heavenly Jerusalem and Orthodox Judaism", in *Donum Gentilicum: Essays in Honour of David Daube*, ed. C.K. Barrett, E. Bammel and W.D. Davies (Oxford: Clarendon, 1978) 222. "Wall" as a metaphor for the people of God is elsewhere attested — the Qumran community made use of such imagery (IQS 8:7).
5. ibid, 222.
6. ibid.
7. Cf. J.C. De Young, *Jerusalem in the New Testament* (Kampen: Kok, 1960) 159.
8. Beasley-Murray, *Revelation*, 322-3.

9. P.R. Ackroyd, "Isaiah I-XII; Presentation of a Prophet", *VTSup* 29 (Leiden: Brill, 1978) 16-48.

10. Verses 18-20 are not placatory in the context. Cf. A.V. Hunter. *Seek the Lord! A Study of the Meaning and Function of the Exhortation in Amos, Hosea, Isaiah, Micah and Zephaniah* (Baltimore: St. Mary's Seminary and University, 1980) 191-9.

11. The connection between thrones set and judgement in the OT is drawn out by R. Knierim "The Vocation of Isaiah", *VT* 18 (1968) 53-4. Knierim also notes the striking correspondences between Isa 6 and the Judgement vision of Micaiah-ben-Imlah at 1 Kgs 22:19.

12. K. Joines ("Winged Serpents in Isaiah's Inaugural Vision", *JBL* 86 [1967] 410-15) has the evidence.

13. Knierim, "Vocation", 54-6.

14. W.J. Dumbrell, "Some Observations on the Political Origins of Israel's Eschatology", *RTR* 36 (1977) 38-9. The material of Isa 2:2-4 is contained in Mic 4:1-5 and thus seems anterior to both.

15. For the presentation of the Zion traditions and their evaluation in terms of their probable historical origins, cf. J.J.M. Roberts, "The Davidic Origin of the Zion Tradition", *JBL* 92 (1973) 329-44.

16. S. Erlandsson (*The Burden of Babylon* [ConBOT 4; Lund: CWK Gleerup, 1970] 102-5) notes this.

17. ibid, 96-97.

18. Roberts, "Isaiah in Old Testament Theology", *Int* 36 (1982) 142.

19. W. Millar, *Isaiah 24-27 and the Origin of Apocalyptic* (HSM 30; Missoula: Scholars, 1976) 30.

20. W.H. Irwin, *Isaiah 28-33, Translation with Philological Notes* (BibOr 30; Rome: Pontifical Biblical Institute, 1977) 30.

21. On the structure of Isa 40:1-11 note K. Kiesow, *Exodustexte im Jesajabuch* (Gottingen: Vandenhoeck and Ruprecht, 1979) 23-66.

22. ibid, 165.

23. ibid, 57-8.

24. As pointed out by W.A.M. Beuken, "*Mispat.* The First Servant Song in its Context", *VT* 22 (1972) 1-30.

25. P.D. Hanson, *The Dawn of Apocalyptic* (Philadelphia: Fortress, 1975) 32-208. Our indebtedness to his dissection of Isa 56-66 is acknowledged.

26. C. Westermann, *Isaiah 40-66* (OTL; London: SCM, 1969) 428.

27. We are dependent upon the outline of J.T. Willis, "The Structure of the Book of Micah", *SEA* 34 (1969) 15-42.

28. B. Albrektson, *Studies in the Text and Theology of the Book of Lamentations* (Lund: CWK Gleerup, 1963) 224.

29. ibid, 229.

30. ibid, 235-9.

31. Porteous ("Jerusalem-Zion", 97) notes this.

32. For the sequence of restoration messages commencing with Ezek 33:21 cf. R. Alexander, "A Fresh Look at Ezekiel 38-39", *JETS* 17 (1974) 157-70.

33. Cf. D. Baltzer, *Ezechiel und Deuterojesaja* (BZAW 121; Berlin: De Gruyter 1971) 28.

34. J. Levenson, *The Theology of the Program of Restoration of Ezekiel 40-48* (HSM 10; Missoula: Scholars, 1976) 25-36.

35. Hanson, *Dawn*, 317-20.

36. ibid, 315-6. So far as the remainder of the OT is concerned Dan 9 anticipates the temporary restoration of Jerusalem achieved in troublesome times. Chronicles is temple-centred, and thus Jerusalem centred.

37. For a survey of hopes built around the new Jerusalem concept in the Inter-testamentary literature, the Rabbinic writings and at Qumran, cf. A. Lincoln, *Paradise Now and Not Yet* (SNTSMS 43; Cambridge: Cambridge University, 1981) 19-21.

38. This is argued more extensively in W.J. Dumbrell, "The Logic of the Role of the Law in Matt 5:1-20", *NovT* 23 (1981) 1-21.

39. The arguments of G. Howard (*Paul: Crisis in Galatia* [SNTSMS 35; Cambridge: Cambridge University, 1979] 46-82) on the place of the law in Gal 3-4 should be noted.

40. A rebuilt and glorified Jerusalem is common in the Intertestamentary literature cf. Tob 13:9ff, 14:7, Jub 4:26 Sib Or 5:250ff, 414-433, Pss Sol 11:8 T Levi 10:5, T Dan 5:7, 12, 1QM XII:13ff 4QpIsa[a]1,7,11. A real correspondence to Paul's thought can be found only in much later Rabbinic literature, cf. B. Baba Bathra 75b, though it is clear that the 2nd century AD apocalypses of 4 Ezra (10:53ff, 13:35ff) and 2 Bar 6:9, 32:4, have a notion of a heavenly Jerusalem. On the question, cf. Lincoln, *Paradise*, 19-20.

41. ibid, 25.

42. A fuller exposition of this important passage is contained in W.J. Dumbrell, "The Spirits of Just Men Made Perfect", *EvQ* 48 (1976) 154-9.

43. For the particular ingredients bound up with the developed Zion theology cf. Roberts, "Davidic Origin", 329-44.

NEW TEMPLE — SUMMARY

In a vision replete with temple imagery, the New Temple is conspicuous by its absence in Rev 21-22. What accounts for this "absent presence"? As with each of our major themes, only a full consideration of its development within the OT, and subsequent refinement in the NT, will illuminate this paradox.

Initial investigation must focus on the tabernacle and in particular on the structure of the narrative which records its details and erection, Exod 25-31. Following the ratification of the covenant a plethora of images converge to identify the tabernacle's significance as nothing less than the seat of divine kingship, fashioned as a copy of the heavenly temple/palace. Thus the golden calf incident interrupts the building of the tabernacle since it entails a denial of Yahweh's rule. But acknowledgement of this lordship will secure peace in Israel's greater sanctuary, the promised land. Here the twin motifs of tabernacle and sabbath intertwine. The tabernacle symbolizes the presence of Yahweh the King who returns Israel to the Eden rest by transforming the promised land into a sanctuary.

Thus the temple can only be built after the gaining of "rest" from all of Israel's enemies. And this is evidenced by the fresh impetus for David to complete the conquest given by the arrival of the Ark, Yahweh's sacred throne, in Jerusalem. Continuity with the older structure is further demonstrated by the transferral of the Sinai traditions to the new building in 1 Kgs 8. But the temple was no talisman. Disregard for Yahweh's kingship could never annul its existence. Rather this same King would turn against his subjects, destroying his throne and profaning his sanctuary. This was the exile — without temple, land, or rest.

Yet as unequivocably as "the prophet astride the ages," Jeremiah, pronounced the temple's doom, Ezekiel projected its restoration. Structured around visions of the temple profaned, rejected and renewed in glory, the prophet conceives of the great King as leaving his throne to demolish it and then to return once more. But despite the appropriateness and relative success of the temple programmes under Haggai and Zechariah, Ezekiel's vision fills a far greater canvas. This structure is the world centre of the New Age, the inner sanctuary of the New Paradise.

How else then could Jesus enter the temple of his day than as the King? Moreover, he is this New Temple "made without hands" — "divinely constructed" by the resurrection. To him the redeemed people direct their worship. He is the one the world comes to in pilgrimage, for by his presence he makes his people a temple. No temple in the final vision of Revelation? Indeed there is, for the Lamb and God have come to dwell with their people.

2

THE NEW TEMPLE

The Presentation in Revelation 21-22

In describing the nature of the end-time city of Jerusalem, Rev 21:22 says explicitly that there was no temple there. However, in spite of this emphatic statement there is good ground for supposing that the symbolism associated with the concept and function of the temple in the OT period is present in these concluding chapters of the Bible. The theology bound up with the concept of the New Temple in the OT and NT also finds an unmistakable place.

First of all, as A.Y. Collins has noted,[1] the Jerusalem appendix to the book of Revelation (i.e., Rev 21:9-22:5) has been carefully constructed on the form and content of Ezek 40-48. Blending temple complex and holy city, the city of Ezekiel's expectation is clearly the New Jerusalem even though it is not named, probably for polemic reasons associated with the period. However, Zion and Jerusalem, temple and temple site itself, had been inextricably bound together in the OT. Thus at the conclusion of Ezek 40-48 the magnificence of the temple description, and the blessings conferred by its presence, is given its rationale by being fitted into the new city structure. The name of that end-time city, Ezekiel indicates, is fittingly *Yahweh Shammah*, "Yahweh is present". City and temple are therefore again associated in that developed eschatological presentation from which Rev 21 draws much of its material.

Secondly, the Holy City comes down as the abode of Yahweh, i.e., as the temple of Yahweh had been in the OT. He is thus enthroned in the New Jerusalem as he was in the OT temple. The point of approach to God is through entry into the New Jerusalem, as it was the temple in the OT. In short, in Rev 21 the concept of the sanctuary is enlarged to be co-extensive with the concept of "holy space" referred to in that

37

chapter. Jerusalem is the sacred shrine of the new heavens and the new earth, the place from which the glory of God radiates throughout the new universe. The New Jerusalem thus not only fulfils the political associations of kingdom (the place to which the tribes go up for decision, etc.) but includes sacral functions as well (the place where God and the Lamb rule and bless).

The association between Rev 21:10-27 and Ezek 40 is underlined. A heavenly guide in Rev 21 takes the seer on tour through the structure, carrying a measuring rod in his hand (v15 cf. Ezek 40:3). The ritual purity of Ezekiel, his emphasis on the exclusion of the profane, is observed thoroughly in connection with the exclusion of all that is unclean (Rev 21:27) from the New Jerusalem. The river of life flows in 21:1-2 from under the throne of God and the Lamb, just as it had flowed eastwards from under the threshold of the house in Ezek 47:1-12 with fertilizing force. Blessings of the same order as in Rev 22 proceed from its course.

Thus the total benefits of salvation associated with the presence of the temple in Ezek 40-48 are now associated with the New Jerusalem in Rev 21. In OT terms the expectation of a New Jerusalem without the rebuilding of the temple would have been unthinkable.[2] Indeed it is the presence of the temple (cf. Ezek 40-48 which makes Jerusalem the city of God (cf. Ps 46:5). In brief, we may assume all aspects of the temple symbolism have come together in this pattern of expectation of the last two chapters of the Bible. We may add as a note of emphasis that the idea of "glory", a temple characteristic (cf. Rev 21:23,26), is associated with the new city.

The Old Testament

i. *Tabernacle and Exodus*

We now review the OT evidence relating to the temple motif. In doing so it is necessary to commence with the concept as given in the projection and building of the tabernacle in the book of Exodus, since it is admitted that the later temple is simply a recognizable variant on this earlier shrine. The temple simply carries further the theological motifs expressed in the earlier structure. It is important to note that the account of the tabernacle is recorded in two sections in Exodus. First, the blueprint for its erection is given in Exod 25-31. We might expect the construction to have followed but for good reason to which later reference will be made it is deferred. Second, the account of the actual erection in chapters 35-40 is the note on which the book closes, and thus is presented as the climax of the book. More specifically the glory of God filling the tabernacle is the point on which the book concludes. Exodus begins with the question of the Abrahamic promises of land and progeny having been partly realized in the shape of Israel as a populous people. They are, however, enslaved but a threat to Egypt and in need of living space. Thus the progress of the book of Exodus to the building of the tabernacle is suggestive; a movement from slavery to the worship of him whose service is perfect freedom.

It has been made abundantly clear through the theophanies of the book of Genesis, that the presence of God was peculiarly associated with the land promised to Abraham. This is especially the case in the Jacob narratives where divine encounters are experienced by Jacob on leaving (Gen 28:10-22) and re-entering (chap. 32) the promised land. Divine assurances to the patriarchs have also served to make it patent that the land would only come to Israel as God's gift in God's time. No human striving would bring possession of Canaan. Moreover the gift of the land was originally made outside of the land itself, as bound up with Abraham's call. In short the promised land is God's land, his to dispose, his to give in his own time.

The book of Exodus thus commences with Israel populous yet enslaved and outside of the land. It concludes with the tabernacle constructed, with the cloud of glory overshadowing it, and the nation poised to march into Canaan. We are moving, as we have noted, from Israel enslaved to Israel at worship. Israel recognizes that her future manifestly depends upon her awareness of the need of God's presence in her midst and the realization of that need. Thus, we are not to see the construction of the tabernacle as an appendage to the book of Exodus. Rather it provides the controlling factor by which the significance of the Exodus event may be assessed. Therefore, far from being a mere priestly digression given over to petty cultic interests, the construction of the tabernacle gives point to the purpose of the act of the Exodus itself. Israel has been redeemed *from* Pharaoh, but redeemed *for* Yahweh. And the response expressing that redemption undergirds the theology which surrounds the construction of the tabernacle.

a. Exodus 15:1-18

However, before we turn to the question of the break in the account of the tabernacle erection, and offer reasons for it, we must discuss the redemption outlined in Exod 15 so far as it bears upon our topic. We will note later in chapter five that the details of this old hymn present the redemption of the Exodus as a New Creation. Our attention is drawn by the features of the hymn to the goal of the Exodus, which is the establishment of Israel in the promised land. This land is viewed in verse 17 as a sacred site, God's own mountain. The reference to the "mountain" does not convey with it an anticipation of later temple centralization at Jerusalem as some have argued, but in terms of Ps 78:54 is a reference to the land of Palestine viewed totally as a divine sanctuary.

Under this concept of a "holy mountain" we are dealing with old and pervasive ancient Near Eastern ideas. In the ancient world the dwelling place of the deity was thought to be on some inaccessible point where heaven and earth met. Such was Mt Olympus of Greek mythology or, nearer the point, the location of El, the head of the Canaanite pantheon on an inaccessible mountain at the "source of the double deeps" (i.e., where the upper and lower waters meet).

Such a cosmic centre formed the point of contact between heaven and earth. This was probably the intent of the Babylonian ziggurats, mountain-like in their configuration. Even in Egypt, though geographically featureless, the notion is found of a cosmic "hillock" where Amun-Re began creation.[3] A frequent allusion to the promised land (Heb. *makon* "place" Exod 15:17 cf. Deut 11:5 etc.), underlies the symbolism of Israel "planted in their place". Palestine is being emphasized as the special point of contact between heaven and earth, the sanctuary setting in which God will reveal himself to his people, and where in effect God will sit enthroned as world King. This point will be further developed below.

b. Sabbath and Creation

On the general question of the tabernacle in Exodus, however, we note that the two accounts (Exod 25-31, 35-40) conclude (in the first case) and begin (in the second) with an emphasis upon the keeping of the sabbath. This is significant. The "sabbath" in Gen 2:1-4a is bound up with the question of a perfected creation. Creation was actually finished or consummated on the seventh day. The seventh day thus brings the creation week to an end and therefore to its goal. While the Heb. root *sbt* can mean "cease" or "stop" the underlying note there is of what completes a sequence and thus gives it point or purpose.[4] Thus the building of the tabernacle, closely associated as it is with the keeping of the sabbath, completes the Exodus redemption and gives it this significance. We will have occasion later to note that in Gen 2:1-4a the concept of sabbath is associated with a notion involving "rest" or "perfection".

It is thus revealing that when the rationale for the keeping of the sabbath is offered in Exod 20:11 this notion of "sabbath rest" is brought into connection with a further important Hebrew theological concept of "rest" as dimension is added to the concept of sabbath and a link is provided between two distinct, but interrelated notions. In Exod 20:11 the Heb. noun $m^e nuhah$ occurs. This root does not occur in Gen 2:1-4a. It is now brought into connection with sbt "to rest". The meaning of this concept is not that expressed under the notion of sbt. It is rather "ease", "refreshment", life in an atmosphere where tensions have been withdrawn.[5]

Since from a qualitative perspective peace in God's presence is the goal of all human experiences, the two notions of rest associated with the sabbath in Exod 20:11 are not remote from each other. Heb. $nuah$ from which $m^e nuhah$ derives primarily has to do with the undisturbed, peaceful nature of the life of the people of God in the domain of God's gift, the land. It therefore conveniently expresses the goal or completion of God's promises and thus symbolizes their wider enjoyment. $Nuah$ and sbt are drawn together not only at 20:11 but also in 23:22. The notion of rest from labour, however, contained in the sabbath arrangement of 23:12 and 34:21 is a derivative idea arising from completion, and therefore not a primary concern.

By placing the tabernacle's erection in close association with an insistence upon the observation of the sabbath, we are reminded not only of the connections between sabbath and creation forged by Exod 20:11,[6] but also of the nature of Adam's sanctuary situation in Gen 2. This, in turn, furthers connections between the Tabernacle and the creation account. It is interesting to observe that in Ezek 28:11-15 the parallelism is clear between Eden as the garden of God (v13) and as the mountain of God (v14). Moreover, fabulous wealth (vv1-5) is descriptive of this situation (cf. Gen 2:6-14). Later, in connection with the temple, we will encounter the notion of the river of God fertilizing the earth, another concept developed from the Eden material.

It is enough, however, for our purposes here to point to the general connection made between sanctuary (tabernacle), creation and rest/sabbath.[7] If it is the presence of God in Eden which permits the garden to function as a sanctuary, then tabernacle/temple theology is designed to enable the promised land as a whole to serve as a sacred shrine. What is more, the resplendent description of the Prince of Tyre in Ezek 28:11-15 has long since been recognized not only to be dependent upon the Eden background, but also to have reference through the precious stones mentioned (v13) to the adornment of the breast-plate of the High Priest, the tabernacle officiant.[8] Indirectly the biblical writers may have thought Adam's role to have been priestly. We recognize that he is also portrayed in Gen 1 in a distinctively royal role.[9]

There is doubtless some connection between all of this and the charge given to Israel in Exod 19:5b-6 to function as a kingdom of priests. In the progressive separation in the OT between king and priest institutionally, both function as representative figures. The high priestly breast-plate points to the function of the high priest as intercessor and as representative of Israel as a whole, carrying the notion of a "royalty of priests" forward in an interesting direction.

c. Sinai Covenant

There is need to return now to the specific function of the tabernacle within the covenant account of Exodus. The blueprint to build is offered to Moses as the conclusion of the covenant ratification in Exod 24. In short, this forms the divine response to that ceremony. The concept of the tabernacle thus expresses the unity of Israel as a worshipping community under covenant, echoing the frequently reiterated OT ideal, "My dwelling place will be with them; and I will be their God, and they will be my people" (cf. Ezek 37:27). This is essentially restated in Rev 21:3. God's presence in Israel, however, is kingly, a point which Exod 19:5b-6 has made clear. As have, it might be added, the possible master/servant features deducible from the ancient Near Eastern treaty format to which we believe the account of Exod 19-34 is substantially indebted. Moreover, the notion of Yahweh's kingship over Israel is explicitly stated in 15:18.

The tabernacle and the later temple thus function as a royal dwelling and it is therefore apparent why its "pattern" must descend from heaven, and why the heavenly genesis of the idea is so emphasized in Exodus. Temple/tabernacle and palace are thus united functions. The intention of this first tabernacle account is now clear. Israel is to respond in worship and this response is to take the primary form of acknowledging sovereignty; God's kingship over Israel and the world. The presence of the tabernacle in Israel's midst is a primary reminder of Israel's role. In other words, worship is the protocol by which one may enter the divine presence, and it is in this connection that we may now notice the interesting gradations of approach reflected in the tabernacle design and furnishings.

M. Haran[10] has argued that the gradation in holiness expressed by the divisions between the outer court of the tabernacle, the holy place, and the holy of holies, corresponded to a gradation of furnishings and dress dependent upon the position of the officiant in the complex or the location of the item of furniture. He has also raised the interesting possibility that ritual acts within the tabernacle took seriously the concept of a present sovereign. Catering to the various senses (smell, taste, touch, sight, etc.,) these rites were designed to provide for all possible divine needs in this anthropomorphic transfer. Haran argues that the nature of tabernacle ritual underscores the nature of the divine presence associated with the tabernacle.

d. Construction Interrupted

The heinous Israelite sin of the golden calf narrated in Exod 32 suspended the intention to erect the tabernacle. In Exod 33 God seems to turn away from Israel in general and to be inclined to continue his Abrahamic call through the person of Moses alone. Though the command is given for Israel to proceed to the promised land under the leadership of Moses, God will not be present in their midst (vv1-6). Verses 7-11 seem to be a slight digression, yet they function to emphasize Israel will now have contact with Yahweh only through Moses, at the tent of meeting (not to be identified or confused with the tabernacle).[11] The Lord makes it plain that his presence will be with Moses personally, but not with Israel generally (vv12-23). Moses appeals for confirmation of this with a request to behold God's glory; God's hiddenness, the depths of what has not so far been revealed, the essence of the divine character. God in effect declines this request (v19) but promises that the revelation of the name given in 3:14 will be renewed in Moses' own experience.

In short, the glory associated with the tabernacle and temple, the dark heavy cloud suggesting immanence and yet transcendence, cannot be penetrated in the OT even by one such as Moses. Yet the name will be revealed, which indicates the gracious openness of God in revelation. The terrifying manifestation of the divine presence through theophany, the clouds and darkness which are round about him, reminds us in the OT that God is the subject of respectful awe. True, Moses' shining face (Exod 34:29-35) is a reflection of this glory, but at the same time when the tabernacle is finally constructed and filled with the glory cloud, Moses cannot enter for that reason (40:34-35).[12]

While God's glory remains hidden, revelation through the name continues. The covenant is renewed with heavy emphasis on Moses as mediator since the commandments are delivered afresh (Exod 34) and the position of Moses confirmed (vv29-35). The sabbath command, which concludes Exod 25-31, is restated at the beginning of chapter 35 to emphasize the continuity of chapters 35-40 with 25-31. As the earthly palace of the heavenly king the tabernacle is then erected and filled with glory (chaps. 35-40).

ii. *Tabernacle and Conquest*

The portable tabernacle borne by delegated priestly families was a feature of Israel's worship until the early monarchical period. Its place in the centre of the camp with the tribes arranged four-square around it (Num 2) emphasized the centrality in Israel's experience of the divine kingship to which it pointed. It also emphasized the manner of Israel's response to this "church in the wilderness" situation (cf. Acts 7:38). No significant move to locate the tabernacle permanently takes place until 2 Sam 7. The reasons for which it is done there are theologically interesting and we will examine them in due course. Nevertheless, a principle of centralization with regard to the tabernacle appears as early as the book of Deuteronomy (cf. Deut 12:1-14). Since the idea of a defined central sanctuary does not accord with the known facts of Israel's pre-settlement experience it is often suggested that centralist material of this kind is really an addition stemming from the later reforms of Josiah (2 Kgs 22-23). It is normally suggested that this concept was written into Deuteronomy at a time when older material was being redated.

Two responses seem necessary here. The first relates to the association of the tabernacle to the centrality legislation of Deut 12; note the clause "God will cause his name to dwell there" (v5). Along with a doctrine of centrality, it is suggested that there was a move by the "Deuteronomist school" to replace an older and cruder immanistic theology of God, as associated with the tabernacle, with a more theologically elevated doctrine. Yahweh himself would not be present at the centralised sanctuary, only his name, his *alter ego* (Deut 21:11 etc.).[13] However, such a degree of sophistication is neither necessary nor warranted to explain the occurrence of the phrase "to cause the name to dwell". For it has become clear that the expression is an old ownership formula attested extra-biblically which says nothing about the nature of the divine presence at the sanctuary. It merely affirms divine ownership and thus asserts the kingship which stands behind the sanctuary.[14]

Secondly, there is no hard evidence to suggest that the central sanctuary of Deut 12 was a sole sanctuary. But the issue of the interpretation of this chapter is still open since it is just as feasible to interpret the wording of the relevant section distributively,[15] i.e., as referring to a principle of centrality which could be expressed for the time being by any one of a number of possible sites (though the evidence of vv15-28 suggests that they may have been few). Centrality for the time being may have been determined by the festival with which a particular sanctuary was associated, by the needs of a particular convocation (cf. Bethel at Judg 20:27), by the location of the ark and tabernacle, or by some other reason unknown to us. Shechem, Gilgal, Bethel, Shiloh all seem to have served in this capacity, each being associated with particular facets of Israel's early experience.

iii. *From Tabernacle to Temple*

We may pass over the intervening historical period and turn now to the transition from tabernacle to temple which comes under David. The books of Samuel have this movement as their theme. 1 Samuel begins with Israel worshipping at a debased sanctuary depicted not only in terms of the irregularities manifested in chapters 1-3; but behind Shiloh also stands the atrocities committed there by Israel in Judg 21. 2 Sam 24 concludes with David's purchase of the temple site from Araunah the Jebusite. This movement has as its aim the re-establishment through temple emphasis of a proper understanding of Yahweh's kingship in Israel.

Clearly the theology of divine kingship declined in terms of public commitment during the period of the Judges. Paradoxically, Israel's survival at that time depended on Yahweh's royal interventions, yet the basic character of these actions had left little lasting impression upon the thought of the age. Nevertheless, miraculously and totally unexpectedly and in spite of all Israelite attempts at self-destruction, the end of the Judges period leaves us with the concept of a divinely preserved Israel (cf. Judg 21:25). All the disorders of the Judges period had made it clear that Israelite governmental structures more expressively demonstrate belief in Yahweh's kingship. The erection of kingship, modified and refined by Samuel and Nathan in 1 and 2 Samuel, was designed to throw into bold relief the nature of the rule that stood behind Israel's institutions. If eventually it had a quite different effect this could not be attributed to an inadequate theological base for Israelite kingship but to human abuse of the institution. We labour this point since in the first place Israelite kingship and Jerusalem temple will be seen as inextricably linked and secondly the movement in the books of Samuel is towards these two entities. How did this work out in Israel's life?

The shrine at Shiloh at which the ark and its habitation were semi-permanently located was debased. Set side by side with this is the emerging figure of Samuel, the man who is being raised up to meet the crisis evoked by such national attitudes to worship. Samuel, as we note in detail, becomes Israel's saviour and is eventually instrumental in the appointment of Saul as Israel's first king. The thoroughly tentative nature of Saul's kingship is made plain by the absence of the ark from Israel for twenty years during his reign (cf. 1 Sam 7:2 and 2 Sam 6). His well-meaning attempts to maintain power are offset by his theological obtuseness in the early encounters with Samuel, which make it clear that Saul was not the carrier of a dynasty. David's rise to power is completed in 2 Sam 5 with his defeat of the Philistines and capture of Jerusalem. This firmer theological arrangement in support of David's kingship eventually resulted in the establishment of the Davidic covenant reported in 2 Sam 7.

iv. *Kingship and Temple*

However, we are interested in the movements of this period only so far as they bear upon the temple theology of the OT. Israel was aware that kingship had come to her later than her neighbours and more limited in its extent. She was also aware that her future was very much in the hands of Yahweh, to whom she turned for guidance. The return of the ark in 2 Sam 6 indicated Yahweh was once again willing to place himself at the centre of Israel's life. This is clear from the manner of the return and Yahweh's clear endorsement of it. The theological interlude of the past twenty years is complete. In that time the ark had been at Kiryath-Jearim and had represented the repository of the covenant traditions.[16]

The events of 2 Sam 6 showed that Yahweh was once again the disposer of Israel's history and was now willing to endorse the city of Jerusalem as sacred space, David's own city. David's attempts to bring the ark back had been initially unsuccessful, in fact disastrous. It was not until a visible sign of blessing accompanied the location of the ark in the house of Obed-Edom the Gittite that David had ventured to move the ark onwards again. The joyful reception which the ark received on its return (v15) defined it as the pre-eminent Israelite cultic object. Its return also heralded a new departure in relationships for the house of David since, in the closing verses of chapter 6, the house of Saul in the shape of David's wife Michal is rejected from participation in the Davidic succession. Thus the ill-based kingship of Saul which had not been associated with the sacral symbols of the kingdom was brought to a formal close by Michal's dismissal from the court.

Ancient Near Eastern connections between dynastic kingship and temple must now be explored. In Egypt the king was divine and represented the basic principle of order. It was he who wielded power to maintain the static order of creation (*maat*) by which world structures were regulated. In Mesopotamia and Palestine the concept of divine kingship did not prevail. Like Israelite kingship, Mesopotamian rule was god-given. The king in the Mesopotamian city-state system was the servant, the steward of the deity whose temple within the city-state complex represented the final locus of governmental order. Since the image of the deity was located in the Mesopotamian temples they were regarded as signifying his presence. Temple, as preserver of stability in the god-given social order, and kingship, as the human arm by which that stability was maintained, were the Mesopotamian order.

From this perspective we may note again the logic of the order of 2 Sam 6 and 7. Yahweh must first endorse Jerusalem before the matter may be taken further by David in 7:1.[17] We note that the impulse for the building of a house for Yahweh arose from the fact that Yahweh "gave rest to David from all his enemies round about" (v1). Just as building the tabernacle was the fitting climax to the Exodus redemption and pointed to its meaning, so here the question of building a temple comes as the consummation of the conquest now finalized by David's defeat of the Philistines in chapter 5. We may also note by way of anticipation that in Ezek 40-48 the building of the temple comes as the consummation of all things, the goal of eschatology and follows the final eschatological battle (chaps. 38-39).

The association of the ark with rest in 2 Sam 7:1 therefore, simply continues the relationship mentioned in Num 10:33 where the ark of the covenant determined Israel's "resting place" (Heb. $m^e huhah$) during the wilderness wandering period. The ark's significance in the allotment of the promised land is noted by R.A. Carlson. He refers to

Josh 3:11 where at the Jordan crossing the ark is named "the ark of the covenant of the Lord of all the earth".[18] The role of the ark in the conquest is also attested by its function in the fall of Jericho (Josh 6). Our attention is further directed to the pointed observation in Josh 18:1 that the distribution of Israel's inheritance of the land coincided with the erection of the tabernacle at Shiloh. Consistently the themes of rest, centrality and cult had been carefully interwoven in Deut 12:1-10.[19]

Additionally, Ps 132 provides a liturgical commentary upon 2 Sam 6 and 7 disclosing the search for the ark and its subsequent return to Jerusalem: a clear endorsement of the Davidic house. Verse 8 may well have a movement to Jerusalem in mind for it may be translated "Arise O Lord, and go up from your dwelling place". From this perspective the Psalm forges a secure connection between the ark and the notion of rest (cf. v14). The Psalm therefore brings together the concepts of ark, rest, dwelling, throne and temple, as interrelated terms bound up finally with the choice of Zion and David. David is thus to understand the nature of this "rest" which is to be related to his present building initiative and he is to realize that Israel's worship structure should reflect this understanding.

a. David and the Building of the Temple

It seems clear that David understands his subordinate role in the political life of the nation after 2 Sam 6. His first concern is therefore to capitalize upon the divinely given stability and to build a temple to symbolize the real factor ensuring national continuance. Only a proper acknowledgement of Yahweh's kingship will promise security as David perceived in 7:1. In this same verse the three key terms of "rest", "dwelling" and "house" are raised, all of them contingent upon divine blessing. Nathan, whose prophetic advice must be sought, is at first encouraging, but then requires modification in the light of further revelation (v5).

The reply in 2 Sam 7:5 functions in two ways. First, it throws into clear relief the nature of the temple builder. It is "my servant" David who is addressed. So far this is a title which has been given only to Moses (Exod 14:31), Caleb (an energizer of the conquest, Num 14:24) and Joshua (as a "second" Moses, Josh 24:29). David's leadership role is further emphasized by reference in 2 Sam 7:11 to the fact that what the Judges had been unable to do (i.e., complete the conquest) David accomplished, or at least had set in motion. David has also been described in surrogate terms as Yahweh's representative (in 5:2) — as Israel's shepherd. The reply (7:5) thus sets David before us in exalted terms. Second, however, the reply refuses David permission to build.

In view of David's stature this refusal is often regarded as puzzling, and reasons for it are usually sought within 2 Sam 7:5. Because of the similarity between verses 5 and 13 (note the emphatic pronouns Heb. *attah* "you" and *hu* "he" in vv5,13 and the verb to build *banah* in both verses) the "you" in verse 5 must bear considerable emphasis. Certainly there is a rejection here of the sufficiency of any human initiative in the matter of temple building. No mere human may undertake this course without prior divine commissioning. The true builder of the temple and indeed the builder of the true temple is God himself. In the more limited sense however it is a rejection of David as builder for reasons still to be discerned, yet is not an outright refusal to endorse a temple; verse 13 makes that clear. Temple building as a human exercise therefore is not rejected in the final sense of the word.

Others suggest it would be offensive to the prophetic consciousness to build a temple, since prophetic theology belonged to the older tribal league whose point of reference in worship was the mobile tabernacle (cf. 2 Sam 7:6). This can hardly be allowed, however, since the movement of Yahweh to Jerusalem (occurring in chap. 6) is the endorsement of Jerusalem as sacred space and was thus the precursor to temple building. Others have located Yahweh's refusal in disapproval of David's understanding of the nature of the temple as merely a house which Yahweh will indwell — or in which he will be enthroned, if we were to give Heb. *yasab* "to dwell" the customary meaning which it has in divine references in the OT. This last point is valid as is indicated by the dedication narrative of 1 Kgs 8, though it does not sufficiently explain the refusal to build. The temple will be a symbol of the presence. However, the divine presence must never be presumed upon.

The detail of the following verses need not be developed more exhaustively except to note that 2 Sam 7:6-9 traces the history of David's rise to power and makes it clear his role and influence are to be seen as the physical fulfilment of the promises to Abraham (cf. Gen 12:2 and the "great name" which God "will make" for David). 2 Sam 7:9b-11 deals with the future of the Davidic dynasty. The establishment of David's great name will be followed by the appointment of a "place for Israel" in which they will dwell securely. Since Heb. *maqom* "place" is the word often used to describe the promised land (cf. Deut 11:24; Josh 1:3), David's great name will also mean Israel's secure occupancy of its allotted territory. All this will be followed by the rest God will give (2 Sam 7:11), a notion clearly associated with the gift of the land in the completed sense of a final conquest (cf. v10). "Rest" (v11) will ensure a stable dynasty for David but more importantly presupposes divine kingship.

We note, however, that the concentration on temple has now been replaced with the Davidic dynasty by a play on the word "house" (Heb. *bayit*), the common word for temple in the sense of "inner shrine" in the OT. Heb. *bayit* can also function metaphorically, and embody the sense of "lineage". Nevertheless, 2 Sam 7 contains all the ingredients of emerging temple theology. The temple in Israel expresses the political rule of Yahweh over his people, necessarily subordinating the messianic king. It does not bind Yahweh in terms of static location, but can only arise from a divine decision and is thus not seen as a mere concomitant of earthly kingship. Given its representative and political role as an endorsement of the promised land as a whole, presumably it may only come when the promised land exists as an entity. The temple will secure the Davidic line but David will not build it (one must not miss the oblique reference to Gen 15:13 in the note of "seed" in 2 Sam 7:12). He cannot, it seems, for David's role is to be the builder of the empire not the temple.

b. Davidic Covenant Promises

The emphasis in 2 Sam 7 is therefore on David as conqueror and provider of "rest". 1 Kgs 5:3-4 indicates, however, that David deferred building because he lacked opportunity. The Kings account is clarified in 1 Chron 22:8 (cf. 1 Chron 28:3) which ascribes the reason to his preoccupation with bloody conquest. This is confirmed in the present sequence in 2 Samuel by the account of David's wars which follows in chapters 8-10, obviously structured theologically rather than chronologically. The eternal kingship to be given to the Davidic line is referred to in absolute terms in 2 Sam 7:13b. Though the line may be chastened in terms of particular individuals (v14), these covenantal promises will not fail (note the use of the word *hesed* "mercy" or, sometimes, "covenant loyalty" in v15).

There is good warrant for supposing that 2 Sam 7 provides the account of the "Davidic Covenant". Even though the word *bᵉrit* "covenant" does not occur in chapter 7 it does in material which reflects upon the chapter (2 Sam 23:5 and Ps 89:33-38). The ambivalence in the OT between the unconditional nature of the promises to David (2 Sam 23:5; Ps 89:33-38) and the conditional nature of the Davidic covenant (Pss 89:29-32; 132:12; 1 Kgs 2:4; 8:25; 9:4-5) does not create difficulties. It simply reflects the absolute character of the promise and the historical situation in which it was applied. In general terms, the line would not fail. Yet in particular terms its benefits might be withdrawn from individuals. Indeed, the result of 587 BC, the fall of Jerusalem, and the contribution of abject leadership to that fall, is the virtual end of the physical line of David. In eschatological terms, however, as we well know, there was to be a "great David's greater Son".

Of course, David appears in 2 Sam 7 as Israel's representative. This note will be picked up elsewhere when Israel in particular is being discussed. One further point must be made for our present purposes from the prayer of David (2 Sam 7:18-29) which responds to the first half of the same chapter. The tenor of this prayer indicates that David well understood the issues involved in Nathan's prophecy. We cannot treat this prayer in detail.

Introduced in 2 Sam 7:18, it is summarized by the important but difficult verse 19 containing the puzzling Heb. phrase $w^e zo't$ $torat$ $ha'adam$ (literally "and this is the law of man"). It needs to be remembered that the Heb. $torah$ is a word with a wide range of meaning basically having the sense of "guidance" or "direction" rather than the full legal overtones of our English word "law". There is some doubt whether verse 19b is to be taken as a statement or as a question (cf. the English translations). By carefully analysing the occurrences of the phrase $w^e zo't$ $torat$ plus genitive, W.C. Kaiser[20] has shown that verse 19b must be taken as a statement and that the Heb. phrase concerned served to introduce or to summarize (as here) a set of divine instructions. Under the "this" David has in mind the promises of the first half of the chapter. That is to say, what must precede the building of the temple and what will result from it. The "law of man" sets forth as far as David understood the 2 Sam 7 promise implications for the future. This puzzling phrase "law of man" has been shown to be paralleled by the similar Akk. $terit$ $nise$ which carries the meaning of a "fateful oracle for man".[21] The Akk. term carries the notion of an utterance which controls or provides destiny for mankind. This sense fits the Samuel context well. Kaiser has thus suggested that the phrase in 2 Sam 7:19b be understood as "this is the charter by which humanity will be directed."[22]

David correctly sees that the future and the destiny of the human race are involved in the promises delivered to him. These promises have been built upon the broad history of covenant concepts developed from creation onwards. David has thus seen the full implications connected with temple and kingship in the history of salvation.

We should not be surprised to find that in 2 Sam 7 we are dealing with a broad cross-section of biblical ideals. The age of David saw the zenith of Israel's historical fortunes. For example, chapters 8-10 detail the impressive extent of the Davidic empire. However, the Abrahamic boundaries were in fact not fully achieved.[23] This serves to remind us that the political hopes which rested upon the temple symbolism were never realized in the OT period. Under Solomon, Israel's heightened political splendour is world-impressive (cf. 1 Kgs 10), a fact recognized by the application of Abrahamic fulfilment terminology (cf. 4:20

which alludes to the united kingdom in Abrahamic terms as multitudinous and happy; note also the "rest" concept in 5:4). But the rest which was to be the reality of the promises for the people of God still remained unexperienced and even the magnificence and pomp of the Solomonic period could not disguise the fact that the kingdom of Israel would not endure politically. The books of Kings are in fact concerned to display its gradual dissolution, as we will note in detail later.

c. Monarchical Period

With 1 Kgs 8 we return to a further important temple item, namely the consecration of the finished structure, seven years in the building. At the dedication of the temple, the ark and thus with it the transfer of the Sinai traditions is deposited in the inner sanctum. The presence of the cloud-glory symbolism stresses continuity in the theology applicable to both Temple and Tabernacle (Exod 19:9-25; 40:34-38; 1 Kgs 8:11). The emphasis in this dedication upon the temple as a house of prayer is an emphasis on God's leadership in Israel's affairs. Prayer is to be directed to the house and to the concepts it enshrines. In all of this, the emphasis of 1 Kgs 8 upon Yahweh's endorsement of Israel's sacred traditions is confirmatory of 2 Sam 7 (the chapter itself makes this clear cf. 1 Kgs 8:15). Yahweh's presence associated with the temple makes it clear that an unbroken covenant relationship with the Sinai structures continues for Israel, thus ensuring a future for national Israel as the people of God. Without that presence there can be no future. Consistently, Solomon's prayer (vv22-61) makes it plain that even when national sin has reached its ultimate end in exile, prayer directed towards the place where God has set his name will be efficacious.

As for the art motifs of the temple, its walls were adorned with figures of the guardian cherubim, palm trees and flowers (1 Kgs 6:29,32). In this way the meaning of the garden sanctuary was graphically transferred (cf. Ps 92:13; cf. Ezek 28:13; Isa 54:12).[24] Yahweh's presence in the temple established it in Zion as the centre of the universe (as many of the Zion Psalms make plain).[25] Also interesting is the old poetic fragment, 2 Kgs 8:12-13, reconstructed with the aid of the LXX, as descriptive of the nature of Yahweh's indwelling. The creator of the universe has set the sun in the heavens but condescends to fix his throne in the midst of his people Israel. His nearness and readily experienced power, however, do not exhaust the revelation of himself. He still dwells in thick darkness hence the association of glory with the temple.

But the building of the temple also confirms the election of Jerusalem. What began in 2 Samuel 6 in terms of both place and dynasty is now authenticated. The Exodus traditions are transferred to this sacred mount which then became representative for all Israel. Zion is now the cosmic centre, the point of contact between heaven and earth. Accordingly, the ark loses its significance and will not be replaced after its presumed destruction in 587BC, since it is clear from 1 Kgs 8:16 that the act of Davidic dynasty centralization is the climax of the conquest just as the building of the temple is the consummation of the Sinai covenant. The Sinai tenor of the dedication is carefully brought out in 1 Chron 29:10-20. David appears in the posture of a second Moses assembling willing givers for the building of God's house (cf. Exod 35:20-29).[26] But the Chronicles account reveals this temple is God's "citadel" (Heb. *birah*, cf. 1 Chron 29:1), thereby pronouncing a patent political note; the temple is built for God not for man.

With the acceptance of this theology of the presence and the supremacy of Jerusalem and its temple in the divine political designs for his people, the importance of Jerusalem begins to grow in prophetic eschatology. This has been dealt with in our treatment of the New Jerusalem. Until the exilic period, however, the temple does not figure largely in the historical narratives. This is an ominous omission in the narratives of 1 and 2 Kings which are concerned with the decline and fall of historical kingship. Clearly the function of the temple was corrupted and diminished, so that mention of it is largely restricted to either the plundering of the Temple by conquerors — (1 Kgs 14:25-26, 2 Chron 12:9 — Shishak of Egypt; 1 Kgs 15:18 cf. 2 Chron 16:2 — Ben Hadad of Syria; 2 Kgs 12:18 — Hazael of Syria; 2 Kgs 14:14 — Jehoash of Israel) — or the association of pious kings with thorough-going temple reforms, predominantly Hezekiah and Josiah.

The historical end of the temple came with the advent of Babylonian power. Early in his reign Nebuchadezzar foreshadowed the end by taking vessels from the house of the Lord to Babylon (Dan 1:2). Total destruction of the temple occured in 587BC. But Judah received fair warning through Jeremiah. Particularly in his temple sermon (Jer 7 and 26, 609BC; cf. 26:1-19), Jeremiah inveighed against the popular view which regarded the temple as a sort of talisman. In the common mind the existence of the temple in Jerusalem guaranteed the inviolability of that city. Yahweh would never destroy the sanctuary which is called by his name! Jeremiah warned Judah, however, that the temple would suffer the same fate as Shiloh (cf. Ezek 8-11). We gather from this that the degree of corruption in the Jerusalem temple in the time of Jeremiah was approximate to that of the Shiloh period! The Josianic reforms notwithstanding!

In Jer 7:1-5 the prophet reverses the popular opinion. They must protect the temple, the temple will not protect them! There is a designed play in this passage on the word "place" (Heb. *maqom*). In verse 3, spoken to the men of Judah who are entering the temple precincts, Jeremiah issues a call to repentance. If they mend their ways then they may expect to continue to dwell in the land; note the further use of "place" in verse 7 in the old Deuteronomic sense of "land". In short, the preservation of the temple by piety protects that which gives the land its character of a promised land.

T.W. Overholt had noted[27] that Jeremiah presents Yahweh's case against the Jerusalem worshippers in the form of a legal brief. Within this form Jer 7:1-2 is an instruction to the prophet, verses 3-4 contain the details of the brief (no trust in the physical presence of the temple), verses 5-11 take note of the social actions generated by a false sense of security occasioned by the presence of the temple, and verses 12-15 expose the character of their false assumptions by the example of what happened to Shiloh under parallel circumstances. In this structure verses 5-7 contain the stipulations of the covenant and verses 8-11 are the prophetic accusation based upon the popular rejection of these basic covenant concepts. Jeremiah is thus calling for a radical reassessment of national direction.

The destruction of the Shiloh sanctuary had been occasioned by a wanton attitude to Yahweh's rule, a contempt displayed by the conduct of worship at the shrine. So also in Jerusalem. This house is called by God's name. In other words it is identified with God's revelation in history and thus with his rule (cf. Jer 7:7,10,11,14). If Yahweh's sovereignty is spurned, then the symbol of that sovereignty must necessarily be destroyed. God would annihilate this temple. Even the ark would never be missed (cf. 3:16) since symbolism without reality is of no value. Nowhere in his prophecy does Jeremiah hold out any hope for the erection of a new temple. God will indwell his people again by a new covenant. In 31:31-34 there is no mention of that presence associated with a new temple. We simply note in passing that a similar silence concerning the Jerusalem temple occurs in the book of Isaiah. Isa 56-66 reports misplaced attitudes to the (restored?) temple (66:1) in keeping with those denounced in Jer 7 although the subject is not elaborated.

v. *Ezekiel*

a. Initial Visions

If restoration only plays a slight role in Jeremiah it is dominant in Ezekiel, a supremely temple-centred book. With Jeremiah, Ezekiel categorically turned his back on those left behind after the initial deportation in 597BC in which Ezekiel was involved. Like Jeremiah, Ezekiel addressed a people who refused to accept the impending reality that God would forsake his Jerusalem sanctuary (Ezek 1-24), even though this symbol of his presence had become so denigrated as to provide a centre for idolatry (8:6). Therefore these two issues, misplaced trust in the temple and its certain destruction, are major issues in the first half of the book. The significance of this message must be evaluated in two ways. First, in the light of the extreme interest Ezekiel displays in the temple. Second, it must be correlated with the fact that the eschatology of chapters 40-48 is almost totally directed towards the erection of a new temple. Our initial attention, however, must be given to the earlier "temple visions".

It is clear temple language and imagery dominate the first chapter of the book. The similarity of the mobile throne vision of Ezekiel 1 to the call narrative of Isaiah 6 has often been noted, and the two chapters are parallel in terms of a common temple perspective.[28] Both passages reveal after a dating reference how each prophet is overwhelmed by a vision of the glory of Yahweh. An ominous mood is present in each at the commencement of the vision. The substance of the visions is basically the same. Ezek 1:1-14 depicts Yahweh's portable ark-throne borne as expected by the cherubim (cf. Ps 18:10; note the precise identification of the "living creatures" as cherubim at Ezek 10:15,20,22). To digress slightly, it is noteworthy that at the commencement of his prophecy Ezekiel's theology is moving in concepts which exalt Yahweh's kingship and which ante-dated the monarchy and the first temple (cf. the ark-throne depicted in 1 Sam 4:4). Such a concept although liturgically preserved (cf. Pss 24, 96, 132, etc.) did not find frequent expression later in the Jerusalem royal court theology.

Thus the throne appears both in Isa 6 and Ezek 1. A heavenly dwelling place from which the vision emanates is clearly implied by Ezek 1:1, just as Isa 6 is best understood as a prophetic vision of a heavenly judgement scene. In Isa 6 the judgement motifs are obvious; on the other hand, in Ezekiel the motifs are clearly inferential. Were we in any doubt, the subsequent course of Ezekiel's prophecy serves to validate the judgement character of this first vision. Both Isaiah and

Ezekiel place great emphasis upon the divine majesty and transcendence by their respective use of background and imagery. Ezek 1:4-28 is bonded by verses 4 and 26-28 as a unit; the details of verse 4 (storm, surrounding brightness, and the gleam of electrum)[29] are described in the reverse order in verses 27-28. The storm images promote continuity with the old theophanic traditions. Further, the northern origin of the theophany, the mysterious place which was the threatening and portentous area in the exilic period, underscores the fact that in this theophany Judah will be called to account.[30] Specifically, Yahweh has moved out from his heavenly palace and is proceeding in imminent judgement. Thus the often cited similarity to Isa 6 is not misplaced.

Ezek 1 sets the tone for the book. The chapter is not only glory centred (emphasizing divine sovereignty) but temple directed and it is not surprising to find that the second prophetic vision of judgement has much the same emphasis. In chapters 8-11 the prophet is brought in Spirit to Jerusalem. These units present a vision of judgement about to befall the Jerusalem temple and serve to place chapter 10 in prominence.[31] Verse 1 is concerned with the arrival of the throne of God at the Jerusalem temple. Since the details almost exactly parallel 1:26 we may deduce that the judgement in 10:1 is the specific continuation of the general vision of chapter 1. As judgement begins in the house of God the incense coals purge (Ezek 10:2) rather than cleanse (Isa 6:6). The glory cloud filling the temple at Ezek 10:4 is again ominously reminiscent of the incense and smoke which filled the house resulting from the divine presence in judgement in Isa 6. A detailed account of the cherubim follows in Ezek 10:8-17 during which our attention moves back from the threshold to the waiting divine chariot. In verses 18-19 the glory of the Lord moves from the sanctuary to the chariot and thus the temple, the most sacred symbol of all Israel, is abandoned.

b. Vision of the New Temple

From this dramatic rejection of the temple, we turn to the grandiose new temple vision of Ezek 40-48, in which a radical break with the political past is asserted. While the high mountain in Israel to which the prophet is brought by the Spirit in 40:2 is not identified, the thought is somewhat similar to 17:22-24 where the scion of the house of David is .to be plucked from the tip of the cedar tree planted on a high mountain. In view of the Davidic tenor of chapter 17, the mountain of Ezek 40:1 seems to be Mt Zion.[32] This conclusion and its application to chapters

40-48 is further confirmed by the activity of the man with the measuring rod (40:5), an activity associated with the measurement of Jerusalem in Zech 2:1-4.

Yet the theology of Ezek 40-48 is hardly Zion or Davidic centred despite the earlier connections. Dealing with the character of the ideal Israel these chapters draw their particular theological stance from the remote past, particularly the period of the tribal confederation. Since the vision represents a new beginning in these terms, a possibility exists that Sinai characteristics are also to be associated with this mountain. This becomes increasingly evident as the blueprint for the new temple emerges from heaven, as the *tabnit* "pattern" for the older tabernacle had. There is probably a confluence of traditions here, all of which underscore the emphasis placed upon divine kingship in these chapters. Just as the building of the tabernacle completed the Exodus and was its logical conclusion, eschatology is dominated here by the construction of the new temple. Just as the meaning of the Exodus was proclaimed in the "cultic" response of Israel to divine kingship, so here the new temple will function as Yahweh's kingly setting in the new holy city.

The vision begins with a precise description of the temple, in fact minute in its precision, emphasizing the writer's absorption with the concept. Moving from the outer wall (Ezek 40:5-16) to the outer court (vv17-27), then on to the inner court (40:28-41:26), returning to the outer court (42:1-14), we finally conclude the tour outside the outer wall (vv15-20).[33] Standing at the centre of the material is the structure of the house itself (40:48-41:26). The elaborate symmetry, its continuity with and yet distinction from the temple of Solomon, the emphasized use of symbolic numbers (etc.), all serve to indicate that we are moving in these pictures from what has been historically experienced to eschatology. Herein the central notion of worship controls the response of the perfected people of God. Thus, at this point, the temple vision serves to emphatically state the general tenor of Ezekiel's eschatology.

H.D. Parunak[34] notes the temple tour recommences with a reference to the divine presence (cf. Ezek 43:2), phrased in clear echoes of the older Sinai encounter. Summaries of that encounter (cf. Deut 33:2; Judg 5:4; Ps 68:8; Hab 3:3,4) have two features which are emphasized in Ezek 43:1-5: one, the Lord approaches from the east since Israel is coming from the west (i.e., Egypt); and two, the manifestation of the divine presence is thunderously audible. Verses 3-4 take us back to the prophet's earlier visions (chaps 1-2, 9-10). The cumulative message of these visions is a presentation of Israel's history and her future. The apostate nation is to be judged and then restored to the land under divine kingship. In the inner court two prophetic pronouncements are delivered concerning the temple (43:5-44:3) and its use in worship (44:6-46:24). In all this there is a careful removal of the temple from any former political associations (cf. 42:20; 44:6-9). It is now an entirely priestly domain which the "prince" (Heb. *nasi'*) may not enter (44:4-8). The emphasis is now clear. Yahweh is the sole ruler in the new age (cf. 20:33). To put it differently, the reality which now controls the future throws the failures of the past into quite clear relief. The movements of the prince in regard to the sanctuary are quite circumscribed. Thus the ideals of the Davidic period have been passed over in the interests of older sacral conventions (particularly the worship format of the desert period).[35]

c. Significance of the Vision

The purifying and sanctifying influence of the building upon the land is then outlined in Ezek 47:1-12 (cf. Exod 15:17-18). Fertilizing waters flowing from the sanctuary heal the land and restore it to paradise; the "garden of God". "Trees of life" are planted on either side of the stream which itself increases to an immeasurable degree (Ezek 47:5). These trees will be for "food" (v12), and one may eat of their fruit unlike an earlier time without fear of judgement.[36] The land, cleansed and renewed by divine possession, is then divided. No prior conquest is needed merely purification. The division of the land is undertaken with regard to the ideal borders expressed in the older traditions (cf. Num 34:1-12). An allotment is given to the seven tribes to be located in the north (Ezek 48:1-7). Then like the division of the land in Joshua the undertaking is interrupted with reference to the sanctuary (cf. Josh 18:1).[37] That is to say, our attention after the first division is directed to the holy site divided among the Zadokites, the purified priesthood (Ezek 48:8-12). The Levites, the public, and the prince then receive attention (vv13-22). Land is allotted to the five remaining tribes (vv23-29). The handmaid tribes (Gad, Asher, Dan, Naphthali) are remotest from the temple. The sacred shrine itself is surrounded by the tribe of Levi, as further sacral protection from contamination. Judah is now directly to the north of the shrine and Benjamin to the south, thus obliterating the old north/south distinctions. It is probable that the tribes share equally in the distribution of land. Thus the new society emerging from this temple description seeks to redress the economic and political imbalances of the past[38] by a return to the egalitarianism of the Exodus period. Though the tribes seem to receive equal allotments, their position in relation to the city has been determined by the narratives concerning their origins. The account concludes with the name of the city, *Yahweh-Shammah* — The Lord is There.

Thus the book of Ezekiel begins with an introductory vision of judgement directly related to the temple, and concludes with a vision of a new society which is temple controlled and theocratically centred. The fact that the shrine and the city are no longer in Judah and that Zion has only been referred to obliquely in these chapters appears to be an explicit rejection of Jerusalem royal theology. No tribe has received land east of the Jordan. In short, it is the patriarchal land promises which are held out to the new people of God in this symbolic presentation. No pattern evidenced in Israel's history accounts for the order of the tribes, a fact which further underscores the reality of a totally new beginning taking Israel back to its patriarchal past. The tribal arrangement, four square around the sanctuary, is a reflection of the older Exodus structure and its theology. There are no special centres for the Levites, i.e., "Levitical cities," thus once again implying a preconquest structure. The theological structures of the monarchical period are totally rejected here, particularly the inviolability of Jerusalem and the first temple.

Clearly we cannot simply speak of a New Temple. This is no mere blueprint for post-exilic restoration. Rather if Israel is to have a future, Yahweh himself must do a new thing with himself at the centre. He alone will be responsible for the future of the people of God. He alone will erect this temple. Ezekiel's role is simply to relay to Israel the shape of the future (Ezek 40:4; 43:10-11). The immaculate symmetry to which we have referred, the holy city removed from direct tribal contact and thus from political tensions, and the centrality of worship in the new age, all point to the exalted doctrine of the presence offered in the book of Ezekiel. From the divine palace there now flows forth the never ending blessings which will be the product of perfect divine rule. The holy city has become the world mountain, the centre of the universe.

Ezek 40-48 makes no provision for Davidic kingship and indeed the term Heb. *melek* "king" is not used for the political ruler in the future age; Heb. *nasi'* "prince" is the preferred term (cf. 44:3; 45:7-8,16-17; 46:2; 48:21-22). This is consistent with the diminished role assigned to David and to kingship generally in this book. All of this is thoroughly consonant with Ezekiel's avowed theocratic aims. In a grand prophetic panorama we are taken from a picture of the temple under judgement to the heavenly temple from which that judgement emerged. This temple is the royal centre around which the new society will be constructed.

vi. *Haggai*

The post-exilic prophets Haggai and Zechariah lean heavily upon Ezekiel's theocratic programme. It is not surprising then to find that a call to rebuild the temple is central to their message. This is not to stamp them as priestly in their emphasis or pedestrian in their handling of lesser issues, nor does it suggest that they present a declining prophetic voice which ignores the pointed social emphasis of the classical prophets. Haggai and Zechariah both preserve the prophetic emphasis upon the fortunes of the nation and deal with issues raised specifically by the exile. With the backing of Ezekiel's theology it is hardly likely that Haggai or Zechariah should be Davidic/messianic revivalists, though doubtless their content would be temple centred.

When Haggai began his ministry to the returned exiles in 520BC, the temple lay in ruins.[39] The Persian kingdom had been wracked by revolts after the death of Cambyses in 522BC[40] and Darius I had assumed firm control only shortly before the opening of the book of Haggai. Thus whatever hopes the returnees may have entertained of deriving some political advantage out of the internecine disorders within the Persian realm vanished. By Haggai's time the community is given over to apathy. The prophet's ministry, therefore, is primarily a challenge to this complacency.

Haggai's message is addressed to the returnees[41] who 'commissioned by Cyrus' were to rebuild the temple. Haggai, in effect, invites them to recommence their history on a similar note to Ezek 40-48 which pursued the idealism of the OT. In Hag 1:4-11 the prophet chides his hearers over the lack of prosperity in the community — a traditional sign of covenant blessings accompanying the occupation of the land. This disputation speech has at its heart the demand to rebuild the temple (v9). Since the denunciations are drawn from the sphere of the Sinai covenant curse material (vv6,9a),[42] the people's reluctant attitude to rebuilding is an expression of political revolt from Yahweh's suzerainty. The rebuilding of the temple must not flow from blessings received, Haggai argues, but must be the act of faith which precedes them. In NT terms they must seek first the kingdom of God.

The response of the people is given in Hag 1:12-14. "Hearing my voice", "fearing", and, principally, "I am with you" (v13) all point to the re-establishment of the divine presence resulting from covenant repentance. Thus in chapter 1 we have the sequence of sin, punishment, repentance and grace.[43] 1:15-2:9 views the temple as a world pilgrimage centre — an older prophetic point which the theocratically dominated Ezekiel did not carry forward. In this section, the frequent mention of "Lord of Hosts" gives the proper focus. It is the centrality of divine kingship which is being expressed by temple rebuilding. We also note that the temple becomes the promoter of the blessing of prosperity (Hag 2:9). Doubtless there is a play upon temple and land with a subtle underscoring of the influence of the former on the latter.

In Hag 2:10-14 the mood changes. Unclean people are addressed in the third person. These are seemingly the ones who had remained in the land, or who had been resettled after 722BC (cf. Ezra 4:1-4) and attempted to join in the rebuilding operations. The remnant community is to keep its distance from these people (Hag 2:15-19). It is to be noticed that on the very day in which pagan approaches to rebuild are spurned, a private oracle is addressed to the Davidide Zerubbabel as temple builder (vv20-23). Usually the messianism of Haggai is said to have been brought into full play at this point. Certainly Zerubbabel is seen as a Davidic restoration figure and as a replacement for the rejected Jehoiachin, the next to last king before the exile (598-597BC) in whom the exilic congregations placed great hope. The language of choice applied to Zerubbabel ("chosen", "signet ring", "servant") echoes Jeremiah's description of Jehoiachin as a signet ring to be plucked off (Jer 22:24).

But Zerubbabel is addressed here primarily as the Persian governor and it is likely that even though we have a note of Davidic continuity here, the Davidic role is severely down-played. He is not associated directly with the temple centred eschatology expressed in the earlier part of Haggai 2. Zerubbabel quickly vanishes from historical perspective and the secondary use of his Davidic connection may only have been to authenticate him as the post-exilic temple builder. Haggai thus both begins and concludes with a temple emphasis.

vii. *Zechariah*

Temple building is even more prominently featured in the book of Zechariah. In the opening address of Zech 1:1-6 the returnees are carefully separated from their "fathers". The threefold use of Heb. *Sub* "repent" in this section indicates the strength of the prophetic desire for the returned exiles to strike out in a totally new direction. The visions which follow (chaps 1-8; chap. 3 stands outside of the sequence[44]) are all temple centred. They are structured around chapter 4, the fourth vision of the seven, which displays the central theme of the first eight chapters of the book.

The interpretative key to the first vision (Zech 1:7-17) is verse 16, which announces the rebuilding of the temple as the motive for the divine return to Jerusalem. However throughout this vision the prophet expresses concern that the "shaking" of the nations has not yet occurred for the patrolling horsemen report that "all the earth is at rest" (v11). Since visions one and seven apparently display the background of the heavenly assembly[45] the setting for the seven visions is clear. The rebuilt temple will point the worshipper to the heavenly realities which undergird it. Perhaps as Halpern has suggested,[46] the second vision (vv18-21) dealing with the totality of political opposition under the form of four "horns" is an allusion to the "horned" altar. The measurement of the sacred space in 2:1-4 leaves us in no doubt (cf. Ezek 40:3) as to the link in this third vision. The fifth vision (Zech 5:1-4) also has temple points of reference in its depiction of the operation of covenant curses in the land as part of the purification process. The scroll on which the curses are written is of the same dimensions as the "porch" Heb. 'ulam of Solomon's temple. In the sixth vision (5:5-11) wickedness in the shape of a woman in a container is removed from the land and consigned (as is fitting) to the "land of Shinar" (i.e., Babylonia), where an anti-temple, a "house", is built for her (v11). The seventh vision (6:1-8) confirms that preparatory action has been taken for building, as the apocalyptic riders take Yahweh's judgement to all points of the compass. It is the converse of the first vision.

As the central vision of the seven, Zechariah 4 seems to be the point of focus of the first eight chapters. Mention must be made, however, of Zechariah 3 where the revestiture of Joshua the high priest occurs in an obvious heavenly council setting. The link between his reclothing and the temple dedication is clear enough given the association of the initial investiture with the tabernacle dedication in Lev 8:1-30.[47]

In Zech 4 the temple is the point of reference in the vision of the lampstand. The account is supposedly interrupted by the oracular material of verses 6b-10a, but this interlude actually serves to throw clear emphasis upon the command to Zerubbabel and grounds the vision firmly in the historical realities of the period. Zerubbabel is thus prominently featured as the temple-builder. The two sons of oil, Joshua and Zerubbabel (v14), are not "anointed ones" (contra RSV) but rather are sources of community blessing by their association with temple building.[48] As always, temple building must proceed by divine authority (v6).

Perhaps, as Halpern has suggested, Zech 4:6b-10a proceeds in two stages. This section is a complete review of Zerubbabel's participation in the rebuilding operation and a total survey of his involvement.

Verses 6-7 appear to represent the first stage in which the "great mountain", i.e., the former temple site, is cleared. In terms of the clear Mesopotamian parallels Zerubbabel as builder then deposits a stone removed from the old temple site[49] as the first stone of the new temple. Perhaps, as had been suggested, this first stone is identical with the seven faceted stone set before Joshua (3:9) who is also involved in the rebuilding process. The second address to Zerubbabel in 4:8-10 reasserts his participation in the rebuilding process.[50] Customary temple rebuilding ritual in the matter of foundation deposits of precious metal may be in view in the reference to the "stone of tin" (v10).[51]

Bound up with the rebuilding of the temple on which Zech 4 lays such heavy weight is the restoration of the social order ushered in by the two "sons of blessing", Joshua and Zerubbabel, priest and prince of the hoped for new age in the Ezekiel blueprint (cf. Zech 3:9). The arrival in that day of total individual well-being is described under the traditional imagery of "every one under his vine and his fig tree" (v10). We should also note verse 8 where the duties of Zerubbabel as "branch" presumptively include that of temple builder.

Following upon these visions directly connected with temple re-erection are questions put to the prophet in Zech 7 relating to cultic usages developed during the exile. Chapter 8 returns to the basic theme of the divine return to Zion and the rebuilt house (v3). Consequently, covenant renewal results in security and peace for Jerusalem (vv4-8). The visionary and prospective nature of the earlier material is translated into the language of exhortation to rebuild (vv9-13), and into an oracle of reassurance (vv14-17). Verses 18-19 return to the themes of cultic observances raised in 7:1-7. The typical prophetic eschatology associated with the temple as a world centre to which the nations come in pilgrimage (8:20-23) completes the first half of the prophecy.

We will treat the second half of Zechariah in association with the later treatment of the New Creation theme. For now we merely note that chapters 9-14 seem to function as an apocalyptic commentary upon chapters 1-8. Later we will have occasion to note that they begin with Yahweh's triumphant march to the temple, i.e., a return to Jerusalem and an assertion of theocratic rule (9:1-8),[52] and conclude on the same note of universal pilgrimage to the temple city (14:16-21) as we have noted in 8:20-23. Zech 9 thus commences with the proposed return and Zech 14 concludes with the restored and cosmically acclaimed temple city, carefully following the order and logic of Zechariah 1-8.

viii. *Chronicles, Ezra and Nehemiah*

Chronicles commences with the genealogy of Adam and ends with the edict of Cyrus permitting the exiles to return to Jerusalem in order to rebuild the temple. Chronicles takes us in panoramic survey from creation to the consummation of divine purposes as expressed in temple reconstruction for the Jerusalem city state. Half the contents of these books are devoted to David and Solomon as planner and builder of the temple respectively.[53] As builder Solomon is the "man of rest" (Heb. *m^{e}nuhah* cf. 1 Chron 22:7-10). This temple preoccupation is the basis for an emphasis on the "reunion" of Israel since the sanctuary serves as the centre point of theological hopes in a manner similar to Ezek 40-48. The history of the divided kingdoms is presented so as to play down division and magnify the reconciling potential of united temple access by north and south.

Cyrus' proclamation (2 Chron 36:22-23) needs to be noted carefully. He is presented as the divine servant and thus in terms of his role in Isa 40-55 as the promoter of the New Exodus ("The Lord, the God of heaven has given me all the kingdoms of the earth", 2 Chron 36:23a). This recognition of divine kingship is followed by the acknowledgement of responsibility to take charge of the temple rebuilding in Jerusalem. Thus there is a fusion of the post-exilic theologies of restoration. Divine kingship, New Covenant and New Creation theology from Isa 40-55 are implied by the "messianic" features of the Cyrus proclamation. In Isa 40-55 Cyrus is the restorer of the people of God to Jerusalem in what is conceived of as an act of new creation wrought through this "divine servant". These features are joined with the kingship and temple notes of Ezekiel by Chronicles. From this perspective we now see the rationale for the detailed emphasis given to the work of David and Solomon in Chronicles. All this was written in the interests of demonstrating continuity between the first and second temples.

It is curious, however, that Chronicles should end on this note of expectancy considering the books were probably written or finally compiled in the early fourth century BC and thus are directed to that age.[54] In other words, this temple theology is in fact eschatology since these books are not written to support the Ezra-Nehemiah reforms. Rather they were written to commemorate the great moments in Israel's history which have been connected with temple or temple service. Thus they are an attempt to provide an eschatological hope for a community whose enthusiasm is flagging after the failed reforms of the Ezra-Nehemiah period. Historically, the return from exile and the decree of Cyrus are long gone. The reality behind the extravagant theological terms of the presentation of the return in Isa 40-66 is yet to come. The close of the books of Chronicles alludes to this theology and thus informs its readers that the best is yet to come, the future is open-ended.

Chronicles reminds the tired community of fourth century BC Jerusalem that the tight priestly bureaucracy imposed after the collapse of the Ezra-Nehemiah reforms and in force until the Maccabaean revolt (c. 175BC) is not a valid expression of the purpose involved in temple rebuilding. That purpose ideally had in mind the reunification of all Israel under divine leadership and held out the possibility of a cleansed people of God. This was centred upon a temple concept expressing a conviction that the building symbolized Yahweh as God of heaven and Lord of all the kingdoms of the earth (2 Chron 36:23). Thus the Chronicler was the great revivalist of his day, enthusing the small city state of Jerusalem by reference to the theological links with the past, provided by the concept of the existent temple, this second temple in Jerusalem. His "historical theology" spoke to them of the manner in which the sanctuary was to be regarded and the hopes which were to be reposed in it.

The Book of Ezra, which falls chronologically prior to the books of Chronicles, commences with the edict of Cyrus. Its connection with the book of Nehemiah is clear. Nehemiah ends with the temple reforms having been undertaken, but the political situation somewhat uncertain. Ezra-Nehemiah seems to have been dependent for their impetus on Malachi, a book which presupposes the existence of the second temple but calls for its reform so that it might reflect the status of Yahweh as the "great king" (Mal 1:14). It is likely that Ezra is the immediate fulfilment of the prophecy of a "messenger" who would suddenly appear in the temple (Mal 3:1), since his commission in Ezra 7 has much more to do with temple and temple service than with the imposition of the law.[55] Like Chronicles, Ezra-Nehemiah project the vision of a cleansed people of God gathered around the sanctuary and thus endeavour to implement, under difficult circumstances, the post-exilic ideals within their own community. Ezra, in particular, is presented as the temple reformer[56] with Nehemiah as his political arm. Ultimately, however, their reforms seem to have fallen prey to priestly disputes so that at the end of the fifth century Jerusalem is in the hands of a Persian governor and an authoritarian state is emerging. It was in these circumstances that Chronicles was written to inspire hope in a weary group.

Space dictates we pass over the intertestamental material in this survey. Although far from uninteresting it does not greatly modify the basic position developed in the OT of the New Temple as the focal point of revelation in the new age.[57]

The New Testament

i. *Gospels*

Mark and Matthew on the one hand, Luke and John on the other each have differing emphases in regard to the role of the temple. Apart from Luke's specific interest in the temple, two main issues occur in the synoptics; the entry into Jerusalem and the cleansing of the temple (Matt 21; Mark 11; Luke 19), and the curious charge at the trial recorded only in Mark 14:58.

a. *Jesus' Temple Entry*

The details of the entry vary slightly in each account and we cannot look at these nuances in this brief survey. The general outline, however, is clear. The entry as described in Matt 21:5 is an assertion of kingship in the language of Zech 9:9, yet with the ominous omission of "bearing salvation". It is not a meek entry Jesus makes. Rather we must see Matt 21 as a reference to the total background of Zech 9. The entry is then Jesus' claim as the divine king to the temple as "his house" (cf. Matt 21:12-13).

However, unlike the background from Zechariah, Jesus' entry does not bear salvation for Israel even though in its own paradoxical way it will result in the release of the captives. In all three synoptics there is a reference to Jer 7:11 indicating the nation is faced with loss of both temple and land. Traditionally in the OT temple cleansing had been associated with the revival of political hopes and restoration (Josiah, Hezekiah, Ezek 40-48 and cf. Judas Maccabaeus). Thus in these NT accounts there is a sombre reversal of usual expectations. Fittingly as foreshadowing divine judgement, therefore, theophanic language is implemented in Matthew to describe the entry (Matt 21:10; the whole city is "stirred"; Gk. *seio* "to shake").

The pilgrim salutation to the temple entrant: "blessed is he who comes in the name of the Lord" (Ps 118:26) is quickly transmuted by Jesus into the language of rejection, drawn ominously from the same Psalm (vv42-43, "the very stone which the builders rejected has become the head of the corner!" cf. Matt 21:42.) Thus the destruction of the temple foreshadowed in this entry will mean the end of national Israel. This rejection is further contextually delineated in the synoptics.

Matthew and Mark bring the parable of the barren fig tree into direct connection with the entry (cf. Matt 21:18; Mark 11:20-25). The intention is thus clear. A prominent OT symbol of peace and security under which every man in the new age will sit, the fig tree is now not only barren (thus reversing the new age expectation) but withers. The Jerusalem temple has not only failed to be the reality which it symbolized, it will be destroyed and its destruction will mean the end of Israel. It is no longer a house of prayer, a point of divine reference (cf. Matt 21:13). More importantly, it never served as the world centre and thus as a potential rallying place for all nations. In the allusion to Isa 56:7 (cf. Matt 21:13) therefore, no mention is made by the synoptic writers of the phrase "for all nations".

b. Jesus' Trial

The matter of the charge against Jesus reported in Mark 14:58 is curious and difficult. What is meant by the charge that Jesus prophesied the destruction of the temple made "with hands" and the erection of a new temple "not made with hands" after three days? In the OT "made with hands" is the regular synonym for "idolatrous". This could be the case here also. However, other possibilities exist. Eph 2:11 contrasts the former state of the Gentiles as characterized by uncircumcision, with the Jew whose circumcision was "made *in the flesh* by hands" (cf. Col 2:11). In this context "made with hands" seems to mean "unspiritual" or "fleshly".[58] Jesus may be pointing therefore in Mark 14:58 to a reality of a different order which will arise as a result of his resurrection. This possibility appears to be confirmed in Heb 9:11 where "not made with hands" means "not part of this creation", i.e., otherworldly, a New Creation. Thus, if this view can be sustained, Jesus' assertion in Mark 14:58 signifies that the resurrection which brings the New Temple into being also gives birth to the reality of the New Creation— God's rule totally demonstrated through Jesus. As a piece of theological symbolism the New Temple imagery will be an important conveyor of the eschatological reality to which the resurrection points. It was eminently appropriate, therefore, that at the moment of the death of Jesus the earthly temple was profaned, the veil was rent (Matt 27:51). Israel's house was thus left to her "desolate" (cf. 23:38).

c. Luke and Stephen's Speech

Temple references abound in Luke 1-2 and 19-24. As such they frame his gospel and underscore the importance of the temple for him. The temple charge does not appear in Luke's version of the trial since he wishes to emphasize the political leaders' responsibility. Having stayed in Jerusalem, the question is put by the disciples with Israel in view as to whether Jesus will restore the kingdom (Acts 1:6). In other words, has the time come for the eschatological pilgrimage of the nations to the temple? The descent of the Spirit (in underlying Sinai terms) in Acts 2[59] answers this question somewhat unexpectedly, and recalls the New "Israel" to its Exod 19:5b-6 vocation.

Stephen's speech clearly shows the attitude of the Jerusalem community to the prevailing temple theology, and constitutes a decisive break with the temple. Paul will still use it as a base but his admission of a gentile into the temple (Acts 21:27-29) will occasion his arrest, imprisonment and voyage to Rome, actions whereby Judaism is finally rejected. Stephen's speech begins by noting that the Abrahamic promise of the land had worship as its aim. That is to say it would be consummated by temple construction (7:7). Israel's remarkable preservation as a (potentially) worshipping nation is then narrated. The Mosaic reference culminates with mention of the building of the tabernacle, the pattern for worship which God gave to Israel (v44). But the desert forefathers rejected Moses and gave themselves over to idolatry. The account of the building of the temple of Solomon closely follows and leads up to the appraisal that the Jews had looked on it simply as a "house" (Gk. *oikos* v47), a purely human edifice. An analogy is thus drawn of constant historical rejection. On the one hand blatant desert idolatry and a more sophisticated idolatry bound up with Solomon's "house" on the other.[60] Clearly, what is required is "something not made with hands", i.e., something heavenly. The account closes with the martyr Stephen directing his worship to just such a site — the heavenly Son of Man, the New Temple (v56).

d. John

John's gospel as in other things goes its own way in the matter of the temple. Its emphasis is on Jesus as the New Temple, the new point of contact and the one to whom divine homage must now be directed. Although he had come to his own (i.e., Israel), they had not received him (John 1:11). The new community who had received him (v12) recognized that in him the glory of God had "tabernacled" (v14). That is to say, the glory theophany associated with the temple/tabernacle in the OT is now manifested in Jesus. The vision of awe and fear before which the people had quailed is now beheld by the "New Israel"! By dwelling among them, by the fact of the incarnation, Jesus revealed himself as the true tabernacle "pitched" by God. Now Jesus fully discloses the previously hidden aspects of the divine nature. In his own person he demonstrates divine kingship (an important theme in John). He is thus the new point of revelation, the new Bethel (v51). Since the Jerusalem temple was no longer the point of contact between heaven and earth, Jesus presents himself as its replacement (2:12-25). Worship would not henceforth be offered at places (Gerizim or Jerusalem) but to the Father in spirit and in truth (4:20-24). This would be possible since Jesus, drawing on new temple analogies provided by Ezek 47:1-12, presents himself as the dispenser of the Spirit, and thus of life and fertility (John 7:37-38).

ii. *Paul*

The New Temple concept is applied to the individual believer by Paul (1 Cor 6:19), though it is possible that the reference here is to the congregation.[61] This temple connotation is a clear mark of God's lordship (cf. 2 Cor 6:16-7:1) since the indwelling of the Spirit, closely associated in both Testaments with the idea of kingdom,[62] makes the believer a temple. God's rule is manifested in him through the Spirit!

Eph 2:20-22 is an important passage in which the images of growth and temple are combined. Christ is presented in the wider context of verses 11-20 as the bringer of cosmic peace in a ministry which reconciles the universe and removes the barriers between heaven and earth.[63] Language of access and citizenship in the new commonwealth of the Kingdom dominates this section. Divisions are broken down and a new unity is created (vv14,15,16,18).[64] The images fluctuate but the commonwealth is presented as a household which grows into a holy temple (v21) built upon the NT apostles whose ministry is also prophetic.[65] Viewed as a building, growth on the foundation stone[66] is still occurring. However, this growth is directed towards the community finally indwelt by God and thus operating as a holy temple (v21). The mention of "holy" temple (v21) both provides the motif by which this result will be achieved (i.e., God's elective purposes fulfilled) and at the same time contrasts this new temple with its OT counterpart.

Whether or not the temple is implied in 1 Tim 3:15 is uncertain, since

Gk. *oikos* "house" is probably used in the sense of "household" in verses 4, 5, and 12. At 2 Thess 2:3-4 the anti-christ sits in the *naos* "temple/shrine". However, this is an eschatological reference and is not related to the growing church.[67]

iii. *Peter*

The "stone" language in this section (1 Pet 2:6; cf. Isa 28:16; 1 Pet 2:7; cf. Ps 118:22; 1 Pet 2:8; cf. Isa 8:14), the Zion reference (1 Pet 2:6), the analogy provided by the Qumran concept of the community as an eschatological temple,[68] as well as the seemingly cultic tenor of the passage (cf. "holy priesthood" "spiritual sacrifices" v5, "royal priesthood" v9) might incline us to take the "spiritual house" of verse 5 as a temple. J.H. Elliott,[69] however, points out that Gk. *oikos* "house" (v5) is never otherwise used in the NT for temple and that by the use of the "stone" references the passage emphasizes the elective purpose of God to construct a new worshipping community (cf. Exod 19:5b-6). As Elliott argues, the "body of priests" (Gk. *hierateuma*, 1 Pet 2:9) will show their role by exhibiting the "spiritual sacrifices" of the type which the following social code (vv11-20) demands. Images of growth and election are in verses 4-10 but temple symbolism is not appealed to.

iv. *Hebrews*

Again the use of the temple concept is mainly indirect in Hebrews. True, chapters 8-10 are given over to a major critique of the worship structure under the Levitical system, but this is in the interests of covenant replacement rather than temple itself. There is a clear reference to the heavenly sanctuary in 8:1 in which Jesus now sits enthroned. This means the automatic rejection of the earthly sanctuary and its ordinances (cf. 9:1-10). Jesus is the high priest of the heavenly sanctuary (cf. "not made with hands" v11) Who by His one atoning sacrifice has passed through the "holy place", the "greater and more perfect tent" (v11) into the holy of holies itself (v12).[70] The earthly sanctuary was merely a symbol of the heavenly (cf. v24, Exod 25:9). The entry of Christ into the sanctuary signifies his heavenly rule (Heb 10:12) and assures our participation in the present benefits of the new covenant and their consummation at the eschaton. 12:18-24 views believers as present members of the heavenly Jerusalem, but this passage serves the interests of covenant conclusion (Sinai and Zion are contrasted) rather than to carry forward the temple concept.

v. Revelation Reconsidered

R.J. McKelvey notes that Rev 4-20 shows little interest in the theology of the heavenly temple but that there is major use of the temple symbolism in these chapters to provide background for the unfolding events of the prophecy.[71] Clearly the heavenly temple is the place where universal worship is offered and thus functions as the symbol of unity under divine kingship. Of particular importance is the throne room vision of chapter 4 where the spectacle of divine rule is seen as the body of the book begins. In the face of the world opposition the book details, this vision will be translated into reality. The long forgotten ark reappears in the heavenly sanctuary (11:19) at the end of the first of the two great cycles of visions (1:9-11:19; 12:1-22:5).[72] This vision of the heavenly sanctuary as the conclusion to the first cycle indicates the direction which the second cycle will take and foreshadows the conclusion of the book.

We have now completed our biblical survey. The NT analysis confirms the OT. A temple in the biblical world was conceived as the dwelling place and manifestation of the deity. This framework coupled with the OT eschatological hope that God would personally indwell his people in full covenant blessing in the final age has prepared us for a theology of Christ's indwelling in the believing community. God would locate Himself personally and corporately in believers and the community of the new age.[73] In the OT worship was offered to God as the Lord of all. Since God's declared purpose in the NT is to sum up all things in Christ (Col 1:20), it is clear that Jesus is the NT point of reference for all the temple expectations of the OT. Primarily the temple has been a symbol of total divine rule. Thus, as the locus of the New Temple in whom believers are constituted as a temple, Jesus on the one hand points to a display of divine rule and on the other hand to the broader motif of a New Creation which incorporates the perfected New Temple. This last point will be taken up in our final chapter. We are not surprised, therefore, to find at the end of a book whose liturgical character has been obvious, the New Jerusalem presented as a city permanently indwelt by God and thus as a place of continuous and joyful worship.

Notes

1. A.Y. Collins, *The Combat Myth in the Book of Revelation* (HDR 9; Missoula: Scholars, 1976) 229.

2. Cf. E. Fiorenza, *Priester fur Gott* (Munster: Aschendorff, 1972) 403.

3. As R.J. Clifford *(The Cosmic Mountain in Canaan and the Old Testament* [HSM 4; Cambridge: Harvard University, 1972] 26) notes.

4. Cf. G. Robinson, "The Idea of Rest in the Old Testament and the Search for the Basic Character of the Sabbath", *ZAW* 92 (1980) 32-42.

5. ibid, 33-37.

6. Deut 5:15 takes the sabbath command up in terms of redemption from Egypt. This has seemed to conflict with Exod 20:11. It does not really do so when it is remembered that creation and redemption are related as source and consequence.

7. It is to be noted that the consecration of the cult was a seven day process, thus extending the sabbath idea in the context cf. Exod 29:37; 34:18.

8. The dependence upon, or narrow relationship of Ezek 28:11-15 with Exod 28:17-20, but with Eden in mind as the ultimate referent, is recognized by W. Zimmerli, *Ezechiel 25-48* (BKAT XIII/2; Neukirchen-Vluyn: Neukirchener, 1969) 684.

9. Cf. recently, P. Bird, "Male and Female He Created Them: Genesis 1:27b in the Context of the Priestly Account of Creation", *HTR* 74 (1981) 137-44.

10. M. Haran, *Temples and Temple Service in Ancient Israel* (Oxford: Clarendon, 1978) 205-25.

11. ibid, 260-75.

12. On the function of the glory cloud in the Exodus, cf. J.G. McConville, "God's 'Name' and God's 'Glory'," *TynB* 30 (1979) 149-63.

13. R.E. Clements *(God and Temple* [Oxford: Blackwell, 1965] 94-9) has taken this basic thesis of G. von Rad a little further.

14. As G. Wenham ("Deuteronomy and the Central Sanctuary", *TynB* 22 [1971] 113-4) notes.

15. This is by no means a novel view, cf. G.T. Manley, *The Book of the Law* (London: Tyndale, 1957) 132.

16. The theological role of the ark in I & II Sam is well treated by A.F. Campbell, *The Ark Narrative* (SBLDS 16; Missoula: Scholars, 1975) 193-210.

17. On temple building as a task for gods, cf. B. Halpern, *The Constitution of the Monarchy in Israel* (HSM 25; Missoula: Scholars, 1981) 19-31.

18. R.A. Carlson, *David the Chosen King* (Stockholm: Almqvist & Wiksell, 1964) 102. We are generally indebted to Carlson for his perceptive treatment of 2 Sam 7.

19. ibid, 100.

20. W.C. Kaiser, Jr., "The Blessing of David: The Charter for Humanity", in *The Law and the Prophets; Old Testament Studies in Honor of O.T. Allis* ed. J.H. Skilton (Nutley: Presbyterian and Reformed, 1974) 311.

21. Carlson, *David*, 125, note 4.

22. Kaiser, "Blessing of David", 314.

23. Y. Kaufmann (*The Biblical Conquest of Palestine* [Jerusalem: Magnes, 1953] 54) points out that the Davidic empire never included Tyre and Sidon but included East Jordan territories which formed no part of the promised land.

24. For the connection of the motifs of temple and ideal garden, cf. H.J. van Dijk, *Ezekiel's Prophecy on Tyre* (BibOr 20; Rome: Pontifical Biblical Institute, 1968) 117.

25. Cf. J.D. Levenson, *The Theology of the Program of Restoration of Ezekiel 40-48* (HSM 10; Missoula: Scholars, 1976) 25-36.

26. As R.B. Dillard ("The Chronicler's Solomon", *WTJ* 43 [1981] 289-300) has pointed out.

27. T.W. Overholt, *Threat of Falsehood* (London: SCM, 1970) 1-23.

28. Zimmerli, *Ezekiel 1-24* (Hermeneia: Philadelphia: Fortress, 1979) 98-9.

29. As H.D. Parunak ("The Literary Architecture of Ezekiel's mar ot 'elohim", *JBL* 99 [1980] 63) suggests.

30. The north in the exilic period was the area from which numinous judgement was thought to portend, cf. B.S. Childs, "The Enemy from the North and the Chaos Tradition", *JBL* 78 (1959) 187-98.

31. Parunak, "Architecture", 66.

32. Levenson, *Program*, 7-19.

33. Our dependence upon Parunak's presentation at this point is acknowledged, cf. "Architecture", 71.

34. ibid, 72.

35. Cf. N. Poulssen, *Konig und Tempel in Glaubenszeugnis des alten Testamentes* (Stuttgart: Katholisches Bibelwerk, 1967) 150.

36. The theme of the temple as bound up with the fountain of life occurs as Ps 36:7-9 and frequently elsewhere (cf. Gen 2:6-7; Zech 14:8; Joel 3:18). The Tree of Life and fateful tree themes are not in Ezek 28 but we note that the beauty of the world tree in 31:1-9 is accounted for because it draws its strength from the underlying waters of life (v4). The stream Gihon ("Gusher") in Jerusalem, the underground spring, may point in the same direction.

37. Parunak, "Architecture", 74.

38. Levenson, *Program*, 124.

39. For the significance of this phrase as indicating that the temple was at least partially built but was being neglected in worship, cf. F.I. Andersen, "Who Built the Second Temple?", *AusBR* 6 (1958) 23-27.

40. K. Galling (*Studien zur Geschichte Israels im persischen Zeitalter* [Tubingen: Mohr, 1964] 48-51) supplies details of this period of Persian conflict.

41. So W.A.M. Beuken, *Haggai-Sacharja 1-8* (Assen: Van Gorcum, 1967) 30.

42. Cf. J.W. Whedbee, "A Question-Answer Schema in Haggai 1": in *Biblical and Near Eastern Studies: Essays in Honor of W.S. Lasor* ed. G. Tuttle (Grand Rapids: Eerdmans, 1978) 192.

43. Beuken, *Haggai*, 27-49.

44. H. Gese ("Anfang und Ende der Apokalyptik dargestellt am Sacharjabuch", *ZTK* 70 [1973] 25) suggests a structure of seven visions. He omits Zech 3 because of the doubtful parallels in content and formal features with the other visions. We believe he is correct and that the symmetry of the visions clearly indicates a number of seven.

45. Halpern argues this way in "The Ritual Background of Zechariah's Temple Song", *CBQ* 40 (1978) 179.

46. ibid, 177.

47. ibid, 173.

48. Heb. *yishar*, "oil" Zech 4:14 is not otherwise associated with anointing in the OT. Thus anointing may not be on view here, cf. A.S. van der Woude, "Die Beiden Sohne des Ols (Sach. 4:14)", in *Travels in the World of the Old Testament, M.A. Beek Festschrift* ed. H.G. Heerma van Voss (Assen: Van Gorcum, 1974) 262-8.

49. A. Petitjean (*Les Oracles du Proto-Zacharie* [Paris: Gabalda, 1969] 258-63) surveys the ancient Near Eastern evidence.

50. The Heb. verb *yasad* used of "laying the foundation stone" in Zech 4:9 has a wider meaning than merely the initiation of a building operation. It can mean "undertake responsibility for the entire work" or the like, cf. Andersen, "Second Temple", 15-21.

51. Cf. D.L. Petersen, "Zerubbabel and Jerusalem Temple Reconstruction", *CBQ* 36 (1974) 366-72.

52. As P.D. Hanson (*The Dawn of Apocalyptic* [Philadelphia: Fortress, 1975] 292-324) has perceptively argued.

53. Dillard draws careful attention to the many connections forged between the Exodus narratives and the Solomonic age, cf. "Solomon", 293-9.

54. For this dating, cf. H.G. Williamson, *Israel in the Books of Chronicles* (Cambridge: Cambridge University, 1977) 86.

55. I have argued this way in "Malachi and the Ezra-Nehemiah Reforms", *RTR* 35 (1976) 42-52.

56. Cf. K. Koch, "Ezra and the Origins of Judaism", *JSS* 19 (1974) 193.

57. The evidence from the Intertestamentary literature, Rabbinic and Qumran sources is presented in R.J. McKelvey, *The New Temple* (Oxford: Oxford University, 1969) 15-41.

58. D. Juel (*Messiah and Temple* [SBLDS 31; Missoula: Scholars, 1977] 143-57) carefully surveys the possibilities contained in the expression "made with hands" in the NT.

59. J. Nolland ("Luke's Readers — a Study of Luke 4:22-8, Acts 13:46, 18:6, 28:28 and Luke 21:5-36" [Ph.D dissertation, Cambridge University, 1977] 97-99) notes the relationship between Pentecost and Sinai. He also draws our attention to the fact that the Messiah in Jewish expectation would be the builder/restorer of the temple, 183-92.

60. Notice this line of reasoning which is advanced by J. Kilgallen, *The Stephen Speech* (AnBib 67; Rome: Pontifical Biblical Institute, 1976) 37-92.

61. Cf. R. Kempthorne, "Incest and the Body of Christ: A Study of 1 Corinthians vi. 12-20", *NTS* 14 (1968) 568-74.

62. I have noted this association in "Spirit and Kingdom of God in the Old Testament", *RTR* 33 (1974) 1-10.

63. Cf. A.T. Lincoln *Paradise Now and Not Yet* (SNTSMS 43; Cambridge: Cambridge University, 1981) 150.

64. Cf. E. Roels *God's Mission* (Amsterdam: Wever, 1962) 145-51.

65. Cf. Wayne A. Grudem (*The Gift of Prophecy in 1 Corinthians* [Washington: University of America, 1982] 93-105) offers a recent discussion of Eph 2:20.

66. As to whether Jesus constitutes the copestone or the foundation stone of the New Temple is a difficult point and the issues are finely balanced. On the whole the context appears to support the latter, cf. ibid, 85-6.

67. When Christians in the NT are described as a "temple" the word used is *naos* cf. 1 Cor 3:16-17; 6:19; Eph 2:21. Apart from the reference at 1 Thess 2:3-4 which refers to the future, the use of Gk. *naos* and *oikos* must be kept apart.

68. For this community concept at Qumran cf. McKelvey, *New Temple*, 128.

69. J.H. Elliott, *The Elect and the Holy* (NovTSup 12; Leiden: Brill, 1966) 157-69.

70. On the exegesis of the difficult Heb 9:11-12 cf. D.G. Peterson, *Hebrews and Perfection: An examination of the Concept of Perfection in the Epistle to the Hebrews* (SNTSMS 47; Cambridge: Cambridge University, 1982) 140-4.

71. McKelvey (*New Temple*, 161-2) points to the use of the heavenly temple background in seven scenes: Rev 4:2-11, where the elders are at worship; 5:8-14, the heavenly concourse worships the Lamb; 7:9-17, the great multitude drawn from all nations who worship God; 11:15-19, the elders at worship; 14:1-5, the Lamb with the gathered elect of 144,000 on Mt Zion; 15:2-4, where the redeemed stand at the edge of the sea and sing the song of the Exodus, the song of Moses and the Lamb; and 19:1-8, where the multitudes celebrate the marriage of the Lamb.

72. Collins, *Combat Myth*, 28.

73. Cf. E. Best, *One Body in Christ* (London: SPCK, 1955) 168.

NEW COVENANT — SUMMARY

There seems to be no end to the intersection and amalgamations of motifs in John's panorama. The New Jerusalem in descent is the realization of the New Covenant, a connection rendered ummistakeable by the use of Lev 26:11-12 in Rev 21:3. The agenda of Sinai and hope of Jeremiah meet in the experience of the Bride.

Thought of a New Covenant did not arise until the threat of imminent exile, for Sinai and nationalism went hand-in-hand. But the end of nationalism seemed the annulment of the Sinai covenant. Although presupposed by the pre-exilic prophets, the covenant assumed prominence in Jeremiah and Lamentations. Straddling the concept of divine fidelity as the basis of covenant theology and the record of Israel's history as warranting the curses of Deut 28, Jeremiah announces the hope of a New Covenant. Not new because it offers a "new heart", but because this heart will be given to all the people. It would mean the end of sin. Solid continuity is in Jeremiah's account married to radical discontinuity.

Ezekiel's restoration vision holds forth similar hopes. After the staging of a New Exodus, Israel will experience the gift of a new spirit. This injection of edenic life is no less than a resurrection of the whole people. Isa 40-66 is just as grandiose. Here the covenant renewal affected by the New Exodus can only have one end — the restoration of all things, the New Creation. The Servant embodies the covenant and ensures the fulfillment of the Abrahamic promises and transferral of the Davidic promises to the entire people.

Ultimately, of course, this Servant is the exalted Son of Man. This fact is clarified at both the beginning and conclusion of Matthew's Gospel, by the emphasis on Jesus' role as the bearer of the Abrahamic and Davidic promises and creator of the New Community. Paul further elaborates this christological focus on covenant in 2 Cor 3 in his exposition of Expd 34. Although originally addressed to all Israel, the fullness of the Sinai covenant narrows to Moses after the rejection of Yahweh in the people's worship of the golden calf. Now Moses must wear a veil whenever he is not acting as mediator and Israel cannot endure the glory of the divine presence. In Paul's own day the Jews still cannot see the glory of Jesus because of the veil covering their hearts. But in Jesus through the Spirit we are admitted to the full privileges of the covenant.

Even so we wait for the total realization of the covenant in our experience. Although possessing a new heart we still remember the agony of sin as we long for the day of John's vision when sin will be no more.

3

THE NEW COVENANT

The Presentation in Revelation 21-22

The fulfilment of the divine covenant with men is a further motif taken up in our portrait of the eschaton. To indicate this association, Revelation 21 consciously employs the language of Lev 26:11-12, itself a strongly covenantal passage speaking of the national conduct appropriate or inappropriate for the maintenance of the covenant. "The dwelling of God is with men, He will dwell with them, and they will be his peoples (note the plural) and God Himself will be with them" (Rev 21:3). This comment interprets the significance of the descent of the New Jerusalem, but also points to the manner in which the promises of the Sinai covenant will be realized in the experiences of these "peoples" of the eschaton.

The Old Testament

God's presence among men is also the hallmark of the New Covenant theology in the OT. Thus the everlasting covenant of peace concluded with Israel at the close of Ezek 37 entails the presence of God's tabernacle with them ("I will be their God and they will be my people", vv26-27). The nations of the world then defer to this established presence and world peace results (v28). The unity of Judah and Israel and the obliteration of former divisions constitute the preliminaries to the imposition of this New Covenant (vv1-14) and in its own way forms a commentary upon the national resurrection of Israel in exile. This is further reflected in Jer 32:36-40, which looks forward to the return from exile, the gathering of all Israel, the indwelling of God in his people (v38), and the making of an everlasting covenant. This last passage is similar to the classic announcement of the New Covenant in Jer 31:31-34, which will be the subject of our discussion throughout this chapter.

i. *Pre-exilic Prophetic Attitude to Covenant*

Before we proceed directly to that passage some attention must be paid
to the historical context of Jeremiah and his theological antecedents via
the prophetic preaching of covenant. In regard to the latter it is
understandable, though initially puzzling, that the pre-exilic prophets
made such little direct use of the covenant concepts.

Amos is no stranger to the idea of covenant,[1] as evidenced by his
thoroughly covenant centred[2] preaching, yet he does not use
"covenant" (*berit*) to refer directly to the Sinai agreement. The
particular social exploitation and abuses castigated by Amos
presuppose that Israel is not honouring the covenant. Indeed, all the
ills of the book are traced to covenant breach. Even the historical
introduction to the oracles against the foreign nations with which the
book commences serves to indicate that the offences to which Amos'
audience would have given ready condemnation are no more severe
and serious than those in which Israel also freely indulges.[3] By her sin
Israel identifies herself with the other nations (cf. Amos 9:7), thereby
forfeiting her elective status and inviting divine punishment in the form
of exile, which stands as an impending reality. Amos' insistence upon
the demonstration of covenant relationships in his demand for
righteousness clearly indicates that whatever else may be unique in his
prophecies it is certainly not the fact that Israel is a covenant dependent
people.[4]

Hosea uses "covenant" (Heb. *berit*) some five times (of the Sinai
compact at Hos 6:7, 8:1, and at 2:18 of what is, in fact, to be the New
Covenant with Israel. 10:4 and 12:1 are non-specific uses of *berit*).
Clearly important for the understanding of Hosea's covenant
background is the extended marriage imagery of his first three
chapters. We do not intend to review these chapters in detail, but their
purpose is to underscore the dominance of the Sinai background which
he brings to his own situation by oscillating between the historical
position of the prophet and his marriage difficulties, and the position
of Yahweh and Israel.

The second chapter of Hosea is bewilderingly difficult to follow and
poetic licence must often be given its free reign. But the overall message
is clear. Israel is indicted for breach of covenant (Hos 2:2-8), inviting
the traditional curses of Deut 28 (Hos 2:9-13), yet not so as to exclude
the possibility of restoration and re-enactment of the Exodus
(vv14-15). Subsequently, verses 16-23 indicate the dimensions of what
seems an anticipation of the exilic New Covenant programme. Within
this cursing/blessing structure verse 18 specifically refers to a

prospective *berit* leading to universal peace and the secure occupancy of the land. With this comes a perfected marriage relationship (vv19-20; note the blessings which will proceed from this relationship vv21-23). The final chapter of the prophecy ends with Israel re-established and the full harmony to which chapter 2 points. Thus the movement of thought controlling the book is from covenant breach to covenant renewal.

Isa 1:2-31[5] begins with a long invective against covenant breach. As we noticed in the New Jerusalem chapter Isa 1-39 is concerned to trace the consequences of that breach; consequences which end in the exile of the Davidic house and the destruction of Jerusalem. We cannot say that the particular emphasis upon covenant is dominant or prominent in the remaining pre-exilic books (e.g., Micah, Zephaniah and Habakkuk). In all of them, however, the concept is presupposed. Probably the specific exposition of the term is not needed since the motif provided the axiom whereby a history for Israel was constructed. Its exilic employment must be understood in the light of the fact that the exile virtually brought the fortunes of the nation to a close. The crises of the exile cast doubt upon the question of historical continuity and had thus brought the matter of the covenant and the nature of its content into clear relief and public questioning.

ii. *Prominence of Covenant Terminology in the Exilic Period*

Jerusalem's fall exposed the radical disjunction between the faith expectations of Israel and the undeniable apostasy throughout the course of her history. As a final prelude to Jeremiah, we note that it is this tension between event and expectation that is confronted in the book of Lamentations.

This tension is developed by emphasizing the Zion theology around which covenant concepts are centred at the time of the exile. Since the promises linked with Zion were inviolate and therefore could not be called into question (cf. Ps 48:2 "the city of the great king") what had to be challenged was the conduct of the nation which had brought about the exile. In this way Lamentations provides the theological axis upon which covenant continuity turns during the exile. It points to the promises, yet also, as we have noted earlier, to the destruction of Jerusalem. This judgement was in its own way an index of Yahweh's consistency. In the historical experience of Israel the covenant promises were necessarily contingent upon obedience and thus Lamentations sees the disaster of 587BC as the operation of the threats

81

of Deuteronomy 28. The book is an extended national confession of sin to Yahweh. Only such a recognition of guilt could generate the faint doctrine of hope on which the book ends. Theologically, the promises of God to Abraham could not fail. The exile would reaffirm this and the prophetic preaching of the period would insist upon it. God would begin again, re-establishing a covenant of everlasting peace with Israel, yet with the world in view. Yahweh would indwell them; they would be his people, and he would be their God.

iii. *Jeremiah*

a. Call and Vocation

It is in Jeremiah that the doctrine of a new covenant emerges consciously (Jer 31:31-34). We have suggested that it is the collapse of the nation that brings the national Sinai covenant under review, and this proves to be the case in Jeremiah. His prophecy and its general background require careful examination to unearth the rationale for propounding the doctrine of a New Covenant, for appreciating the necessity of its development at that stage in Israel's history, and for understanding its peculiar content.

Depending upon the interpretation of Jer 1:2 (i.e., whether it refers to his birth or to the beginning of his ministry) Jeremiah's prophetic activity may have extended from 627BC to c582BC. Thus it spanned the Josianic reforms in which a covenant of some sort had been re-affirmed by king and people (cf. 2 Kgs 23:3) and continued throughout the reign of Josiah (640-609BC) and the reigns of four descendants of Josiah (three sons — Jehoahaz 609BC, Jehoiakim 609-598BC, Zedekiah 597-587/6BC, and one grandson — the son of Jehoiakim, Jehoiachin 598-597BC). The prophet therefore knew first-hand the period of hope engendered by the reforms of Josiah and the subsequent fall of Jerusalem in 587/6BC which revealed the superficiality of those reforms. The prophet also knew the ultimate inadequacy of political attempts by reforming kings who sought to impose change from above. Jeremiah's ministry saw the fall of the Assyrian empire (initially with the fall of Nineveh, 612BC; totally with the defeat of Assyria's Egyptian ally by Babylon at Carchemish, 605BC) as well as the rapid ascendancy of the Babylonian empire (begun with Nabopolassar, 626BC, and peaking with the victory of his son Nebuchadrezzar at Carchemish).

For our purposes an understanding of the nature of Jeremiah's call is crucial. Jeremiah comes before us as a prophet of a new age and as a prophet to the nations (Jer 1:5,10). This manner of his call is emphasized by its repetition in chapter 1. Thus the international character of Jeremiah's ministry is introduced. His call is unique among the vocational calls of the OT prophets, for the others are all sent solely to Israel/Judah. Jeremiah's word is meant to relate Judah to the world of its day. It is designed to provide for a transition from the previous narrow nationalism to the concept of a people of God existing within a pagan world framework.

It is not insignificant that oracles against foreign nations conclude the prophecy in the Hebrew text. Admittedly, these oracles are placed between Jer 25:13a and 15 in the Greek OT, but this seems to have risen from a desire for a more consistent historical structure, as well as from the purpose of ending the book with the account of the fall of Jerusalem and what immediately preceded the fall. But the Hebrew placement of these oracles at the conclusion of the book, viewed together with the nature of the prophet's call, draws into obvious focus the internationalism of the prophecy. This broader political perspective recognized that all the organized world as Jeremiah knew it was involved in a new societal structure under the leadership of Babylon.

Moreover, from a formal structural perspective, Jer 51:64 forms an inclusion with 1:1. In chapters 46-51 the oracles against the foreign nations are arranged geographically (Egypt, Philistia, Moab, Ammon, Edom, Damascus, Arabs, Elam and finally Babylon) and have the common theme of failure to submit to Babylon. Finally, Babylon herself is punished for *hubris*. These oracles underscore the tenor of Jeremiah's constant prophecy of Judah's need to recognize Babylonian hegemony as the new factor in the world situation.

b. Structure

Jeremiah's structure is complex with numerous peculiar difficulties which cannot be given a detailed analysis here. However, within the major sections of the book a certain pattern occurs to which it may be helpful to refer. The first major section of the prophecy runs from Jer 1:5 to 20:18 and is framed by inclusions referring to Jeremiah's birth. This break at the conclusion of chapter 20 is confirmed by the fact that chapter 21 is the first datable oracle in the book. It has been suggested that chapters 1-20 comprise the material read by Baruch before

Jehoiakim (cf. chap. 36) and it is generally agreed that these chapters represent Jeremiah's earliest prophecies.

In general terms, Jer 2-3 confronts covenant infidelity, referring principally to Judah's constant lapses into idolatry. This can only lead to a call for repentance (4:1-4), followed by the threat of Yahweh's own warfare against Judah (a reversal of holy war), and the constant theme of terrible punishment (4:5-6:30) to be exacted in this case by the as yet unnamed "foe from the north" (a theme continued generally in 8:14-10:25). As a summary of his prophetic stance, Jeremiah's famous temple sermon in chapter 7 (cf. its repetition in chap. 26 where it serves to announce a new phase in the prophecy) declares that a right attitude to the temple, and thus to divine kingship, would secure the promised land. Therefore, the absence of this covenant response prompts Jeremiah to surrender cult, priesthood, temple and land and to foreshadow their end, thus pointing to the conclusion of an era. Chapter 7 also indicates that the Josianic reforms had been reversed (v31 cf. 2 Kgs 23:10). The shocking presentation of an abandoned Judah is continued (Jer 8-10), while her ills are directly related to a breach of covenant (11:1-13:27). It matters little whether Jeremiah is referring here to the Josianic covenant (2 Kgs 23:3) or the Sinaitic since the former was the renewal of the latter. Whatever the case, the crimes of Judah are to be punished by the typical covenant curses of drought and exile (Jer 14:1-15:9).

Throughout the section Jer 15:10-20:18 the prophecy assumes a particular personal slant, including the so-called "confessions" of Jeremiah. The struggles of his ministry, the introspection to which he was given, his isolation and depression, and the various plots against his life all emphasize his distance from and difference to his prophetic predecessors at the end of this first major section of his ministry. These earlier messengers, while foreshadowing punishment and generally urging repentance, had for the most part presumed the continuing integrity of the nation based on either repentance or eschatology. Jeremiah, however, preached the end of the state, the demise of all the external features by which Israel is identified, even the abandonment of the ark (Jer 3:16).

Jer 21-25 assumes a somewhat different tone. A review of Judaean kingship is conducted after the Davidic house is summoned to submit to Babylon (chap. 21). This review in turn precipitates a definition of Judaean kingship in terms of Jeremiah's model, Josiah (22:1-9). But the model also served to pronounce condemnation upon his successors. Even the boy king Jehoiachin, son of Jehoiakim is condemned, and goes into exile in March 597BC after reigning for a period of only three months. He is written off in the genealogies as "childless" (vv24-30, i.e., without a throne successor) though in actual fact at least five sons were born to him in exile. This attention to Jehoiachin is calculated to extinguish all the hopes of the popular anti-Babylonian party who viewed the young sovereign as the soon to be restored rightful king.

Davidic kingship is in fact sweepingly dismissed by Jeremiah (23:1-4). Yahweh will establish his own leadership, and it will be totally unlike that of the ruling Zedekiah in whose time the oracle was uttered. Only when God restored Judah in the uncertain future would the ruling king of the house of David be named "Yahweh is our righteousness" (Jer 23:6). Again, since this name is the reversal of the name of the then king Zedekiah ("my righteousness is Yahweh") it clearly suggests a rejection of empirical kingship in favour of eschatological kingship.[6]

The denunciation of Judah's leadership shifts to the prophets in Jer 23:9-40 where the true prophet who has stood in the council of Yahweh (vv18,22) as Jeremiah has done is set over against the imposters. The stage is set for Jeremiah's rebuttal of popular "prophetic" theology in chapters 27-28. On the other hand, valid prophecy is indicated by the tenor of its remarks concerning the future of Judah (chap. 24). True prophecy will preach exile with the possibility that from this judgement Yahweh will do a new thing and raise up a new people. Exile is the necessary purging of the nation. Thus it is the exiles who are "good figs" (v5) as opposed to the "bad figs" who remain in the land. They are not good because they are exiled, but because in exile Yahweh will give them a heart to know him (v7).

Judah, however, is placed among the world of nations who are called upon to submit to Babylon (providing a rationale for the LXX to include Jer 46-51 after 25:13a as we have noticed). The prophecy continues with Judah's own failure to submit, resulting in her exile, while the fate of the nations who fail to heed this summons is deferred until chapters 46-51. Thus all the institutional fabric of Judah is now demolished. The world has been handed to Yahweh's servant Nebuchadnezzar (25:9), thus ushering in the age of the gentiles. Israel will cease from this time to be a geographical reality, never in fact to be restored to her promised-land borders. The small city state which will arise after the exile will serve simply to remind the people of God of the eschatological promises which they continue to bear.

The repetition of the temple sermon in Jeremiah 26 (cf. chap. 7) opens a new phase of the prophecy. Jeremiah now becomes more overtly political. Current prophecy which sought to promote misconstrued Zion ideals and which saw the temple as a talisman guaranteeing the existence of Jerusalem is condemned in the sermon and throughout chapters 26-29. The sustained judgement theme is then broken by the "book of consolation" (chaps. 30-33) which includes Jeremiah's proclamation of the New Covenant (31:31-34). A note of castigation returns in Jeremiah's survey of the social abuses which made the fall of Jerusalem both necessary and inevitable (chaps. 34-35), and in his presentation of Jehoiakim, who destroys Baruch's scroll, as a counter Josiah exhibiting national misconduct necessitating a New Covenant (Jer 36).

Jer 37-45 reviews the year and a half of siege before Jerusalem fell in 587/6BC. As indicated the oracles against foreign nations (chaps. 46-51) virtually conclude the book (chapter 52 is an historical appendix relating to the fall of Jerusalem). From start to finish the great prophet's ministry is shaped by a call to announce the end, its rationale and the hope which lay beyond it. Through the fires of exile Israel would re-emerge as a community of faith, albeit a non-national entity. We recognize that this emphasis was to be fulfilled through the death of Jesus and the emergence of the church. However, the constant attempt by post-exilic Judah to revive the past continually reminds us of Israel's tragic history. Nothing less than a new understanding of God's purposes for Israel within the hearts of the people could solve her dilemma. Jeremiah understood this and we now turn to his God-given insistence on the necessity of a New Covenant.

c. Jeremiah 31:31-34

1. *Continuity and Discontinuity.* The review of the Sinai covenant in Jer 31:31-34 reflects the internationalism referred to above. Though there is no mention of a world pilgrimage of the nations that is so characteristic of the prophetic eschatology, there is emphasis in verses 35-37 on the certainty of God's New Covenant as grounded within the order of creation itself. The (muted) note of the New Jerusalem in verses 38-40 combines to suggest the function of Jerusalem as a world centre, and thus to affirm an international context.

Jer 30-31 is almost exclusively given over to material dealing with the return of the exiled and divided nation and its re-establishment. With his understanding of the New Covenant Jeremiah builds a theological bridge connecting Israel's past to her future hope; a link forged between history and eschatology. The structure of 31:31-34, namely the contrast via paired verses of future hope (vv31,33) and the negative recital of the past (vv32,34), suggests elements of continuity and discontinuity are found within the passage. All this reinforces Jeremiah's position as the prophet astride two ages.

"Behold, the days are coming," the opening phrase of Jeremiah's prophecy of the New Covenant (Jer 31:31), indicates that the ensuing pronouncement points to an age in transition. While the phrase could (superficially) be taken as fully eschatological, the wider context must be determinative for us (it occurs some fourteen times in Jeremiah and only four times elsewhere). It is difficult to invest this vague phrase with precision. It does not necessarily refer to the remote future, but rather to the uncertain future whether near or remote. We have noted elsewhere that a distinction in time frame of this character was not generally operative within the prophets.[7] Like the NT writers who looked for the parousia in the near future, eschatology for the Israelite prophets was imminent. They believed in the re-establishment of Israel and in her future. And so the prophets of the exile expected that the return from exile would see the ushering in of the ideal age they predicted. Later, in exposition drawn from their material (cf. Dan 9), the exile itself is seen to be open-ended. Thus the transference of hope from a physical return to an eschatological belief did not prove difficult. This type of modification did not falsify the prophetic predictions, particularly those concerning the second exodus and a resultant covenant renewal; it simply postponed them.

2. *Unilateral Nature of the New Covenant.* There is no problem involved in understanding the meaning of "covenant" (Heb. *berit*) in this context. In our later presentation of the Sinai covenant material we argue a divine covenant followed the establishment of a relationship in Israel's experience (cf. our discussion of the New Israel). It did not call the relationship into being but affirmed its existence and served as a divine pledge of its endurance. Thus it gave quasi-legal backing. The sense of a unilateral commitment always existed in the divine covenants of the OT. In no case was Israel ever the initiator of the series of divine covenants (cf. Abrahamic, Sinatic, Davidic, Jeremianic). Covenant was imposed upon Israel; her part was simply to maintain the relationship to which it attested. In Jer 31 the language of covenant is distinguished by two features. First, we note that the theocentric character of the covenant is underscored by the consistent use of the first person maintained throughout verses 31-34 by Yahweh (e.g., "I will make", "I will put", "I will forgive their iniquity"), leaving no doubt as to the unilateral, and thus the promise dimension, of this covenant.

The second feature is the language of covenant initiation, "I will make" (Heb. *karat*, "to cut"). Heb. *karat* is the only verb employed in the OT for covenant making. It is often suggested that there are a number of synonyms for *karat,* i.e., that it is simply one among many verbs which can be used to indicate the beginning of a covenantal arrangement. But closer examination of the evidence indicates that this is an unwarranted suggestion.[8] Here we are speaking of a new arrangement, something which presupposes two partners, and also of the device whereby this future relationship is confirmed. The suggestion of a covenant affirming a future relationship points to some new divine redemptive intervention, some new divine movement in history. Since the Sinai covenant is clearly the model for the New Covenant, one most naturally thinks of a major redemptive event after the analogy of the first exodus. Unlike Isa 40-45 and Ezekiel, however, Jeremiah does not employ language suggesting a return from exile in terms of the new exodus expectations. Nevertheless, the connection with the Sinai covenant suggests such a redemptive model.

3. *"New" Covenant.* Jeremiah's prophetic covenant is described as "new" (Heb. *hadas* Jer 31:32). Here the element of ambiguity enters again since *hadas* can mean absolutely new or novel (cf. Exod 1:8, Deut 32:17, 1 Sam 6:7, Eccl 1:10) or carry the sense of renewed (cf. Lam 3:22-3). Perhaps we are to balance both uses of the word here. The LXX has chosen Gk. *kainos* here over Gk. *neos* as the translation of Heb. *hadas.* While there is no doubt that the two Greek words are sometimes used synonymously, *kainos* carries a qualitative dimension of "freshness" which *neos* lacks etymologically. It is perhaps too much to deduce the character of the covenant from references of this nature, but the LXX adjective is certainly appropriate to the context. What is intended is the importation of a new dimension so radical as to constitute a complete break with the past. In the immediate vicinity of this context we note Jeremiah's use of Heb. *bara'* "to create", a verb which refers to a totally unprecedented initiative, to describe the reversal of deeply rooted human tendencies and propensities in the new age; "the Lord has created (*bara'*) a new thing on the earth: a woman protects a man" (Jer 31:22). The word "covenant" would have recalled for Jeremiah's hearers a familiar set of experiences and relationships. Indeed, sufficiently familiar to become trite in the national experience, thereby necessitating the exile from which this new arrangement must arise. By the addition of the adjective "new" and its ambiguity, Jeremiah's audience is given opportunity for thought. Will this "new" covenant be more of the same, or of a completely different character?

The language and context permits both nuances. For instance, continuity surfaces with the explanation that this "new" covenant will be made with the traditional geographical entities, the north and south referred to under the terms "house of Israel" and "house of Judah" (Jer 31:31). Much of Jeremiah 30-31 is given over to this question of the kingdom division resulting from Solomon's time, and thus assurance is offered that both exiled or deprived entities would benefit in the new age. Prophecies of hope in these chapters are directed, sometimes alternatively, to both Northern and Southern kingdoms. It is sometimes argued that "house of Judah" in 31:31 is a scribal addition since only the house of Israel occurs in verse 33. But the thought is rather that the imposition of the New Covenant will mean the healing of the breaches long since existing between the two kingdoms. It will give expression to the prophetic conviction that there can only be, and has only ever been, one unified people of God. Like the notion advanced in Ezek 37:15-28, the return from exile will be a divine grafting operation making the two warring brothers one.

Jer 31:31, therefore, may be understood as largely operating within the framework of continuity. Certainly Jeremiah's hearers would have been familiar with the theological concepts advanced. The eschatology of a New Covenant implies a new divine intervention to rescue Israel from oppression just as it had in the past. Thus the tenor of Jeremiah's announcement is quite in keeping with the hope of a reconstituted Israel existing in history as a geographical entity, an idea that came to be expected by Israel as the focus of prophetic eschatology.

Yet the content of Jer 31:32 also moves us sharply away from a prophetic doctrine of continuing national hope. We are thus brought to distinct discontinuity. The New Covenant is not like the Sinai covenant in its tenor or type. Is this a contrast of law and grace? But Sinai was based upon a great act of redemption which called Israel into existence as a political, historical entity. It was characterized by the intervention of Yahweh who is described in the course of the Exodus narratives as "great in mercy" Heb. *hesed* (Exod 34:6). We can hardly expect, therefore, that the New Covenant will display a greater dimension of grace than the Sinai covenant given the extent of Yahweh's commitment to Israel offered at that time. It would be quite mistaken to see Sinai as a demand in contrast to the New Covenant as promise. We will take this point up in detail in the course of this present discussion. But for now it must be emphasized that Yahweh's Sinai commitment arose out of a sheer act of redemptive grace. Thus the question of discontinuity in Jer 31 can hardly be yoked to a different display of the divine character.

What is "new" is the avoidance of the fallibility of the old covenant. That covenant was breachable by Israel ("my covenant which they broke"). The pathetic national response to the reforms of Josiah is living testimony to this fact in the minds of Jeremiah's hearers. But it is not possible to breach the New Covenant. Yahweh had maintained his fidelity to that earlier commitment in spite of Israel's unceasing provocations. In the new arrangement *both* parties would be loyal. The divine faithfulness to the Sinai arrangement is referred to in Jer 31:32 by the familiar prophetic language of marriage. Jeremiah's use of the metaphor is persuasive and apt, reminding Israel of the real nature of the arrangement. Yahweh wooed Israel and drew her with bonds of love. As the bridegroom he initiated this relationship which transcended natural ties, as the marriage bond does. The relationship was conceived of as permanent for in its ideal sense the OT entertained no notion of divorce. In the social context of the day the marriage metaphor pointed to a relationship in which parity did not exist.

The marriage figure emphasized that expectations by both partners existed within the relationship, expectations which had been given legal status by the marriage bond. Thus although Israel had broken the arrangement, the bond still held. The newness of the New Covenant would therefore result in the cessation of Israel's desire to breach the bond. Her heart would be changed and so she would finally be loyal.

4. *Law in the Heart.* Jer 31:33 takes up the note of "law in the heart". This idea of "inwardness" is often thought to provide the element of newness in the New Covenant as the appropriate response to this new arrangement with the implication that the law in the heart will assure the demonstration of constancy in conduct. The basic inability of the old arrangement was the frailty of the human partner. The problems under the old covenant arose on the human level. Would not the inward and transforming relationship to which Jeremiah refers guarantee the distinctiveness of the new arrangement spoken of in the previous verse? Obviously, this is undeniable. But it would be wrong to suggest that the Sinai covenant, which obviously is again in view here with reference to *torah*, had not had its appropriate degree of inwardness.

That inwardness to which we now refer had not led to a national transformation. Nevertheless the Sinai covenant was in conception an idealization which aimed at transformation. The references to "law" in Jer 3:33 cause us to reflect upon the relationship of covenant and law in the OT. Both terms were interdependent: covenant indicating prior relationship; law implying response. It would be a mistake, however, to think in terms of covenant law as a theology of demand since "law" (Heb. *torah*) points to the contours within which the relationship operates. Law was guidance for living in OT terms, not an outward arbitrary demand. One did not come to covenant through law as Exod 20:2 makes clear. In Sinai terms law was the relationship in operation. No demand could be expected where grace had not first operated. And there could be no separation of *torah* from the whole covenant framework.

Later in Israel's history a tendency developed to regard the law as purely demand. Such views took law out of its original context and externalized it. Yet it was not so in the beginning. The book of Deuteronomy makes it perfectly clear at all levels that obedience to the law was incumbent only upon those who stood within the framework of redemption (cf. Deut 6:20-25). This obedience, therefore, was prompted by prior grace. Moreover, in Deuteronomy especially, it is always presumed that the place of the law is in the national and the personal heart (6:4-6; 11:18). Indeed the stylistic oscillation between second person plural and second person singular exhortation which characterizes the book (sometimes suggested to reflect its composite character) was a device utilized in the author's desire to address Israel through individual Israelites.

Certainly in Deuteronomy the notion of the law in the heart is usually advanced imperatively (cf. Deut 6:4-5). But such references point to what is the ideal or desired, and presumably the possible, state for the individual. The demand for the circumcision of the heart is made in similar contexts (10:16), and it seems as if these are all requirements to which Israel must respond. But in Moses' moving final address the possibility of Israel in exile is surveyed (chap. 30). There the recall of the nation is anticipated, but only as a result of a divinely wrought circumcision of the heart (v6). Such passages indicate the ideals underlying the Sinai arrangement from its inception. Ideally the law is always meant to be in the national and individual heart, and we now turn to the wider OT evidence which indicates this.

The OT salvation experience of the individual presupposed the premise of the "law in the heart". The demand for purification of the heart, the creation of a clean heart for personal renewal, is frequent in OT thought. Contrition always stems from the heart (cf. Pss 51:10,17; 73:1; Prov 22:11; Isa 57:15). Jeremiah clearly states a national change of "heart" means a return to Yahweh (Jer 3:10) and uses the circumcision language in this connection (4:4, cf. 9:25-26). The law in the heart is always required for the possibility of spiritual experience in the OT. It is axiomatic that this should be so, cf. Pss 37:31; 40:8: in the latter reference to do the will of God depends upon the placing of the law in the heart. In Isa 51:7 the exiles are addressed in the prospect of a return to Jerusalem and the enactment of a New Covenant. Those addressed are the faithful and are termed "you who know righteousness, the people in whose heart is my law". Of course, there are tensions between the placement of the law in the heart and the obedience arising from it.

However, such tensions are not confined to the OT. They are also inherent in the flesh/Spirit struggles of the NT, tensions which are common to the reception of a biblical faith and its expression. It would thus be to go beyond the evidence to suggest that the newness of the New Covenant has been exposed only in the emphasis upon the inwardness of the law. If the OT assumes that the law in the heart is the basis of faith "experience", it does not suppose that the individual has created this prerequisite. This inward experience comes by divine act, and while the emphasis upon the law written on the heart in Jer 31:33 is compelling it does no more than guard against the ever-present threat of externalism in the OT. Additionally, it stresses that divine grace is the constituent upon which all spiritual experience is based. We are not denying that Israel is being recalled to spiritual idealism in verse 33. But to go further and to suggest that Jeremiah is breaking new ground at this point may be to advance too far. Moreover, verse 33 closes with the contentional covenant formula, "I will be their God and they will be my people". Such a statement merely seems to anticipate the renewed, ongoing relationships in which Israel always was held. Jer 31:33 thus may plausibly be viewed as simply saying Yahweh is returning to the idealism of the Sinai period in the New Covenant relationship.

But a problem remains. If it is more of the same how will the new arrangement adhere? How will the people of God give vent in the new age to the perfect expression of the relationship demanded implicitly by Jer 31:32? Here verse 34 is designed to take us further. As the major concluding statement of the pericope it indicates where the "newness" of the New Covenant is to be found.

5. *"Newness"*. In Jer 31:34 we enter a new phase of human experience. The divine initiative of verse 33 issues into something more than was possible through Sinai. A connection with what preceded continues to be presumed, but the wording "no longer" creates the radical character of the change which is contemplated. Since the old system was mediated, it required the re-iteration of constant

instruction, priestly meditation, prophetic admonition, confession and contrition. None of these will exist or be needed in the new situation. No more instruction, no institutional support will be required to bolster the system grace promoted in the new age! Exhortations will no longer be needed to evoke constancy in the relationship. All will be deeply and totally involved in the new expression of the covenant in the coming days (cf. the use of Heb. *yadac*, "know" a verb often employed in the OT to convey deep intimacy). The basis of this new dimension of covenant experience is the same as in the old; namely the presupposition of experience will be "law in the heart". We have already seen this in verse 33 where internalism was sharply contrasted with the externalism which characterized Jeremiah's day. However, it reoccurs to highlight what follows in the latter half of verse 34. More than a mere reference to the regenerative activity of Yahweh is in view! The experience of the OT and NT believer had coincided in verse 33; namely, without a new birth there is no possibility of the Kingdom of God experience (John 3:5). Read from one point of view, the implicit demand for law in the heart in Jer 31:33 endorsed this. However, in presuming this, verse 34 sets forth the series of circumstances which takes us beyond the range of spiritual experience possible within the framework of human limitations, of "life in the flesh".

The "newness" in the New Covenant appears in the phrase at the end of Jer 31:34. This phrase also seems to account for the possibility referred to at the beginning of that verse. In the new age, says Yahweh, "I will forgive their iniquity and I will remember their sin no more". Forgiveness is normally granted in the OT through the sacrificial system. Generally speaking, this system was efficacious for sins which had been confessed. Unconfessed sins, sins "done with a high hand" stood outside of the system. Of course, from time to time there were departures (cf. the forgiveness of David in 2 Sam 12:13), but these extraordinary acts of forgiveness simply underscored the point that forgiveness in the last analysis depended upon Yahweh's willingness to forgive and not upon any institution. God gave the sacrificial system, it was the normal means of approach and it was properly deemed by the OT believer to be efficacious. The ancient believer was fully aware, if spiritually perceptive, that it was not the blood of bulls and goats which forgave sins. But, as the writer of Hebrews remarks, the system required repetitive approaches and continual confession even though it always looked to the same basis for forgiveness, the free grace of God.

But now in the new age sin will be more than forgiven, it will be "forgotten"! This is a remarkable statement and its complete tenor needs to be appreciated. There is a (technical) usage of the vocabulary, for "remembering" in the OT is not simply limited to the power of psychological recall. In these instances, particularly when predicated of Yahweh, remembering implies reactivating an issue, or taking action on behalf of someone to effect a new set of circumstances whose rationale stems from some past act. Commenting on Jer 31:34 in association with other OT references, B.S. Childs remarks "although (in Jer 31:34) in the majority of cases the subjective element is included, there are no examples where this reflection does not issue in the objective intervention towards that which was remembered. Memory is not identical with the action, though it is never divorced from it".[9] So God remembered Noah (Gen 8:1) and caused the waters to abate. He remembered Hannah (1 Sam 1:19) and the promise of a son became an actuality for her. In the context of Jer 31:34 for God "not to remember" means that no action will need to be taken in the new age against sin. Yet we are not only pointing in this verse to the action of God in Christ as he reconciled the world unto himself, for the text does not merely mean that God's forgiveness will be so comprehensive as to cover all sins, both witting and unwitting, confessed and unconfessed.

We look here for the work of the cross in the *final* experience of the believer. In the eschatological age of which Jeremiah is speaking, sin will not be a factor, it will be foreign to all human experience. Thus the point advanced here is not a contrast between the restrictions under which the old covenant had laboured and the freedom which is dictated by the Spirit in the new. In the age to which Jeremiah's prophecy progressively is looking, sin will neither need to be confessed, nor forgiven. Jer 31:34 moves beyond the course of present human experience to the perfected unfettered fellowship of the New Creation; to harmony prevailing within creation, and between creation and God; to the time when the tensions of human experience within the historical age will have finally been overcome. We will later note how the death of Christ will inaugurate this New Covenant which will assume its full operation at the "redemption of all things", i.e., in the New Creation.

In short, the New Covenant of Jeremiah points to God's final gift. It does not point to a new measure of divine forgiveness since God's forgiveness is offered freely within both testaments. But it points to a new apprehension of that forgiveness within human experience, an apprehension which will mean perfected service in the presence of Him whose service is perfect freedom. Jer 31:31-34 thus looks beyond the community of the NT age to the operation of life within the framework of a revealed New Creation. The new heavens and the new earth will have arrived and the New Jerusalem descended. The dwelling of God is then with men and they will be his people and he will be their God (Rev 21:3-4).

iv. *Ezekiel*

The remaining material in the OT endorses Jeremiah and amplifies what is stated therein. In Ezek 36:16-38 the matter of the way in which the redemption from exile and the return to the land is to be accomplished is examined. Verses 16-20 look back to the loss of the land and the causes of that loss. From this it becomes clear that any restoration which will follow must be completely a divine undertaking dependent upon divine faithfulness (vv21-23). The series of events whereby the return and the renewal will be effected are indicated in verses 24-27. A new exodus will take place (v24) and the manner of the return will involve Israel's cleansing and ritual preparation (v25) for the Edenic sanctuary to which they will return. All of this has overtones of a New Covenant, the more so when we compare what is offered in verse 25 with the covenant ratification ceremony of Exod 24:1-8. This negative separation is then complemented by a positive endowment designed to fit Israel for new life in the now cleansed land.

In Ezek 36:26 the question of a new heart is investigated. A factor which in itself presumes the point to which reference has been made earlier; that it is from within the heart that the issues of life and spiritual response are to be determined. To be sure it is not stated specifically that the law will be put into the heart. However, since an ensuing obedience is pointed to in verse 27 it is clear that the requirements referred to in Jer 31:31-34 are similarly presupposed (that in the new age the law will be in the heart).

Yet Ezek 36 is not merely repetitive. A new element is introduced in Ezek 36:26-27, namely the gift of a "new" spirit (the use of Heb. *hadas* "new" entails the same ambiguities discussed in relation to Jer 31:31). Ezekiel's use of language here is as extraordinary as Jeremiah's. The democratization of the Spirit upon which this new reformation depends suggests a concept of the Spirit which hitherto was unheard of in the OT. Previously the gift of the Spirit was spasmodic and associated with Israel's leadership, generally confined to judges, kings and prophets. Now it is extended to the people of God as a whole.[10] While the Spirit is clearly the vitalizing element in the experience of the new age, the reference to universality can also mean nothing less than a democratization of leadership in the new age where all will be "kings and priests".

While his emphasis is thus slightly different to that of Jeremiah, the goal of Ezekiel is certainly the same; the experience of new life within the New Creation. This is the direction in which Ezek 36 heads, since in verses 28-38 we have a virtual return to the garden scene of Genesis 2. Indeed the comparison is made plain at Ezek 36:35 where it noted that "this land that was desolate has become like the garden of Eden". Thus the renewal of Israel is associated (as we should have expected) with the renewal of Israel's land, with consequent influence being exerted upon the surrounding nations (v36).

From another point of view the same process is reflected upon in Ezek 37 in terms of a national resurrection. The processes of judgement contemplated by the prophet in the "valley" of vision (cf. 3:22) is now accomplished in apparently this same valley (37:1). All that is left of national Israel is the charnel house of bleached bones which lies before the prophet. But transformed by the Spirit of God, a New Israel arises (vv1-14). This in turn is translated in verses 15-28 into the obliteration of all former national divisions, the creation of one new people of God under common Davidic leadership. An everlasting covenant of peace is concluded (v26) by which the creation blessings are renewed ("I will bless them and multiply them" — note that the Heb. has "give them" though the Aramaic Targum supplies "bless"). The Sinaitic covenant promises are revived in verse 26, and the sanctuary, Edenic, character of the land is recaptured in verse 28. After the interlude of Gog from Magog in chapters 38-39, the unfolding of the nature of the divine indwelling in the final age proceeds in the new temple prophecies of 40-48.

Earlier God pledged himself to take New Covenant action in ushering in the new age (Ezek 16). When the question of covenant renewal is raised in 16:1-52, Yahweh undertakes to "remember" the covenant concluded with them in the days of their youth by re-establishing it and setting up an everlasting covenant (vv60-61). The Sinai covenant is broken (v59), yet continuity remains (cf. Heb. *heqim* "re-establish, confirm" in v62). Somewhat puzzlingly, verse 61 remarks that the reception of the two erstwhile erring daughters, Jerusalem and Samaria (surrogates for north and south), will not be "on account of the covenant with you". Perhaps this must be interpreted to mean that there will be no easy mechanical transition into the new age. Along with continuity there will also be a very serious difference. The efficacy of mere reliance upon old connections by Israel must not be presumed.

v. *Isaiah 40-66*

As the opening sentence of Isa 40:1 indicates ("Comfort, comfort my people, says your God"), these chapters are entirely devoted to covenant renewal and the New Jerusalem. Only the major features of these verses may be discussed here.

Covenant renewal is linked in these chapters with the theme of the restoration of all things. Final end-time renewal is a sustained emphasis in Isa 40-66. Note its occurrence in 40:1-11, which serves as a general introduction to chapters 40-66 and in particular to 40-55. Thus the transformation of nature is expected in 40:3-5, in the conclusion of 40-55 (55:12-13), and again in the final chapters of the prophecy (cf. 65:17). The emphasis of a New Creation through covenant in chapters 40-66 is affirmed by the agency of the divine word, which is prominent in 40:6-8, repeated in 55:6-11, and dominant in the assessment of the ministry of the servant (52:13-53:12). Elsewhere we have noticed the heavy second exodus emphasis of chapters 40-55 (cf. Isa 42:16; 43:16,19; 49:9,11; 51:10). Its connection with covenant renewal and entry into the promised land is clear from the application of first exodus analogies.

Older covenantal promises are revived through recalling the Abrahamic traditions (Isa 41:8; 51:1-2). For instance, Abraham was once a dweller in the land in which Israel now receives the call to return. Through his call he became the father of a great nation (51:2). Now Israel is poised to become a great people (49:20-21; 54:3) dwelling in the promised land (49:8,19), and serving as a blessing to others (vv5-6, cf. Gen 12:1-3). Thus the full extent of the Abrahamic covenant commitment is envisaged in the summons issued to Israel by the prophet to prepare to come home.

But we should note that it is only faithful Israel who is in view. Thus, they are exhorted to look to the rock from which they were hewn, Abraham (Isa 51:1). This is the Israel who "follows righteousness" and "who seeks the Lord". Isa 51:1-6 proceeds in the best traditions of prophetic eschatology. The faithful are urged to look back to the history of salvation for assurance (v1) since Yahweh is now moving to comfort Zion (v3) and to make her the new Eden, the world centre, the oasis from which blessing radiates (v3). This in turn will mean the incorporation of the nations within the salvation promises (vv4-6). After further reassurance to the redeemed, the links between creation, exodus and the second exodus are further forged in verses 9-11.

It is in the ministry of the servant that the covenant expectations which Isaiah cherished are best seen. The language of the first servant passage (Isa 42:1-4) is carefully analysed by W.A.M. Beuken.[11] Kingly and prophetic features are to be found in this enigmatic figure, thus uniting all previous leadership traditions, though his ministry will be superficially unimpressive. Yet as Beuken remarks, with "covenant fidelity in view" (a fair implication from Heb. *le'emet* "for faithfulness" v3) the servant's ministry will effect the changes in the course of history for which Israel is now looking as an answer to her complaints, and to which, commencing at 40:12, Yahweh had responded.

The express link between the servant and covenant is made by Isa 42:6 (vv5-9 may be a continuation of vv1-4; certainly they are a comment upon the earlier section)[12] as well as by 49:6. Both references include the difficult and disputed phrase "covenant to the people" (Heb. *berit am*). The translation "covenant people" defies the Hebrew order. But "covenant of the people" with the individual servant as the carrier of the older traditions and as a pledge for them is possible. As is a "covenant of the people" where servant Israel (Israel and the servant are identified in 49:3) is a pledge of Yahweh's world intentions. A fourth suggestion which relates "covenant" Heb. *berit* to a root meaning "splendour" or "brightness", thus avoiding the translation "covenant", fails to do justice to the covenant tenor of this passage and prophecy.

In either of the two views preferred above the servant is a covenant embodiment. He perpetuates the past and guarantees the future. He is the link between what is jettisoned and what is proposed. What he will do will have reference to Israel and to the nations through restored Israel. After further assessment of the servant's ministry in Isa 49:1-6 and 50:4-9, its final elaboration occurs in 52:13-53:12. Foreign kings who recognize the scope of the deliverance can only marvel (52:13-15; they appear to be assessors of his ministry, 53:1-9).[13] The extent of this deliverance brought about by the atoning ministry of the servant, a ministry which finds its final fulfilment in Jesus, is then surveyed by chapters 54-55 which logically depend upon the detail of chapter 53.

Isaiah 54 in particular, as Beuken[14] has pointed out, takes up a sustained series of salvation history images. Verses 1-3 are obviously Abrahamic in tenor. Note the symbolism of the barren woman who now conceives, the multitude of children which will be hers, the consequent need to enlarge the tent, and the possession of the gates of the enemy by her seed (cf. Gen 18:10 where Sarah hears of the seed promise, and 22:17 where dominance is accorded to Abraham's seed).

In its fuller context Isa 54:1-3 infers a revival of the Abrahamic promises, a revival resulting from the servant's ministry which brought a renewed Israel into being. The image of the barren woman changes dramatically to the related image of the forsaken wife in verses 4-8. This reference, together with the marriage imagery and exodus terminology (cf. "Holy One of Israel", "Redeemer" v5, "everlasting *hesed*") has the Sinai event in view, although the mention of Yahweh as the "creator of Israel" in verse 5 interlocks with the Abrahamic promises of the previous section.

A comparison of the exile to the flood begins at Isa 54:9. The reference to the "covenant of peace" in verse 10, a most comprehensive reference given the wealth of connotations which underly "peace" (Heb. *salom*), serves a two-fold purpose. First, it points to the exile as an interlude which prefaces a new beginning. In the second place it affirms that God's creation purposes expressed in Noah[15] will not be negated but will in fact be given complete expression through this covenant of peace. Never again will the position of the people of God be threatened (v10). In the new order their security will be as unchallengeable as the most fixed elements of the natural order.

Although the flood imagery is continued we move into a new domain with Isa 54:11-17. The new factor emerging in verses 11-12 is a city of resplendent foundations which God has laid, thereby assuring the stability and permanency of the new structure. Yet the earlier material imagery is revived somewhat paradoxically in a bewildering fusion of imagery, since this city is the possessor of offspring who in covenant language "will be taught by the Lord". The imagery of the New Jerusalem, the city for which Abraham looked, is drawn magnificently and the new arrangement of blessing for the community is laid bare in verses 14-17, an address which is enclosed by the note of righteousness characteristic of the new age (Heb. vv14,17), as Beuken notes.[16]

However, this does not mean that Israel involves herself in the New Covenant. Rather it is divine fidelity which assures the fulfilment of commitments in the history of salvation and the continuance of blessings projected for the people of God throughout the new age. Isa 54:17 uses the older covenant promised land language of "inheritance" (Heb. *nah^{a}lah*). Thus the covenant tenor of this wide-ranging chapter is not only endorsed but its goal is foreshadowed. Implicitly a reference is made here to the dominant covenant blessing of "rest", a prominent ideal of covenant fulfilment in Deuteronomy as fulness of life in a sanctuary land indwelt by God (Deut 3:20; 12:9; 25:19; 28:65). Therefore, the survey of the array of covenant promises in Isa 54 points to a continuity with these past traditions but foreshadows the radical character of the future. Under a series of multiple images the age of the New Covenant and the perfection of the people of God are treated. All of this it must be emphasized has stemmed from the ministry of the servant whose sufferings must perfect the new age.

The New Jerusalem notes of Isa 54 have implicitly raised the question of the place of Davidic kingship in the new era, and this theme returns in 55:3-5. Immediately preceding this, 55:1-2 summons faithful Israel to participate in the new life which will flow forth from the New Jerusalem (cf. Ezek 47:1-12). Here the abundance of water, wine, and milk herald the blessings of the new paradise. The everlasting covenant referred to in verses 3-5 further explicates the "covenant of peace" (54:10). This New Covenant will mean a democratization of the Davidic promises with the benefits of the Davidic position being extended to all believers in the new age. All will be kings and priests, therefore enjoying the particular relationship which characterized the special position of David in the historical period. Thus the Davidic promises, now devoid of any political significance, are transferred to the total people of God. World leadership is now the office of the new community, which the nations recognize in their pilgrimage to Jerusalem, the world centre (cf. 2:2-4).

In Isa 40-55 the servant's ministry is directed to faithful Israel. Perhaps he is to be seen as their representative; perhaps he was a prophetic figure in the exile; perhaps an idealization of Jesus who was to come. The lines of interpretation in this matter are still disputed. Remaining at the perimeter in this new internationalism, the nations are summoned only to participate in the blessings which are essentially Israel's, when her future is certain.

The remainder of Isa 40-66 takes the covenant question no further. These chapters do emphasize however, as P.D. Hanson notes,[17] that salvation is not for the whole nation but for the faithful within the nation. There is no mention here of a Davidic figure for like chapters 40-55 their tenor is to stress the kingship of God. Thus, in the whole of Isa 40-66, the covenant renewal of Israel proceeds in Abrahamic terms with Israel at the centre. Indeed, covenant renewal proceeds in terms of a New Covenant which ushers in a New Creation. This is an emphasis which the NT will carry further. Of course, the extravagance of the prophetic projections of the return from exile, the transformation of nature and the immediacy of fulfilment, all contrast markedly with the actual nature of the return. But Isaiah, Jeremiah and Ezekiel are united in their emphasis. The position of Israel in exile can only be reversed by divine intervention of the character which, while preserving continuity with the past, broadens out in future prospect to a totally new era of salvation. Nothing less than the inbreaking of the rule of God.

vi. *Post-Exilic Period*

In the post-exilic period there are desultory attempts (particularly reported by Haggai and Zechariah) to implement the programme of Ezekiel. Messianism at this time receded into the background. Haggai particularly is very much covenant orientated and his work is couched in familiar covenant language.[18] We have already noted in dealing with the "New Temple" the theme of sin and the operation of the covenant curses (Hag 1:4-11), the people's repentance and the divine acceptance of this response (vv12,14). All of this anticipates the inflow of nations resulting from the rebuilt temple assuming its place as the world centre (2:1-9), a state which demands a "purified promised land" (vv10-19). Davidic expectations are kept alive in the form of Zerubbabel, but he is only a continuity figure, being presented as the Persian governor (vv20-23).

A note of covenant renewal opens the book of Zechariah (Zech 1:1-6). The sustained use of "return" Heb. *sub* (1:3,6,6) points in that direction through its extended use in OT covenant contexts, with the transferred sense of repent.[19] Zech 1-8 has as its principal theme the building of the temple. Consistent with Zion and temple expectations delineated elsewhere 8:20-23 reports Jerusalem's role as a world centre. Yet earlier covenant traditions are also present. Thus the asseveration of the pilgrim foreigner who takes hold of the robe of a Jew distinctly echoes the words of Abimelech, the first foreign contact with whom Abraham regularly associated (v23 "Let us go with you, for we have heard that God is with you" cf. Gen 21:22). The second half of Zechariah is concerned with the manifestation of divine kingship and temple occupancy and ends on the same world pilgrimage note as 8:20-23 (cf. chap. 14).

Malachi, best understood as written on the eve of the Ezra-Nehemiah reforms teems with covenant allusions or dependence. The issue in Mal 1 is the acknowledgement of divine rule by Judah. Divine rule is rejected by God's people now but will be acknowledged by the world (v11). We cannot be sure about the precise significance of the covenant reference of Mal 2:1-9, nor whether the priesthood to whom the rebuke is directed is being rejected in favour of a wider covenant with Levi. Verses 10-16 with their reference to "one father" (v10) appeal to the Abrahamic base of Israel's relationship. Whether in verses 13-16 divorce or apostasy is on view is difficult to decide. The covenant emphasis of the passage is clear, however (vv10,14).

Covenant breach invites response (2:17-3:5). God Himself will come as judge, judging those who ridicule the absence of His judgement (v17). Perhaps the "messenger of the covenant" (3:1) whose ministry will have some connection with the return to the land (cf. the allusions in Mal 3:1 to Exod 23:20 and Isa 40:3) had immediate reference to the ministry of Ezra which was about to occur. More fully, however, the role of this messenger will be taken up in the Elijah figure of Mal 4:4-6. Mal 3:6-12 refers to God's constancy despite provocation. Mal 3:13-4:3 repeats the basic charge of abuse of the temple and sacrificial system. A remnant group who responds to the prophetic preaching is mentioned in verse 16 and to them the promises of Exod 19:3b-6 are virtually repeated in 3:17. The division between the wicked and the elect when judgement comes is referred to in 4:1-3. The point of the book is brought out in Mal 4:4-6 (Heb. 3:22-24). Yahweh is faithful to his covenant but requires a response from the community of the day. Before the final Day of the Lord an Elijah-type figure will come who will expose the real issues and place them before Israel. After this recall to Sinai (which the coming of Elijah will mean, cf. 1 Kgs 18-19) the coming of God then superintervenes. If the Elijah initiative fails then final covenant curses will fall upon Israel for covenant breach. Of course these closing verses are fulfilled in the ministry of John the Baptist which was followed by the Day of the Lord, judgement through the ministry of Jesus.[20]

Ezra the reformer returned from the exile in 458BC. Traditionally he is depicted as the post-exilic law-giver, the reviver of legalism within the community, the father of later Judaism. But as K. Koch[21] notes, the evidence points in a different direction. The temple emphasis and only peripheral mention of the law in chapter 7 places Ezra in direct continuity with the earlier leaders of the return, Joshua and Zerubbabel, and highlights his concern for the creation of a new community. Moreover, Ezra's emphasis upon a purified promised land occupied by a culturally united people offers all the ingredients of the second exodus theology to which Isa 40-55 had pointed.

The emphasis of this book, together with that of Nehemiah, in which Ezra also figures, is, as already noted, upon the endeavours of these two reformers to implement the return programme outlined by the exilic prophets. This programme had earlier failed, the efforts of Haggai and Zechariah notwithstanding. Thus a further review of Israel's covenant history occurs in Nehemiah with a final plea for renewal based upon Yahweh's fidelity to his prior promises. Arguing from an Abrahamic base (v8), chapter nine goes on to detail the history of salvation before presenting Israel's present position of bondage. But now the bondage is within the land of promise (v36)! The best efforts of these two reformers to create a new covenant community (cf. the renewal ceremony of Neh 8-10), however, are thwarted by political divisions and the power of the Jerusalem priesthood. And so the Ezra-Nehemiah period ends on a sad note.

Chronicles appears to have been written as support for the Ezra-Nehemiah reforms[22] and perpetuates the tradition of a new exodus community looking for the fulfilment of the prophetic hopes. Following the close of the canon (c350BC), the small city state of Jerusalem, in which nationalistic hopes were still foolishly cherished, lapsed into tight priestly control persisting for some two hundred years until the progress of the Maccabaean revolt loosened it. But the OT is the record of a spiritual failure. Much had been given to Israel and high expectations were entertained. Yet she had not achieved them and it was clear that she could not. The nation would retire from history with the destruction of the second temple, but the longing for the kingdom of God as the inbreaking of the New Creation forged by her prophets under divine inspiration continued as the goals towards which the NT community would direct its gaze.

What has surfaced in all the biblical materials on covenant is that the shape of the New Covenant is controlled by the parameters of the past. Elsewhere[23] we have argued that though there are many expressions of the covenant (a point that Paul appears to make by the plural in Rom 9:5) there is only one biblical covenant, that made implicitly by the fact of creation itself and re-established in the details of Gen 6:18 and 9:7-13. What this means is that covenant theology is always promise theology. Thus it is consistent in view of the national failure found in the OT that Rabbinic Judaism appears to have recognized the promise tenor of covenant. Rabbinic Judaism saw God as the initiator and upholder of the covenant and believed in its permanence despite Israel's defections. Even when faced with national disobedience God remains faithful to his undertakings, for covenant promises were not finally dependent upon Israel's performance.[24] Of course, the Jerusalem destruction in 70AD may have produced this later Rabbinic emphasis but as we approach the NT the misunderstandings of the relationships between law and promise may not, as E.P. Sanders points out,[25] have been due to Jewish misunderstanding of the covenant relationship.

The New Testament

i. Matthew

In our OT survey we have hinted at the significance of christology for new covenant formation in the NT. The full significance of the LXX use of "covenant" (Gk. *diatheke*) as divine disposition or imposition[26] becomes clear in the presentation of Jesus' death in the synoptic Gospel narratives as ushering in the New Covenant (cf. Mark 14:24; Matt 26:28; Luke 22:20). These institution narratives view his death as the cup of suffering drunk to initiate the new age.

Matthew's Gospel is thoroughly covenantal in orientation; it is important to consider points of contact with OT covenant theology in some detail. Only very general remarks will be offered on the other two synoptics. Luke views the new age as one of Abrahamic fulfilment (Luke 1:72). Mark's witness is kingdom centred and thus indirectly covenantal. Some reference will be made later to John's Gospel which is concerned, as we point out in our discussion of the New Israel, with documenting the emergence of the new community.

We will survey the impact of Matt 1 and the covenant renewal ministry of John the Baptist in material relating to the New Israel. Therefore, details need not be pressed at this point. Matthew's Gospel appears to be structured around a framework of Abrahamic promise and fulfilment. This may be demonstrated by referring first to the conclusion of the Gospel and then by noting the inclusion that the final verses form with the first chapter.

Matt 28:16-20 takes place in Galilee, the scene of Jesus' eschatological teaching where the messianic light had first dawned (4:12-17). As the exalted Son of Man (cf. Dan 7:13),[27] Jesus commissions his disciples on the mountain (i.e., the world mountain) from which ministry will now proceed. The enthronement of Jesus to full authority is not presented here since we are dealing with a commission and not, as some have argued, with an enthronement formula. Although hardly convincing in its totality, H. Frankemoelle's relation of Matt 28:16-20 to the structure of 2 Chron 36:23 via a common background in OT covenant renewal formulas is interesting.[28] Covenant renewal is certainly part of the content presentation of these verses, as is made clear by the use of the phrase "I am with you" (Matt 28:20). Frankemoelle's approach to Matt 1, a chapter clearly linked to Matt 28, from the basis of his conclusions in regard to Matt 28:16-20 is also helpful. He has highlighted a similarity of emphasis in Matthew 1 to the genealogies of Chronicles (cf. 1 Chron 1-9), whereby the tone for the thrust of the subsequent narrative is set in each case through the genealogies. But the precise covenant formulary equations which Frankemolle postulates between Matt 28:18-20 and 2 Chron 36:23 are not only unconvincing and forced, but fail to account for the total form of Matt 28:16-20.[29] These verses do contain elements of a commissioning narrative, as B. Hubbard has noted.[30] There are difficulties, however, with too precise an attempt to locate this section formally, and we agree with the suggestion that the Matthean redaction in this closing junction of the Gospel makes it fruitless to seek for exact formal parallels.[31]

What we are required to observe, however, are both the breadth and limitation of Jesus' ministry for these points are made within the narrative itself. All power, Jesus asserts, is now his by divine gift. The background of this assertion, as we hinted above, is the allusion to the heavenly Son of Man of Dan 7:13 who appears in a context of judgement as the books of destiny are opened and the histories of all men and nations are controlled. A further background is also evident since the command to the disciples to go "into all the world" discloses a clear affinity with the Abrahamic promise framework, which once again strengthens the conviction that Matthew has used the Abrahamic theme as a basic structure. The promise of "I am with you to the end of the age" vividly recalls the Immanuel statement of Matt 1:23 in which a new people of God is foreshadowed. Thus in this closing statement of the Gospel the victorious Son of Man brings together key elements of the Davidic and Abrahamic promises as the basis upon which a new community will be formed.

The Abrahamic character of Matthew's conclusion is undoubted, refracted though it may be in the variegated expectations linked with the giver of the commission. The "New Israel" is here sent into all the world and the universalism incipient in Matthew's first chapter is now made clear. True, the contours of the Abrahamic covenant are altered by this commission. Israel goes out to the nations, rather than the latter comes in, as the eschatology and implications of that covenant had seemed to demand. The developed prophetic eschatology of the OT is based upon the Abrahamic covenant in ultimate terms. It presupposed the existence of a national framework into which the nations of the world could be incorporated: a geographical Jerusalem into which they could come; a feast of the tabernacles (etc.) which they could attend. But the possibility of all this has now passed and the people of God are only identifiable in terms of their close association with the inaugurator of the New Covenant, Jesus himself. Given the altered circumstances, they must necessarily go out; and they go out with his power transferred to them. But Christ goes with them for it is his ministry that they exercise ("I am with you until the end of the age"). They will be the extension of him in the same way that Luke understands the early apostolic church as the continuation of Jesus' ministry in Acts.

All the promises of the Abrahamic covenant have been clearly fulfilled in Jesus. That is the message of the Gospel of Matthew. Blessing for Jew and Gentile; one new people of God; one new man; one new image. The new people of God without national base must necessarily go out from the Jerusalem which is about to be destroyed. And so the removal of the commission from Jerusalem to Galilee simply underlines the fact that physical Jerusalem no longer has a place in the history of salvation.

Earlier we mentioned not only the comprehensiveness of the Son of Man's ministry, but also a limitation. This is underscored by the closing phrase of the Gospel. His ministry through the disciples will only remain to the end of the age. The proclamation of the death and resurrection of the Son of Man and the significance of that event for the opening of the book of human destiny is a ministry which belongs to this age. Beyond this age, in the age to come, we may expect that proclamation will give way to reality. Thus the full dimension will be realized of all the possibilities entertained in the eschatological event of the advent of Jesus Christ. We must now turn to the beginning of the Gospel.

The genealogy of Matt 1:1-17 opens the future to a new divine intervention in the history of salvation (this point is also made in the chapter on the New Creation). But the function of such a genealogy (as with the opening of the book of Chronicles) is to provide for continuity with the past. In this case it is continuity between the two testaments, and suggests that the Abrahamic promises are continued and fulfilled in Jesus. The genealogy begins with Abraham, thereby emphasizing the salvation history connections. Thus the universalistic tenor of the Gospel in its salvation history context is established. Admittedly, we do not frequently encounter this emphasis within Matthew's Gospel yet it clearly re-emerges at the conclusion. In underlining the further note of Jesus' fulfilment as Son of David (v1) the order of salvation is preserved, to the Jew first and then the Gentiles. Matthew's opening christology is far from exhausted at this juncture. As Son of Abraham and Son of David, Jesus was also Son of God by the manner of his birth and its association with the Spirit. In this way verses 18-25 emphasize the full significance of the nature of Jesus and the prospect which his ministry will bring.

As Immanuel (Matt 1:23) he will save "his people" from their sins (v21).[32] Particular attention must be paid here to the phrase "his people". Throughout the course of these studies we have advanced reasons to suggest that the redeemed, the new people of God, are in mind here and not in any way the resurgence of national Israel. D. Senior has pointed out[33] that Matthew's Gospel offers us a review of salvation history in the manner of some of the major historical works of the OT, particularly the books of Chronicles. Thus we are not surprised to find John the Baptist offering a final platform of covenant recall to all Israel assembled once again in the region round about the Jordan as the last and greatest of the prophets of the old era. It is unheeded and a new people of God is erected in the Gospel. We finish with their commissioning by Jesus who enters into ministry with them until the close of this age.

ii. *Paul*

a. 2 Corinthians 3

Although Paul constantly takes up the question of Jesus as the fulfilment of the Abrahamic promises and thus the One who continues the covenant traditions (cf. Rom 1:1,16-17 and especially Gal 3), a full covenant exposition is rarely offered by him. The covenant blessing of sonship is freely available to believers and Gal 3 makes the point that the role of the law as an "addition" to the Abrahamic promise structure was to throw the nature of sin into clear relief. Freedom, sonship and the function of law, all OT covenant emphases, find frequent mention in Paul. But the Pauline position is most clearly presented in the rather detailed exposition of the significance of the New Covenant offered in 2 Cor 3:7-18.

In regard to the general context of that discussion it is customarily agreed that 2 Cor 3:18 concludes the argument which had begun in 3:7. This discussion involved the significance of the New Covenant and included an exposition of the allusive but interesting detail of Exod 34:29-35. The OT episode dealt with the veiling of Moses' face when he functioned as covenant mediator in the presence of his fellow Israelites. It is further recognized that the detail of 2 Cor 3:7-18 is prepared for by the comparison between the ministry of the letter and the ministry of the Spirit as evidenced in verses 1-6. The implications of his conclusion reached in 3:18 are then drawn out in 4:1-6.

Several points however are still disputed. What is the precise nature of the comparisons and contrasts Paul draws between the new and old covenants? Is the New Covenant confirmatory of the old or does Paul point to the obsolescence of the old in this new phase of salvation history? Is it merely the case that he asserts the old is the covenant of the letter and the new that of the Spirit? Is this the point of comparison or contrast? Was the glory of the old covenant merely transitory just as the glow on Moses' face was "fading"? Who is the "Lord" of 2 Cor 3:16 — an important question in the interpretation of this chapter. What is the "same image" of verse 18 into which all Christians are being transformed? Since the argument of 2 Cor 3:7-18 begins with an appeal to the experience of Moses, it is at that point that we must begin also.

Paul's appeal to the Mosaic experience, and therefore the Sinai covenant, is dominated by the details of Exod 34 (cf. 2 Cor 3:7-10,13,16,18). The argument based upon Exod 34 moves into two stages. First, in 2 Cor 3:7-11 there is the question of the relative glory of the old and new covenants with the note that a "glory" motif is common to both. Secondly, the "veiled" nature of experience under the old covenant and the openness for believers associated with the New Covenant is the theme of verses 12-18 (note the inclusion formed by vv12 and 18 on the theme of access and openness).[34] Some, however, have suggested that in his use of the "glory" (Gk. *doksa*) and "veil" (Gk. *kalumma*) motifs, Paul moves beyond the OT context, since there is no indication that the glory "faded" in Exod 34:29-35. Before taking up this question the account in Exod 34:29-35 needs to be examined carefully.

Exod 34:29-35 operates as the conclusion of the covenant narration begun in Exod 19. It is thus positionally significant. We will also argue for its contextual significance. Although some of the interpretations given for this passage are fanciful, its details are clear. The veil or mask (the meaning of Heb. *masweh* in Exod 34:33 is unclear) is worn by Moses whenever he is *not* acting as a mediator (cf. vv33-35). In other words, Moses wore the veil except when he was actually reading the law or communicating the substance of the covenant to Israel, or whenever he was before the Lord in the tent of meeting. The narrative makes it plain that Moses had first read the commandments to Israel unveiled (v32) and only then did he veil his face (v33, cf. v35). Thus the necessity of the veil is not simply due to the Israelites' fear but to Moses' position as communicator and mediator. The glory which shone from Moses' face appears to have authenticated the revelation which he brought. The glory which suffused his face must be necessarily seen for what it was in the delivery of this "glorious" revelation. Thus the word came to them "unveiled". This is the precise point which the narrative is making. While we are virtually dependent upon Paul for the application of this OT passage, there are also some important clues to be had from its placement in the overall context.

As it stands Exod 34 completes the covenant delivery. This began in Exod 19 with a clear delineation of Israel's vocation as a covenant people (vv5b-6). There the rationale for Israel's call to function as a special separated people, a holy nation, is Yahweh's universal lordship (v5). That is, Israel is called to be the vehicle through which the world may be reached. The substance of verses 1-6 may be reduced to a particular application of the more basic Abrahamic promises in Israel's political experience. We have taken up this question in detail in our analysis of the New Israel theme.

The ten "words" which follow the theophany of Exod 19 are addressed to each Israelite individually. This is the clear meaning of 20:18 (cf. Deut 5:4,22). They came without the aid of any intermediary, a fact which stresses their primacy over all other legal prescriptions. Of course, the following social legislation is mediated by Moses (Exod 21-23). But these are described as "judgements" rather than the more significant term "words" (20:1). In other words, mediation at this point may be designed to indicate a lesser function, an exposition in social terms of the more primary decalogue. Finally, we may note that a free approach to Yahweh by the representatives of Israel remains in the covenant confirmation episode (Exod 24:1-11) though the special position of Moses is again emphasized (vv1-2).

Exod 25-31 deals with the erection of the tabernacle. This is not a digression as we indicated in the discussion of the New Temple. Rather it serves to emphasize the fact of Yahweh's kingship by reference to the building of a portable "temple"/throne and thus to give expression to the political constitution under which Israel now stands. Between the offering of the blueprint and the actual erection (chaps. 35-40) comes the account of Israel's great national apostasy through the golden calf (chap. 32) and the subsequent difficult task of covenant renewal. On this occasion the covenant is effected for Israel solely as a result of Moses' mediatorial efforts.

When the covenant had been renewed in Exod 34, the mediatorial role of Moses assumes prominence in the presentation. Israel's former position of openness to the divine word has now disappeared. Direct communication with Yahweh seems no longer possible for Israel after this time. The national sin of Exod 32 in some form or other will be repeated in Israel's ongoing historical experience. Yet the unveiled face of Moses in reception and communication of the divine word (Exod 34:29-35) continues to express to Israel the potential of the Sinai covenant while the veiled face of Moses proclaims the Israelite inability to receive the covenant blessings in which Moses still shares (cf. Exod 33:12-17 where the blessing of Exod 3:14-15, the giving of the name and the promise of the presence, are virtually transferred to Moses from that point onwards). The veil thus speaks of lost opportunities and yet also of the glory to be associated with divine revelation. As a summary of what Sinai both could have been but yet had become for Israel, this closing episode of Exod 34:29-35 is an eloquent commentary upon the history of Israel in the OT.

Returning to Paul's exposition in 2 Cor 3:7-18, we may understand that his contrast of "letter" and "spirit" is not something intrinsic to the NT. Rather from the very outset it has been part of Israel's national experience and part of the potential experience for each Israelite. The Judaism of Paul's day continued the attitude of national Israel in that they too failed to perceive the real nature of the revelation which had come to them at the "end of the ages". By their attitude to Christ they betrayed the same spiritual obtuseness which their ancestors had shown at Sinai. Thus, by contrasting the ministries of the two covenants as death and life, Paul is commenting upon the effect they have had in national and personal experience to this point. What is central in his exposition throughout verses 7-18 is the relationship between the law of Moses and the gift of the Spirit. From verse 7 Paul documents Israel's national experience under the old dispensation of the letter, which kills. Indeed, it is inevitable the code would kill, when objectified and removed from its context of grace. The ministry of death under the older order was exemplified by the fact the Israelites could not gaze on the face of Moses (v7). Because of national sin the glory associated with Moses' experience could not be Israel's. Throughout the remainder of this chapter (vv12-18) Paul contrasts to this the Christian's access, in which we "all with unveiled face could behold the glory of the Lord" (v18).

However, Paul does not suggest that the glory attached to the old covenant is transitory. The Gk. verb *katargeo* "abolish" is to be understood as passive in 2 Cor 3:7 — referring to the glory of the old covenant, in verses 10 and 13 — referring to the old covenant itself considered as a totality — and in verse 14 — referring to the removal of the veil.[35] This passive use indicates the old covenant was "about to be abolished" or was "in the process of being abolished", i.e., it refers to the gradual replacement of the old covenant with something new. The point of transition between the old and new covenants is the work of Christ.

The old covenant was limited by the inability of human agents to keep it. But the New Covenant inaugurated in Christ provides, through the Spirit of Christ, for the prospect of the complete transformation of the believer into a new man, a prospect to which Paul refers as this chapter progresses (cf. 2 Cor 3:18). Limited as the Sinai covenant had been by human inability it nevertheless embodies the potential the New Covenant expresses, as we have previously argued. In itself, the old covenant lacks the power to confer life, yet it points to the life which could be conferred by a covenant arrangement. The use of the perfect tenses to describe the glory of the Mosaic covenant in verse 10 indicates that the authority which it bore and the eschatological reality to which it pointed were still valid in Paul's day and awaited final fulfilment.

At 2 Cor 3:12 Paul turns to the question of access under the New Covenant. Here the issue of the veil becomes important. Paul argues that the christian has moved beyond the position of the Israelite standing before Sinai. In other words, beyond one who could only see flashes of the divine glory attached to the covenant revelation, a glory seen as an authentication of its nature. Moses was not able to share with Israel the nature of the revelation in complete openness. The Israelites could not look upon Moses' face since it declared the result of an experience which was not or could not be theirs. In verse 13 "end" (Gk. *to telos*) could mean the "high point of OT revelation"[36] indicating there would be a gradual declension in Israelite experience from that point. By the time of the Exod 34 experience, national Israel's mind was already hardened (note the Gk. aorist (past tense) of *poroo* "harden" in v14).

The historical position to which Paul refers still remains in his own day since Jewish obtuseness to revelation prevails. Reading the old covenant narrative (2 Cor 3:14) in the synagogues still fails to produce its real effect upon the Jewish hearer. But the real effect of the Sinai experience is now understood by the Christian, and demonstrated in Paul's message. The Jewish position remains since they are unaware that the significance of the old covenant is revealed in Christ (v14). Perhaps Paul is speaking more generally in verse 15, indicating that the removal of the veil from revelation as a result of Christian exposition does not mean the lifting of the veil from the heart of the Jewish hearer. Unbelief has become, as it were, "canonized" in Jewish experience. Indeed, the persistent opposition to Pauline ministry by Judaism eloquently demonstrates this.

Paul partially returns to Exodus 34 and the experience of Moses as veiled in 2 Cor 3:16, but at the same time he is thinking of the barriers to belief his own ministry encountered among the Jews. Thus the Mosaic experience, referred to by the loose quotation from the LXX is the basis from which Paul begins.

But the change in 3:16 from the narrative imperfect tenses of the LXX to an aorist subjunctive and a present indicative (*epistrepse* "turn" for LXX *eiseporeueto* and *periaireitai* "remove" for *periereito*, LXX Exod 34:34) emphasizes the attitude of the believer, who in conversion (aorist subjunctive) realizes the unique situation of a prospective New Covenant and the passing away of the old one (note the present tense of *periaireo*) with which he is now in contact.

Yet there is still reference in all this to the Mosaic experience. Turning to the Lord, Moses' veil was constantly removed. Turning to Christ for the believer means veiled understanding is progressively being done away with. Thus an analogy between the experience of the christian convert and Moses in the tent is being constructed in 2 Cor 3:16.

2 Cor 3:17 sums up the argument to this point by way of application. The Lord, the Yahweh of the OT, to whose presence Moses possessed unrestrained access, and who provided the content of covenant experience, is now the Spirit who likewise assures our relation to the New Covenant. It is the Spirit who admits the christians to all the privileges in Christ made available through the New Covenant. Yahweh is not remotely situated on the mountain top nor is covenant openness a very limited possibility. He now dwells through the Spirit in the hearts of all christians. The Mosaic Lord of Exodus 34 is now the Spirit of the NT. It is not the conversion of Israel which is in view here, but access under the New Covenant. Thus Paul is directing his attention to the continuation of the argument between the letter and the spirit. It is the contrast between the position of the Jew under the old covenant maintained by Judaism and that of the christian under the New Covenant. Just as the old covenant was revealed in all its openness to Moses, so the Spirit admits us to all the privileges of the new. And so verse 18 suggests that "we all" (i.e., Jewish and Gentile christians alike) are now in the same position of immediate contact with God as Moses.

In this new age, "we" are being progressively changed into the likeness of what we behold. The believer experiences a radically inward renewal (cf. Gk. *metamorphoo* "transform") which is gradual and ongoing (note the present tenses in 2 Cor 3:18). We are being changed "from glory into glory" into the "same" image. Yet no image has been mentioned so far making the use of the adjective "same" puzzling. True, the connection of "glory" (Gk. *doksa*) with "image" (Gk. *eikon*) is close,[37] but we cannot be certain the context of 2 Cor 3:18 immediately refers us to Christ as the image into which we are changed, though this must ultimately be in view. In the closely associated passage of 4:1-6 however, a passage which appeals heavily to creation imagery, Christ is identified as the image (v5). But it is somewhat of a strain upon the context of 3:18 to suggest the immediate reference is to 4:5.

Perhaps the underlying thought of the "same image" of 2 Cor 3:18 is eschatological. It would then be the one and the same image which is the goal of christian experience. This is the one new man of Eph 4:24, a notion which is both corporate and individual. Finally, the comparative "even as" (Gk. *kathaper*) in 2 Cor 3:18 refers to the Mosaic position again (cf. v13). However, it is a reverse comparison for we have advanced beyond the glory even of the Mosaic position. Our access is unfettered and all impediments have been removed.

The point in Paul's exegesis of Exod 34:29-35 is clear. Christians are now put in the ideal position the Sinai covenant intended for historical

Israel, a position only briefly and relatively realized in the experience of Moses. But it is a progressive change that is pointed to here. There are tensions implied; for we are only "being changed". The full range of the experience which Paul contemplates is yet to be. Although in Christ we are a New Creation, we possess this treasure in earthen vessels. In short, the very same problems of continuity and discontinuity identified in Jer 31:31-34 are present in a somewhat different form in 2 Cor 3. 2 Cor 4:1-6, which continues as the explanation of 3:18, reminds us that God has shone out of darkness into our hearts, bringing the light of the knowledge of the glory of God to us (4:6). Thus we are still several stages removed from the actuality which is signified. The New Covenant is in operation as a result of the death of Jesus. But that death points forward to the fulfilment of divine purpose which is to be associated with the constitution of the new man and the ushering in of the New Creation. Paul sees plainly that the New Covenant is associated with an eschatology towards which the christian is being directed.

Throughout his epistles Paul sees the believer as one on whom the end of the age has come. Pauline phrases abound which are reminiscent of the New Covenant and the promise of Gentile incorporation into the Abrahamic covenant.[38] But all this falls short of the full picture sketched by Jeremiah. 1 Thess 4:9 (cf. "taught by God" Gk. *theodidaktai*) is an allusion to Jer 31:34,[39] as Paul offers an exhortation to love one another in fulfilment of this "God-filled" concept. There is also a possible allusion to Ezek 36:27 at 1 Thess 4:8. Certainly the inward gift of the Spirit by which believers are now all sons of Abraham (Gal 3:14) also speaks for the operation of a new dimension, since this Spirit is the Spirit of Christ who is the new man. Yet admonition and exhortation, repentance and forgiveness are still part of our present lot. Paul is well aware christians are exposed to moral fault and sin (cf. Rom 6:12). They have died to sin, yet must be urged not to let sin have dominion over them. The tensions of this struggle in which we are presently engaged are evidenced in the fully developed Pauline teaching.

b. Galatians

Our final treatment of Paul concerns Gal 3-4. Here Paul seems to make an abrupt separation between the Sinai covenant and the New Covenant (which he contemplates); basing one on law and the other on promise. However, these chapters are directed towards his opponents' misunderstanding of law (and thus covenant) and are not a rejection of the concepts. Paul's argument has to do with the establishment of spiritual descent from Abraham, i.e., with the identification of the true people of God. He is concerned with the entry requirements for the christian faith, and not with a faith versus works debate.[40]

Paul argues that the law plays no role in the justification of believers, for acceptance depends upon divine faithfulness.[41] Law reliance brings a curse for all, not merely for the Jews (cf. Gal 3:10-14). Covenant and law are different but related entities (vv15-18). Covenant confirms promise. Law is given to make clear the need for faith (vv19-25). The function of the law was always pedagogical; to point us to faith, to God's fidelity and Christ's faithfulness.[42] Thus resort to law cannot be a means of excluding Gentiles from the promises of salvation. All divisions are broken down by the concept of promise (vv26-29), for Christ's faithfulness which exemplified divine fidelity has made us all sons. Any attempt to put law in a paramount position is tantamount to a lapse into idolatry (4:1-11). Paul's personal appeal (vv12-20) precedes the summary of his position contained in the allegory of verses 21-30. Here he insists upon an Abrahamic connection with the Gospel, and the covenant contrast which he employs here perhaps takes up the language of his opponents and turns it against them. Of the two covenants in verse 24 only one is named, Sinai. An old versus "new" covenant is not intended here, rather it is a perpetuation of the law versus promise argument.

In short, Paul is basically speaking of two perspectives on one covenant, and his appeal in Gal 4:27 to Isa 54:1 to bolster his two-covenant stance makes an absolute rejection of Sinai unlikely. The point of issue in this passage is what Sinai has come to be in the Gospel of his Jewish christian opponents.

iii. *John and Hebrews*

So far as the remainder of the NT is concerned we may briefly refer to John and Hebrews. The new commandment of love Jesus gives his disciples (John 13:34) presupposes the introduction of a New Covenant.[43] This new commandment, an anointing through the word as a result of which no intermediatory teacher is needed (1 John 2:27), will operate through the inner gift of the Spirit and will bring into being the new community under "love" (Gk. *agape*). Such knowledge of God and forgiveness of sins are intrinsic to the new relationship as elaborated by John, particularly in his first epistle. Yet the situation still remains one of expectancy for the christian. We are sons of God, but it is not clear what we will yet be. What is clear is that when "he appears, we will be like him" (3:2). Though our future is certain we work out our salvation with fear and trembling.

The presentation of the epistle to the Hebrews is entirely similar. Institutionally, the covenant is *becoming* obsolete (Heb 8:13). The imperfection to which the writer points in chapters 8-10 as he contrasts the old and new covenants with special reference to Jer 31:31-34 is at all points clear (particularly in regard to the abandonment of sacrifice). This old covenant is being made "old" (Heb 8:13); it is being superseded. Therefore the institutions associated with it are to be rejected (chap. 9). But Christ is the high priest of "good things that have come" (9:11) and his death has brought the promise of eternal life attached to the New Covenant (v15). Sins have been remitted on the basis of the death of Christ (10:18), thereby foreshadowing the time when sins will no longer be "remembered". Encouraged by a cloud of witnesses (chaps. 11-12) believers are to "draw near" to the new situation: i.e., to recognize the freedom inherent in their present position. Believers have come near to the counterpart of Sinai, the heavenly Zion (12:18-24). Therefore they are already a part of the New Covenant framework, whose mediator is Jesus. The sprinkled blood which inaugurated the new bond speaks for better things (i.e., reconciliation); Abel's only spoke of division. Believers are redeemed and perfected; in the language of the epistle, they are able to draw near. The New Covenant has been concluded but in 12:18-24 we are only dealing with Zion as a counterpart to Sinai and the analogy stops at that point. We do not seem to have advanced in this schema to the promised land. Canaan still beckons us on, for in this pilgrim epistle there still remains a rest for the people of God. This in fact is the theme of the epistle and has dictated its presentation from the third chapter (cf. 4:9).

iv. *Revelation Reconsidered*

In short, the biblical witness is clear. The superstructure of the New Covenant, if we may put it that way, has been erected. Its basis stands secure, namely the vicarious and representative death of Christ. Access to the divine presence is assured. But like the biblical witness in general Hebrews calls us to perseverance.

The NT age surveys the tensions of the "now" and the "not yet". But Jeremiah's New Covenant goes beyond that. It looks to the completion of the historical situation. This is the prospect Jesus shared with his disciples in the upper room. His death inaugurates a New Covenant, and believers are members of it. And so Paul, in pointing to the New Covenant aspects of the Lord's Supper, saw it proclaimed the Lord's death "till he comes". The finality of our experience of the New Covenant is bound up with that triumphant return. Therefore Rev 21:2-3 directs us to that great event as the tabernacle of God comes down to men. At that time the very great hope attached to the OT covenant promises becomes a reality in human experience. For God will dwell with them and "they will be his peoples and God himself will be with them".

In this survey of the NT we have for the most part confined ourselves to obvious allusions to the inauguration of the New Covenant. We hope we have offered some bare guidelines, yet are conscious that we have done little more than that. The matter needs careful and detailed research to bring into play the many NT nuances bearing upon the general theme. That is a study in itself, however, and must await another time or another person.

Notes

1. Cf. F. Seilhamer, "The Role of Covenant in the Mission and Message of Amos" in *A Light Unto my Path: Old Testament Studies in Honor of Jacob M. Myers* ed H.N. Bream, R.D. Heim, C.A. Moore (Philadelphia: Temple University, 1974) 435-51.

2. Cf. Amos 4:6-12 where the covenant exposition of Lev 26:3-46 is depended upon yet reversed.

3. Cf. J. Barton, *Amos' Oracles Against the Nations* (SOTSMS 6; Cambridge: Cambridge University, 1980) 49-50.

4. R.E. Clements (*Prophecy and Covenant* [London: SCM, 1965]) has demonstrated how axiomatic the covenant idea was to Amos.

5. Cf. S. Niditch, "The Composition of Isaiah I", *Bib* 61 (1980) 509-29.

6. Cf. J.R. Lundbom (*Jeremiah: A Study in Ancient Hebrew Rhetoric* [SBLDS 18; Missoula: Scholars, 1975] 31-2) draws attention to this fact.

7. In my monograph *Covenant and Creation* (Sydney/Exeter: Lancer/Paternoster, 1984).

8. W.J. Dumbrell, "The Covenant with Noah", *RTR* 38 (1979) 4.

9. B.S. Childs, *Memory and Tradition in Israel* (London: SCM, 1962) 33.

10. I refer to my article ("Spirit and Kingdom in the Old Testament", *RTR* 33 [1974] 1-10) where this matter is discussed fully.

11. Cf. W.A.M. Beuken, "Mispat. The First Servant Song in its Context", *VT* 22 (1972) 1-30.

12. As H.C. Spykerboer ("The Structure and Composition of Deutero-Isaiah" [Ph.D. dissertation, University of Gronigen, 1976] 85-92) notes.

13. ibid, 177-8.

14. Beuken, "Isaiah liv: The Multiple Identity of the Person Addressed", *OTS* 19 (1974) 28-70. We acknowledge our dependence upon his article in our presentation of the character of the covenant concepts involved in this chapter.

15. Dumbrell, "Noah", 1-9.

16. Beuken, "Multiple", 61.

17. P.D. Hanson, *The Dawn of Apocalyptic* (Philadelphia: Fortress, 1975) 32-46.

18. Cf. Beuken, *Haggai-Sacharja 1-8* (Assen: Van Gorcum, 1967) 27-49.

19. On the covenantal use of Heb. *sub* "return" in Zech 1:1-6 Cf. A. Petitjean, *Les Oracles du Proto-Zacharie* (Paris: Gabalda, 1969) 29-37.

20. On the pronounced covenantal emphasis of Malachi Cf. S.L. McKenzie and H.N. Wallace, "Covenant Themes in Malachi" *CBQ* 45 (1983) 549-63.

21. K. Koch, "Ezra and the Origins of Judaism" *JSS* 19 (1974) 173-97.

22. W.J. Dumbrell, "The Purpose of the Books of Chronicles", *JETS* 28 (1985) 257-66.

23. idem, *Covenant*.

24. Cf. E.P. Sanders (*Paul and Palestinian Judaism* [London: SCM, 1977] 95-6) has assessed the Rabbinic evidence.

25. idem, *Paul, the Law and the Jewish People* (Philadelphia: Fortress, 1983) 154-62.

26. On Gk. *diatheke* "covenant" as indicating the declaration of the divine will in the NT Cf. J. Behm, "*diatheke*", *TDNT* 2 (1964) 126-7.

27. On the interrelationship of Matt 28:16-20 and Dan 7:13 Cf. J.P. Meier "Two Disputed Questions in Matthew 28:16-20", *JBL* 96 (1977) 407-24.

28. H. Frankemoelle, *Jahwehbund und Kirche Christi* (Munster: Aschendorff, 1974) 46-61.

29. As Meier ("Questions", 420) notes.

30. Cf. B. Hubbard, *The Matthean Redaction of a Primitive Apostolic Commissioning: An Exegesis of Matt 28:16-20* (SBLDS 19; Missoula: Scholars 1974) 69-99.

31. We note here the review of Hubbard by H.J. McArthur in *CBQ* 38 (1976) 107-8.

32. On the parallelism between Matt 1:21 and 23 Cf. G.M. Soares Prabhu, *The Formula Quotations in the Infancy Narrative* (AnBib 63; Rome: Pontifical Biblical Institute, 1976) 239.

33. Cf. the review of Frankemoelle in D. Senior, *CBQ* 38 (1976) 230-2.

34. Cf. the valuable article by W. van Unnik, "With Unveiled Face; An Exegesis of 2 Corinthians iii, 12-18", *NovT* 6 (1963) 153-69.

35. Cf. D.W. Oostendorp (*Another Jesus* [Kampen: J.H. Kok, 1967] 37, n.24) who puts cogent arguments as to why the use of Gk. *katargeo* "abolish" in 2 Cor 3 is passive.

36. Gk. *telos* could bear this sense since the meanings of "goal", "end" in the sense of "result", "conclusion" are semantically acceptable.

37. Gk. *doksa* "glory" and *eikon* "image" at 2 Cor 3:18 seem virtual equivalents, Cf. S. Kim, *The Origin of Paul's Gospel* (Tubingen/Grand Rapids: Mohr/Eerdmans, 1981/84) 230.

38. W.L. Lane ("Covenant: The Key to Paul's Conflict with Corinth" *TynB* 33 [1982] 3-29) sees Paul's use of the New Covenant motif as prominent throughout 2 Cor. Particularly he draws attention to the appropriation of Isa 49:1-13 in 2 Cor 6. However, while the use of servant imagery by Paul may indirectly refer to covenant it seems to be employed to depict the nature of his ministry.

39. It is suggested by T.J. Deidun (*New Covenant Morality in Paul* [AnBib 89; Rome: Biblical Institute, 1981] 18-28) that Gk. *theodidaktoi* "taught of God" (v9) in the context of 1 Thess 4:1-12 is a reference to the New Covenant of Jer 31:31-34.

40. Sanders, *Law*, 154-62.

41. G. Howard, *Paul: Crisis in Galatia* (SNTSMS 35; Cambridge: Cambridge University, 1979) 57.

42. ibid, 64-5.

43. Undoubtedly the question of a "new commandment" in 1 John presupposes a theology of a New Covenant to which one can be referred. Cf. E. Malatesta, *Interiority and Covenant* (AnBib 69; Rome: Biblical Institute, 1978) 160-1.

NEW ISRAEL — SUMMARY

It is abundantly clear that the presentation of the New Jerusalem of Revelation 21 includes in its symbolism the New People of God. This in turn provokes the suggestion of a "New Israel", an association confirmed by the fusion of tribal and apostolic imagery later in the same vision. But what was Israel? What was its status and function? And why a New Israel?

OT eschatology of Israel retains a Sinaitic flavour, since Israel is defined as a worshipping community under divine kingship. Given perfect expression this Israel exhibits ideal political forms attracting the entire world. All future hopes are in many ways only the realization of the deepest significance of the Sinai arrangement. The Abrahamic promises set the agenda for the reversal of man's attempt to achieve unity under the banner of a rejection of the created order. God will establish a vast people to be a blessing to the world. Sinai gives substance to this programme by the creation of Israel, a priestly royalty and holy nation; a light to lighten the world. Through the specifics of the covenant Israel models divine kingship before the whole earth. As Israel inhabits the promised land the principle of Edenic life, life at rest in the sanctuary, returns to the creation.

But the nation's sin ensured that Sinai was only ever an ideal. Even at conception the status, functions, and privileges of Israel pass to Moses as the people reject Yahweh's rule in the incident of the golden calf. Israel's sin thereby guarantees continual turmoil within her political system. The later introduction of the monarchy highlights that the reality only resides in ideal kingship. Understandably then, the expectations of God's faithful people are increasingly associated with Mosaic revivalists such as Elijah, or in a developing prophetic doctrine of a remnant. It is clear that not all Israel are indeed Israel.

With the demise of the people and their institutions in the exile, the question of Israel's identity and future assumes an utmost urgency. Historically the startling retort of Jeremiah was that from the exiles God would choose "good figs", the true Israel. But far more remarkable is Ezekiel's prospect of a wholly recreated Israel. And as if this were not significant enough, the schema of Isa 40-66 sees this New People as issuing from the Servant, the representative of the remnant community. This is as far as the OT takes us.

Jesus rejects the nation of Israel and creates a New Community. As Son of Abraham he is the source of blessing to all nations. As Son of David he gathers the people under an ideal of perfected leadership. As Son of Man he delivers the final judgement on historical Israel. With the inauguration of the New Covenant all the people are now as Moses was on Mt Sinai (Exod 34) beholding the glory of God. In Christ the new community fulfils the Exod 19:3b-6 role of Israel.

4

THE NEW ISRAEL

The Presentation in Revelation 21-22

Rev 21-22 presents the vision of a new people of God, some would say, a New Israel. The mention of the New Jerusalem in itself suggests this, but there are yet more definite indications. In 21:12-14 the foundations of the new city bear the names of the twelve apostles of the Lamb and the twelve gates the names of the twelve tribes of Israel. Here is an indication of continuity between the testaments as well as a denotation of the uniqueness of the new people of God in Christ. To appreciate both parameters we need to go back and examine the nature of the Old Israel, noting its function and history in the OT. Only then will we see what contribution the OT expectation has made to this NT fulfilment. We will then be able to establish in what sense, if any, the NT continues the OT notion of Israel.

The Old Testament

The point at which we begin is with the Sinai narratives, for most of the expectations surrounding the OT Israel are located there. In particular, we will commence with the description of Israel's status and function in Exod 19:5b-6.

i. *Sinai and Israel*

Exod 19:3b-6 is self-contained. Note the inclusion formed by the introduction ("thus you shall say to the house of Jacob" v3), and the conclusion ("these are the words which you shall speak to the children of Israel" v6). Verse 4 contains a threefold summary of the Exodus. First, "You have seen what I did to the Egyptians" refers to Israel's enslavement in Egypt with which the book commences. There is also a reference to the plague narratives, which serve to demonstrate the character and the authority of Yahweh and to magnify him in the presence of Pharaoh and the Egyptians. Second, "how I bore you on eagles wings" indicates the effortless nature of the redemption from Egypt which followed the subjugation. It speaks of the leading out of Egypt, the crossing of the sea, and Yahweh's general redemptive protection of Israel. Third, the clause "and I brought you to myself" reminds Israel of the purpose or goal of the Exodus. This last statement foreshadows what is about to be disclosed at Sinai. Further, overtones of worship in Yahweh's presence implicit in the clause "brought you to myself" ought not to be overlooked.

Thus before her role and its concomitant responsibilities are delimited, Israel is directed to the meaning of the Exodus for the past, present and future. Therein a great redemption was exercised for Israel by Yahweh. The servitude of bondage to which Israel constantly referred in her early formularies was cancelled. That redemption had projected the notion of Israel as a worshipping people of God. In short, these three statements summarize the content of the entire book of Exodus. The book commences with Israel enslaved and ends with Israel potentially at worship, since the last five chapters (Exod 35-40) deal mainly with the construction of the tabernacle and the accompanying institutions of worship. But the movement from slavery to worship is only possible because of the Exodus redemption, and this is the axis on which the book turns.

In putting all this before Israel on Sinai, Yahweh is indicating the overriding consideration in any survey of the nature or vocation of Israel in the OT. We must be clear on this point before we go further. Israel in the OT will denote a worshipping community of faith based on a great act of redemption. It is this salvation which makes them a people of God able to declare the praises of him who brought them out of the darkness of exile into the light of a liberation experience. Therefore whatever is advanced as an analogy for Israel in the NT will need to exhibit this same structure. The "New Israel" of the NT must therefore be a worshipping community called into being by a great redemption, whose ideal role will be to reflect through worship the nature of God, the Redeemer. We may now examine the content of Exod 19:5-6, reflecting carefully on verse 5 before turning to verse 6.

Exodus 19:5 begins with the conditional phrase: "if you will obey my voice and keep my covenant". Most interpreters relate this statement to the covenant offered at Sinai, and therefore associate the elements of conditionality to the Sinai covenant. However, there are difficulties inherent in this position which now need to be discussed. The condition of the opening phrase is probably synonymous with the second element "keep my covenant," thus giving the concept of location. But one must be wary here as to what is in mind by the introduction of "my covenant". Which covenant is in view? Nothing explicitly covenantal has so far been advanced in this book. Indeed, to this point the notion has only been associated with the Abrahamic covenant (cf. 6:1-8). Most, as we have noticed, take the reference prospectively, referring to what will follow. But a very strong case can be made for interpreting the phrase as reference to an already existing relationship.

First, the phrase "keep a covenant", when used of human response to a divine covenant, only occurs in the OT where obedience to a prior divine commitment by covenant is in view (cf. Gen 17:9,10; 1 Kgs 11:11; Pss 78:10; 103:18; 132:12; Ezek 17:14). If a prior covenant is in view in Exodus 19:5,6 it must be the patriarchal covenant for continuity with promises given to the patriarchs had been presumed in Moses' call (Exod 3:13-15). Secondly, Israel's withdrawal from the world (implied in the remainder of 19:5-6) was designed to allow Israel to become the "light to lighten the gentiles". Herein we find further continuity with the Abrahamic covenant. We will have to take this point further but we may say by way of anticipation that the call of Israel (vv3b-6) appears to set Israel in relation to the world in a position analogous to Abraham (Gen 12:1-3). This will be confirmed in a closer examination of the content of Exod 19:5-6.

The definitive term in these verses is "possession" (Heb. s^egullah Exod 19:5). The term refers to the exclusive nature of private property, with emphasis upon the personal nature of the ownership.[1] Most of the OT references to the word are dependent upon this Exodus context (cf. Deut 7:6; 14:2; 26:18; Ps 135:4; Mal 3:17). There are two further uses of the word which warrant our attention. In Eccl 2:8 the word is used of personal royal property. Even more important for our purposes is 1 Chron 29:3. Therein David declares his intention to devote to the building of the temple not merely the resources of the empire which are his to summon, but also his own personal property (his s^egullah). Thus in keeping with the concept of general ownership inherent in David's kingship, is the notion of special attachment this word embodies.

If we apply these results to the Exodus context then clearly "possession" (Heb. s^egullah) is operating as an elective term in Exod 19:5. This is further substantiated by the prepositional phrase "among all peoples", which plainly adds a separative emphasis. "Among" (Heb. min) can hardly be comparative here, as R. Mosis[2] has pointed out, because the tenor of verse 6 confirms the elective mood of verse 5. Israel is not merely a priestly nation elevated above a world of like qualities. Rather by separation Israel will come to be (cf. Heb. hayah "to be" in v6) a uniquely priestly nation.

By means of Israel's separation the universal sovereignty of Yahweh is being expressed, for he accomplishes the separation. Yahweh's omnipotence is further explicated in the creational relationship of all peoples to Yahweh: "all the earth is mine" (Exod 19:5bB). Israel is now "crown property"; personally Yahweh's. The term at once points to Yahweh's kingship as well as to Israel's vassalship. Taken from these "peoples" (Heb. ᶜammim), Israel is to become special.

A superficial reading of Exod 19:5 often makes this final phrase anticlimactic or parenthetical and some modern versions render it that way (e.g., NIV "*Although* the whole earth"). It thus seems almost a divine apology for the choice of Israel. But Yahweh chooses simply because he is Yahweh, not because he is accountable. No reasons for His mysterious series of choices within history are ever offered. It is much more likely that the Heb. conjunction *ki* "for" works to introduce not the right to choose, but the reason or goal of choice (e.g., "because the whole earth"). Exod 19:6 begins with "and you" (Heb. *we'ᵃttem*) suggesting by "and" (Heb. *waw*) a slight break (cf. LXX *de*) with what has preceded. But verse 6 explicates the content of "possession" (Heb. *sᵉgullah*) adding nothing in its own right which is not potentially already there in the noun. It is doubtful therefore whether Fiorenza[3] and others are to be followed in interpreting verse 6 as the climax of the movement which is to result in the worshipping community to which verse 4 has referred. On the other hand, verse 5 which is pivotal, deals with the Exodus redemption in terms of divine choice and eschatological goals.

In these circumstances the translation of Heb. *ki* "for" in Exod 19:5bB is of some importance. It may well have a summarizing role and here we may basically agree with Mosis.[4] Yet we disagree with his suggestion that verse 6a is merely a restatement of the content of Heb. *sᵉgullah* "possession".[5] The *ki* "for" of verse 5bB brings the argument to its conclusion, and states Yahweh's final goal. Israel is called; she is to be a worshipping community; and her election is emphasized.

The goal Yahweh has in mind is the recognition of his lordship by all peoples. This is the important note on which Exod 19:5 ends. The call of Israel has the world in view. It is not an end in itself. The alternative to this is simply a world of politically nondescript, loosely structured "peoples". To this world the fashion of divine rule over Israel is to be the model of Yahweh's universal lordship. This is the point being made by verse 5bB. The eschatological goal towards which the history of salvation is directed is the acknowledgement by the world beyond Israel of the reality of divine kingship. This is implicit in the phrase "for all the world is mine". In view of the universality of the context there can be no restriction of "land" Heb. "*eres*" (v5bB) to Canaan. Verse 6 will continue with its application of Israel's function.

This brings us to the interpreter's minefield represented by Heb. *kohᵃnim mamleket* "kingdom of priests". We will argue that these words are synonymously paralleled by "holy nation" Heb. *goy qados*. But we admit that the phrase provides an interpretative crux. It is not our intention at this time to review the wider range review the wider range of options which have been presented as translational possibilities for these two phrases. The main difficulty is whether "kingdom" (Heb. *mamleket*) is to be taken absolutely with the following word "priests" standing in apposition, thus yielding the translation "a kingdom, namely priests" or whether *mamleket* is in the Heb. bound or construct form, and hence, "kingdom of priests". If it is the latter then *mamleket* would normally be the dominant word with "of priests" to be taken adjectivally, providing the translation: "priestly kingdom". R.B.Y. Scott,[6] who among others presents the interpretative options available to the translator, inclines to the general sense of "a kingdom set apart like a priesthood in the ancient world is set apart". This captures the note the passage demands. The concept of kingly rule presented earlier in "possession" (s^e*gullah*), is predominant in the passage. One might expect Exod 19:6a would emphasize this royal sense, for it seems to elaborate what is involved in s^e*gullah*. This makes it unlikely that *mamleket koh^{a}nim* "kingdom of priests" simply represents a part, with *goy qados* "holy nation" representing the remaining element (i.e., that a royal priesthood + a holy nation = Israel).[7] It seems more probable the second phrase (*goy qados*) explains and clarifies the first *mamleket koh^{a}nim*. *Mamleket* "kingdom" is generally agreed to refer to the institution of kingship as such, and not to the holder of the office. Royal authority, power to exhibit such authority, and status conferred by this authority are all within the word's normal semantic range. After a very careful examination of the relationship these two terms share in the first phrase, Fiorenza takes *koh nim* "priests", (correctly we feel), as the attribute (i.e. "of priests" = "priestly"), and translates: "priestly royalty".[8] What follows then provides a nice parallel.

Curious in the Heb. phrase "holy nation" *goy qados* is the noun "nation" *goy*. The adjective *qados* "holy" sustains the idea of separation and purity detected throughout this passage. This is both expected and consistent. Yet the use of the political term "nation" *goy* is somewhat puzzling in such an elevated context. The normal election term used of Israel is the familiar ^{c}*am* "people". *Goy* "nation" usually refers to political superstructures, national boundaries, political associations, cultural factors, etc.[9] Perhaps the term indicates Israel's call to move on to the international scene. But in view of the use of "peoples" (^{c}*ammim*), to refer to the remainder of the world, more may be intended.

Within this passage Israel is called to be a kingdom, and that refers to political responsibilities. The point which is being made by the use of the expression "nation" (Heb. *goy*) over against the term "people" (Heb. ^{c}*am*) may be identical to that made in Gen 12:2. Therein *goy* is used of Abram's seed in contradistinction to the remainder of the world, which are merely "clans" (Heb. *misp^{e}hot*). The inference from verses 2-3 is that outside of the structure imposed by the kingdom of God there exists no acceptable political model. Thus Israel is called in Exod 19 onto the world stage as a light to the Gentiles. She assumes this role resulting from a new exodus later in the biblical period (cf. Isa 40-55), but it was nevertheless implicit in her initial political encounter with Yahweh. Exod 19:5b-6 makes it clear that the other political entities in Israel's world are merely loose associations ("peoples").

Of course "priestly kingdom" does not merely indicate separation from society, but also points to the embodiment of values intrinsic to the development of the priesthood in Israel. Purity and holiness are intended, but supreme is the worshipping community, whose life is evidenced in her relationship to her patron. A priestly kingdom is first a worshipping fellowship of priests who are also kings. It is the ideal government, attractive by its difference and distinctiveness, providing a model for what true political alignment in the world is to be. Israel is to be the community which by its manner of life displays the political harmony intended by Yahweh for all society.

a. Moses and the Giving of the Legal Codes

Exod 19:7-8 registers the assent of the elders and the people to the divine proposals of verses 3b-6. The concept of "doing" in these verses underscores the idea of provisionality within the promises, just as "if you obey my voice/keep my covenant" did in verse 5. It now remains to survey Exod 19-34 briefly at various levels. Our main purpose is to establish how the declaration of Yahweh's unconditional purposes which the Sinai covenant contained would work its way out in the history of the nation of Israel. Indeed, provisionality seemed to mark the history of Israel with her national existence always threatened by her apostasy. As the OT continues the unconditionality of Sinai will find its expression in a remnant community of faith. The seed of such a community is contained, as we shall see in Exod 19-34.

The remainder of Exod 19 is concerned with the special preparations for the reception of the divine theophany during which the law codes, the decalogue, and the covenant codes or case law will be delivered. Following the theophany, the decalogue, the basis of Israel's system of jurisprudence and the code from which all else stems, is given in Exod 20:1-17. According to verse 2 the decalogue clearly comes within a framework of grace. Moreover, the overall context makes it equally plain that the ten words come to each Israelite both separately and corporately. In all of this, Moses' position is an elevated one. However, at this point in time his role is not essentially mediatorial. True, verses 18-21 seem to call upon Moses to play such a role, but this is at the request of the people, it is not initiated by Yahweh. The request stems from fear, a fear immediately allayed by Moses. What follows in verse 22 is further admonition to Moses for all Israel. Then in chapters 21-23 a legal code of a different character to the decalogue in 20:1-17 comes through Moses.

There is almost universal acknowledgement and acceptance of the formal differences between the two codes, hence there is probably no need of elaboration. The case law of Exod 21-23 is contingent, providing specific penalties for detailed offences. In contrast to the lofty,, imperatival delivery of 20:1-17 this version speaks to a mundane background of crime and punishment. The decalogue seems intended to reflect what flows naturally out of the relationship effected by redemption. As such it provides the parameters within which the relationship will operate, and offers the guidelines which indicate whether or not the relationship is broken. Law in this sense is the reflex of covenant, not its precondition. There is no indication it can be performed independent of the acceptance of the full implications contained within the relationship.

The covenant codes of Exod 21-23 are derivative (as their delivery through Moses indicates), and they follow admonitions to avoid the dominant national sin of the OT, idolatry, the root of all evil. Whereas the decalogue came unmediated, the covenant codes did not. Rather than stressing Moses' mediatorial role, the distinction is probably meant to underscore the essential character of the one type of law, and the derivative nature of the other. The decalogue points us to the values which the acceptance of the relationship will reflect; the covenant code reminds us of the murmuring Israel seen in the wilderness as they approached Sinai. This tempers the idealism engendered in chapters 19-20 with realism. Therefore the present editorial arrangement of these codes reminds us that both the challenges of Exodus 19-20, and the references to potential social failures in chapters 21-23, are tensions within the entire history of Israel throughout the OT.

Moses is thrown into prominence by his role Exod 24, particularly through his separation at verses 1-2. However, the fact that at the ratification of the covenant in verses 1-11 seventy elders along with Aaron, Nadab and Abihu, accompany Moses onto the mountain and eat in the divine presence, implies all Israel is still considered capable of being addressed without a mediator, and on the most intimate level. The note of promise is still hopefully there. Thus when Moses finally goes up on the mountain (at the end of chapter 24) and into the more immediate divine presence to reduce the commandments to writing, whatever mediatorial role he has assumed to this point is not emphasized. So far, the idealization of Israel has been very carefully presented in Exod 19-20, though the material of chapters 21-23 draws our attention to more basic realities inherent in Israel's national nature.

Exod 25-31 is often overlooked in the assessment of chapters 19-34, yet is really an integral part of the unified whole. The section comes directly after the ratification of the covenant, and may be said to interpret it. This material has already been assessed in detail under the

New Temple concept and need not be taken further here. We have argued in material dealing with the New Temple that the blueprint for the tabernacle provides a natural endorsement of Yahweh's kingship and indicates at the same time the goals of the Exodus, namely the creation of a worshipping community.

b. Covenant Renewal

In our discussion of the "New Covenant" we observe the import of Exod 32-34 and need not repeat the detail here. Suffice it to say the prospect for Israel detailed at 19:3b-6 had now been contracted to Moses and the community of faith which he represented. Moses provides Israel with the possibility of a history, but we have no illusions now as to the outcome of that history. We may expect within it that further ideals will be erected which will contribute to the final kingdom God purposes. We do not expect, however, that it will be the historical Israel of the OT who will enter the blessing of "rest" attached to those promises.

Thus it comes as no surprise in Exod 33:14 to find that God tranfers the notion of his presence to Moses in particular (cf. the singular "you"). He is now the bearer of the name, the mark of the Israel who has found grace in the wilderness. It becomes obvious that the vehicle through which God will work his final purposes is no longer Israel as a whole, as a nation, but individuals whom Moses now represents. When the commandments are given for the second time in chapter 34, they come through Moses. No longer does all Israel stand before the mountain, no longer is the address to Israel, and no longer are the commandments repeated in the presence of the people. The closing section of verses 29-35 is impressive. It is Moses alone who draws near and whose face shines as a result of the indirect contact. Additionally, Moses' face shines before Israel as revelation is offered. Israel as a whole does not enter into this experience, for, as Paul remarks (with apparent reference to the Sinai situation), "their minds were hardened" (2 Cor 3:14).

Exod 19-34 thus prepares us both for Israel's failure and for Moses' role as an Israel within Israel, and 34:29-35 operates as a comment upon the Sinai covenant. This will not be fulfilled in Israel's national history, but will continue within the OT period in an Israel within Israel. To be sure the analysis of Israel in the book of Deuteronomy puts the law in the national heart and calls for the circumcision of the national heart when the nation has strayed (Deut 10:16). After Sinai, however, there is no real hope the possibility being sketched in Exod 19-34 will ever become a *national* reality.

c. Exodus 19:3b-6: Abrahamic Emphasis

There is yet another point which needs to be made from Exod 19:3b-6. Israel's distinctiveness is not unanticipated. The separation of Israel from its environment, its invitation to obey a covenant already existing, its call to be a light to lighten the gentiles, the model for the world that its role would provide, the use of Heb. *goy* "nation" (cf. Gen 12:2) — all of this is confessedly Abrahamic in its tenor. As the continuity of the Exodus narratives (Exod 3:13-15; 6:1-8) suggests, the Sinai covenant is in fact a particularization of Gen 12:1-3 in the experience of Israel. Like Abram, Israel was called outside of the land which would be. Like Abram, Israel would be a great nation (*goy*). Like Abram too, the world would find its source of blessing in Israel.

Thus, another factor emerges endorsing more than a *limited* concept of unconditionality. The strand of covenant theology, begun with Abram, continued with Sinai and adding kingship to its ambit in 2 Sam 7, would climax in the new covenant of Jer 31:31-34. On two counts, therefore, that of the remnant on the human side and divine design on the other, a worshipping company among whom God dwells is bound to emerge. They *would be* priests and kings. We are now in a position to take this Abrahamic theme further, look at the tenor of Gen 12:1-3, and the genealogy of Shem with which it is interwoven.

The genealogy follows hard upon, and seemingly in response to the Tower of Babel account (Gen 11:1-9). Abraham is juxtaposed not only to the Babel builders who have sought a "name" for themselves (cf. 12:2 where the great name is God's gift to Abraham), but also to the prior narrative in Genesis 3-11. The spread of sin narratives in chapters 3-11 climax in the fall of society recorded in 11:1-9. That spread had its provisional climax in the flood which, although it seemed to be the end, offered a new beginning in terms of 1:26-28 to the human race at 9:1-7. Yet Babel is clearly the end of the road. All the tensions which affect our modern world, the ethnic, linguistic, social and cultural divisions etc., are erected as a divine reaction to man's search for the centre of his world within himself and his society. The call of Abraham thus offsets Babel and is designed redemptively to restore the world to its pre-Gen 3 situation.

Insofar as it throws light on the biblical intention for Israel, the structure of Gen 12:1-3 is of interest to us. We may note that promises are given in verse 2 to what appear to be Abraham's lineal descendants.

This verse (Gen 12:2) should probably be divided into two clauses only; namely, "I will make of you a great nation", and "I will bless you by making your name great". It is virtually introduced, by the imperative in verse 1, just as verse 3 is introduced by the imperative with which verse 2 concludes (lit. = "be thou a blessing"). Verse 3a has two subordinate clauses ("I will bless those who bless you", and "him who curses you I will curse") before the final clause is presented in 3b as a result or consequence of the whole sequence. The RSV takes the verb in the last clause of verse 3 as reflexive ("and by you shall all the families of the earth bless themselves"). In a context which appears, by its structure, to be moving to a climax, this rendering appears to be decidedly anti-climactic. It is preferable therefore that the verb (in the Heb. Niph^cal theme) should be taken as either passive ("in you will all the families of the earth be blessed", with the older expositors) or as a middle form ("in you will all the families of the earth win for themselves a blessing").

This latter rendering seems desirable in view of Israel's position with respect to the other OT nations, who come into her structures rather than Israel going out to them in any missionary sense. Thus if Gen 12:2 deals with the erection of Israel at closer range, verse 3 in a very similar manner to Exod 19:6 deals with Israel's function.

However, one must note the unusual application here to Israel of Heb. *goy*, "nation" (to which we have already briefly referred). Normally, when predicated of Israel it is used pejoratively (cf. Deut 32:28; Isa 1:4, 10:6; Jer 5:9). As we have noted the more usual word to describe Israel in relationship to God is Heb. *^cam* "people", a kinship term expressing the intimate relationship Israel and Yahweh share. Why would the more political and "neutral" *goy* have been chosen here? It could be readily argued it is Israel's political structure of the future which is in mind and that the use of the adjective "great" is only relative, designed to set Israel off from her world. In the OT *goy* is normally reserved to describe a people as a political entity, and the use of such a governmental term may have the later Israel immediately in mind. Perhaps more can be said, however.

Gen 12:1-3 is the obvious rejoinder to Babel and the consequences of the Fall in general. Babel had expressed a naive yet total confidence in what human achievement could effect in its world. Babel looked for one world, one language, one common social and economic platform from which human association could proceed. In short, it was the beginning of the utopian humanistic dream to which mankind has always aspired. The Bible means these unities to be achieved, but this is impossible prior to the advent of the New Creation. It is towards this the biblical theology of redemption looks from the Fall onwards.

In the light of the background provided by Gen 1-11 the significance of the use of *goy* "nation" here may be more expansive than a mere political reference. It may be that the course of development for all future redemptive eschatology is introduced. If these verses (Gen 12:1-3) offset the Fall, then they aim at the restoration of all things. Here we are reminded that God's cosmic purpose was for a divinely regulated world in which his authority was recognized and honoured by all. If these final aims are in mind in Gen 12:1-3, then it may be that the use of *goy* here is a studied one. Certainly, the call of Israel and her constitution may be immediately in mind, but only as a pledge of what is still to come beyond that call; namely, the final political reality — the Kingdom of God — a fact with which the Bible begins.

In contrast with the use of "nation" (Heb. *goy*) in Gen 12:2 we have noted that the remainder of the world can be described as mere "families" — as units with no permanent political structure, and in which no system of final political headship fully operates. 11:1-9 shows us world government designed to produce or continue unity in the human situation must be a God-given structure. Presumably, it would come among men if and when God chose to impose it. Israel as a nation may later exhibit features of this since her constitution is God-given, but the true political structure aimed at in Gen 12:1-3 will not come into being until the whole company of the redeemed are gathered together in a New Heaven and a New Earth. Doubtless, the use of "nation" (Heb. *goy*) in Exod 19:6 exploits the full range of intention which we have discerned in the context of Gen 12:1-3.

H.W. Wolff[10] notes the word "blessing" occurs five times in Gen 12:1-3. In the OT development of the term, God is always the giver or the indirect giver of blessing. Space permits us only to generalize, but the evidence suggests blessings are manifestations of solidarity in creational relationships, whereby the natural or personal capacity for the fulfilment of God's purposes is furthered. Thus at Gen 1:28 God blessed man and said, "be fruitful and multiply". This powerful word of God prevailed and thus confers potential power whereby man is able under God to fulfil the aims for which he was created. If these assumptions are followed in 12:1-3, then blessing is bound up with a theology of history. God blesses Abraham by enabling through his call the goal of redemption, the construction of a great nation. Blessing in Gen 12:1-3 encompasses all humanity, as well as the domain in which they live. It is therefore a matter of interest to note that when the later Abrahamic narratives first have occasion to refer back to Gen 12:1-3, and explicitly to Abraham as the carrier of blessing, it is Abraham's relationship to the world in the shape of the coming destruction of Sodom and Gomorrah which is being referred to (19:19).[11]

It is significant[12] that the fivefold occurrences of blessing in this section are contrasted to a fivefold occurrence of "curse" (Heb. 'arar) in Gen 1-11 (viz., 3:14,17; 4:11; 5:29; 9:25). Whereas blessing integrates, and thereby enables the realization under God of potential received through creation, curse alienates and estranges. Curse, as Wolff notes, means loss of freedom (3:17), alienation from the soil (4:12), and shameful degradation (9:25). Bound up with all this is the on-going deprivation which led man from Eden to Babel. However, this fivefold reiteration of blessing in 12:1-3 stresses the fact that in Abraham and his call broken relationships are potentially repaired, and are to be progressively expressed as having been restored. The distance between man and God in chapters 3-11 will be reversed by this call and thus initially through Israel. A new, powerful word has commenced with the call of Abraham and will be extended through the ministry of Israel, to annul the curse of chapter 11. Of course this new word will find its fulfilment in Jesus, for he alone destroys the curse imposed by the Fall.

ii. *Patriarchal Narratives*

Before returning briefly to the covenant context of Exod 19 we will look at the origins of patriarchal Israel during the Genesis period. We are referring here to the birth and history of Jacob and the cycle of narratives associated with him. These reach their turning point[13] in Genesis 30 when Rachel bears children, and Jacob's prosperity in Haran is recounted in some depth. The whole series of alienations characterized in the first half of the cycle now give way to the reconciliations of the second. We should note the important role the concept of the promised land plays in these cycles.

It is made clear to Jacob by the divine theophany received at Bethel, the last notation before he leaves the land (Gen 28:10-17), that he will return. He vows to worship God in Bethel again (cf. v22) and the Abrahamic promises are repeated in this context (vv13-15). Even more significantly, when Jacob does return to the land, he is met at the very border (in chapter 32) by an angel as he pauses at the "two camps" (v2), and the account of his nocturnal encounter with this angel is as perplexing as it is fascinating.[14] The "two camps" is an ominous introduction portending hostility, and the subsequent course of the chapter bears this out. Thus as we face Genesis 32 we wonder if with Esau before him and ostensibly hostile, Jacob the progenitor of Israel will in fact see the promised land. Yet this is not a struggle between brothers which the chapter will disclose. In verse 9 Jacob reminds God of the blessings promised at Bethel, humbles himself (for the first time in the whole cycle), and admits he is at the end of his resources. Nothing, however, comes of the last attempt at trickery he makes via the "present" (Heb. *minhah*) to Esau, or from splitting his own "army" into "two camps".

The setting of the chapter, the movement from night to dawn, from darkness to light, is consonant with Jacob's mood. His struggle with God (i.e., what is in effect an analysis of his life to this point) is resolved and as dawn breaks Jacob receives a new name. The etymology of the term "Israel" is more than likely "God fights".[15] Jacob had striven with men and as a contender he has now striven with God, or rather, God has striven with Jacob. God has moved him into a personal situation from which a set of authentic relationships with his brother may emerge. Throughout Jacob's life he schemed for blessing and manipulated circumstances, but now he must surrender and be led.

In its own way this chapter is a paradigm of national Israel's own experience in the land. When she resorts to devious means to ensure her future and/or struggles politically to maintain herself, Israel fails. Thus paradoxically the future shines on Israel only when she is prepared to yield to God's design. For historical Israel this never in fact results. However, for Jacob the confrontation of Gen 32 results in a changed personality and thus a new name. For him the dawn breaks on a future filled with new possibility.

This change of name theme is repeated in Genesis 35, the narrative which brings the Jacob cycle to an end. Clearly, therefore, we are meant to understand that with this change a new era dawns in the history of the people of God. Yet the Joseph narratives which follow find Israel once again outside of the promised land, and in a situation of dependence. Paradoxically, however, in the patriarchal narratives that is precisely where blessing for the people of God begins. In Egypt, Israel is preserved by the providential placement of Joseph. In the narrative Joseph is presented as the bringer and giver of life. He is at the centre of Egypt, the land where life is sustained, and he is the dispenser of this life.[16] Thus the book of Genesis ends with Israel preserved and populous. Curiously, blessing, or the promise of it, comes to each of the three patriarchs (Abraham, Jacob, Joseph) outside of the promised land, but with reference to the land.[17] Thus at the period when the Exodus seems most likely to take place (i.e., about 1450BC[18]) Israel is potentially a great nation and a threat to Egypt. With the revelation of the name of Yahweh to Moses a new phase in Israelite history begins (Exod 3:13-15).

We may summarize our presentation to this point. We have noted the language of Exod 19:3b-6 and its general familiarity with an Abrahamic background. Called from among the sea of "peoples" (ᶜammim Exod 19:5), Israel as Yahweh's "nation" (goy) offers political hope to the world. She is thus the bearer of the promises given to Abraham in Gen 12:1-3. But that hope is quickly dissipated by the following narrative. The problem of "two Israels" surfaces in Exod 19-34, and the OT will attach itself for the most part to the fortunes of national Israel. From this point on an extended community of faith will gradually become more visible, particularly after the exile of 587BC. We continue now with a fairly brief review of the remainder of the OT.

iii. Deuteronomy

The book of Deuteronomy supplies important details for our investigation. It is essentially comprised of three covenant addresses delivered by Moses in the plains of Moab (Deut 1:6-4:43; 5:1-28,29). All commend the Sinai covenant and aim at its fulfilment in the promised land. The consistent theme throughout is the manner of life to be enjoyed in the land. Somewhat analogous to John's Gospel, Deuteronomy's emphasis is upon the quality of life to be enjoyed if one responds to God's promises.

This land is God's gift to Israel. Yet since it was taken from others by God it is in itself also a warning. The land is presented in extravagant terms; it is the very quintessence of fertility and fruitfulness. Not only will it yield heavenly fare (i.e., milk and honey) but it is actually watered from heaven (Deut 11:11). It is a land of brooks and water, fountains and springs which flow into soft valleys (cf. 8:7). Not merely potentially rich, it is furnished with cisterns which Israel did not dig, houses which she did not build, fruit trees which she did not plant, etc. (cf. 6:10-11). In such a land fullness of life will be enjoyed and Israel will be blessed above all peoples (7:14). All sickness will be removed as well as every threat to Israel's security. God's care of this land is sure, for his eyes are ever on it and his concern for it is continual (11:11-12).

By means of such references the concept of the land as "Eden regained" comes through strongly. This is in keeping with the expectation voiced in Exod 15:17-18 that the land is God's sanctuary, in which Israel is in effect continually at worship. Everything which threatens to pollute must necessarily be removed, for God and Israel inhabit it together.

N. Lohfink[19] draws interesting parallels between Adam's and Israel's positions with respect to the land. Like Adam, Israel is formed outside the "garden" (an inference for Adam from Gen 2:8) and later placed in the "garden". This garden land in Israel's case promises to satisfy every desire. Like Adam, Israel is given rules by which the garden land is to be enjoyed. Yet also like Adam, curiously, Israel breaks every rule — she rejects God as her King. Called to be a "second Adam" she is finally excluded from the garden sanctuary, from the promised land. It is hardly surprising, in view of these parallels, that when we come to the concept of the new community in Rev 21 the Edenic images are sustained. They are coupled there with the presence of God and the Lamb before whom the redeemed are to rejoice forever.

Rest in the land, a notion developed more fully in our New Temple discussion and related to sanctuary concepts, is the great promise accompanying the gift (Deut 3:20; 12:9; 25:17-19; 28:65). God provides rest by his victories on Israel's behalf and thus, as we will note in our New Creation material on Exod 15, a theology of Yahweh war develops. The expected response was Israel's grateful obedience. Thus law objectified by "love" is the conduct which Israel is required to display. Love is not treated in the book as a mere emotion. It can be commanded and is presented synonymously with God's choice (4:37; 10:15). Love in Deuteronomy is primarily associated with activities such as "walking in his ways" and "obeying his voice" etc.[20] Here the great summarizing passage of 10:12-22 is instructional in its initial demand of Israel to fear God. The reference is to the Sinai reaction, to the awe adopted before the revelation of the divine character. This is then the inner attitude to be espoused. But rather than pursuing fear, the passage develops a theme of love as the outcome of fear. If fear is therefore the required interior reaction, love is the outward and visible demonstration. In NT terms fear is faith and love is works. Coerced obedience is not described in Deuteronomy, however, for the theology of this book ultimately presupposes that obedience springs from a heart in which the law finds a home. There is a joyful and a filial note ringing right throughout the book.

With all of this, Deuteronomy adopts a realistic tone in terms of appeal to statutes and ordinances to which Israel is to be subject. There is a dichotomy established in the book similar to that of Exodus. Israel is confronted with choices of life and death (Deut 30:15-20); to love and serve the God of the covenant or to be drawn aside into idolatry.

Blessings follow the one and curses the other (chaps. 27-28). The remainder of the Bible simply discloses the ill-advised path which Israel chose to follow.

iv. Pre-Monarchical Period

We may pass over the book of Joshua simply noting it implements the plan outlined for conquest and occupation in Deuteronomy and Joshua is presented as the Mosaic successor. At this critical point in Israel's history, the covenant is reaffirmed (Josh 24).

Judges, however, raises important questions for the identification and continuation of Israel which can only be touched on here. The book of Judges is written in reference to the problems of the period — the broken covenant. Chapters 1-16 repeat the cycle of apostasy: repentance after domination by a foreign aggressor, and rescue. In the last chapters (17-21) there is à revealing insight into the internal corruption of the society. Moreover, the closing verse of the book is illuminating and informative for an understanding of Israel's reason for existence in the OT. "In those days", we are told, "there was no king in Israel, every man did what was right in his own eyes" (21:25). This is a frank confession of the private and public indiscretions of the period. The absolute chaos produced by this lawlessness and excessive individualism within the tightly structured tribal confederation brought Israel continually and perilously close to the brink of dissolution. Though the foreign threats are mostly directed against one tribe or another, it is plain the weakening of one member within such a small territorial state meant the dismemberment of all.

There is no denial by the author that the period for Israel was a degrading one. Patterns of society were established from which it was very difficult to recover. It may seem from Judg 21:25 that kingship is being recommended as the antidote to the sort of social anarchy and immorality that the book displays. A tight bureaucratic monarchy would remedy the evils which threatened to undo the confederation. Yet Judges condemns attempts to implement kingship and thus implicitly rejects it. Gideon, the great hero, piously refuses an offer (Judg 8:23-24), pointing out it is Yahweh who must reign. When kingship really emerges it is in the lampooned form of a tyrannical half-Canaanite rule which Abimelech the son of Gideon exercised over Shechem.[21] Since Abimelech is the antithesis of everything that a Judge of Israel should be, it would seem that kingship generally, and especially of that kind (which came in under Solomon later), was inimical to Israel's interests.

More likely, the point made by the final verse of Judges is the cohesion of Israel in spite of everything done to effect self-destruction. In spite of the prevailing tendency to disintegration within Israel, in spite of the fact that the social face of Israel presented such a chaotic aspect, the remarkable thing is that during some four hundred years of threatened dissolution of the tribal confederation, Israel held together! The paradox is that at the conclusion of Judges there remains an Israel! In short, the book of Judges reveals the remarkable preservation of Israel. It was not Israel's own self- determination which kept her relatively intact!

Although she had not acknowledged God's kingship with any constancy, what kept her was God's determination not to let her go. From time to time God raised up saviours for her, unwilling to let the concept of a political Israel fall. The message we glean from the book is that Israel's political survival never depended upon her ability to counter the circumstances of the period, or to modify her forms of government to take account of changing social circumstances. It did not depend upon resolute efforts on her part to promote social efficiency. It did not even depend upon gifted or inspired leadership, for in the last analysis such leaders were raised by God. What would and did account for the continuance of a national Israel in the OT was the willingness of God to persevere with that nation. Throughout her history Israel assumed many political guises: patriarchal leadership; charismatic guidance; monarchical rule; and, later in the post-exilic period, a tight hierocracy. None of these permutations, however, accounted for her preservation. God alone accounts for Israel's continuance. He supplies the saviour; Israel must simply depend upon His fidelity. Such faithfulness adheres to the Exod 19 charter.

This is what makes the OT such a curiously modern book. Successful political leadership did not and could not solve the problems of that age. For in the end Israel was an elective concept. What always accounts for Israel is the fact that God is reliable, constant, steadfast. He does not let his promises fail. Judg 21:25 reminds us, however, that we are now on the verge of a great social change within Israel. Kingship will come and leave its stamp upon the developing political formularies of Israel, which in their own way would be transmuted into eschatological expectation.[22]

v. *The Advent of Kingship*

Kingship is anticipated and legislated for in Deut 17:14-20 and this, in fact, is the very form of the request which Israel puts to Samuel in

1 Sam 8:5 (cf. Deut 17:14). It does not surprise us that it should come in a period of increasing urbanization in Palestine. What surprises Samuel, however, is the blatant nature of the request put forth by the elders of Israel (1 Sam 8:5). "You are old", they tell him, "and your sons do not walk in your ways; now appoint for us a king to govern us like all the nations." It is not the request for kingship as such which provokes Samuel's concern, but the ignorance of Israel's vocation which the request displays. True, the request of the elders merely repeats Deut 17:14, but the misuse of the right of appeal to Deut 17 within 1 Sam 8 is pointed to by the repetition (v19) of the request after Samuel's warnings on the dangers of the new office. Moreover, the request comes from the people as a whole in Deut 17:14 and it is modified by the tenor of verses 15-20. Called to be a light to the world and marked off to witness by her separateness, the elders nevertheless request in 1 Sam 8 a king to govern (Heb. *sapat* "judge") her like all the nations. In other words they call for conformity in social patterning to the custom of their world. Israel's political forms are to be those which are generally shared, which presumably will also operate in her as they do in others. There are two factors here which we must consider.

In the first place, a request for dynastic kingship (i.e., self-perpetuating) attempts to undercut divine control. In the era of the Judges, God spontaneously raised up men of his choice to meet the crisis of the time. No longer could such an element of charisma predominate in the contemplated kingship for which Israel asks. It is the control which is being placed upon the gift of the Spirit, if it may be put that way, which is the disturbing element. Second, the request attempts to co-ordinate two widely differing concepts of national leadership. Dynastic kingship is autocratic, self-perpetuating and potentially anti-social. Judgeship (for which Israel also asks, cf. "to govern us" Heb. *sapat*) as exercised by Samuel, the last and greatest of the figures of the period, is episodic, limited and inspired. Thus these two concepts of leadership are diametrically opposed in their political outlook. Indeed Israel's request here for identification with the world is virtually a call for the undoing of the Sinai covenant! What is in mind is the substitution of earthly for divine kingship.

1 Sam 8-12 is concerned with refining the nature of kingship requested into conformity with the Sinai kingdom background. This is finally done in a ceremony which appears to be held at Gilgal, the details of which have been recorded in chapter 12. The reassociation occurs within the context of Yahweh's kingship over Israel, having first been reaffirmed at the conclusion of Saul's inspired victory over the Ammonites (11:12-15). Thus kingship and covenant are linked in

general terms, even though kingship requires further adjustments and a Davidic covenant before it is finally absorbed. But the general principles of covenant/kingship compatibility are laid down in 1 Sam 12.

We need not delay over the details of Saul's kingship except to note two factors important for Israel's development in the OT period which surface at this point. The first concerns the prophetic movement's rise to prominence. The second concerns the nature of the kingship which Yahweh grants and the personal connection to Yahweh's rule which this kingship is to assume.

Prophecy in Israel is as ancient as Abraham (cf. Gen 20:7). It is closely associated with the Sinai covenant (cf. Deut 18:15-22) and with Moses (cf. Num 12:8). Moreover, the prophetic function is disclosed, if not identified, in the period of the Judges as the Mosaic office continues through the charismatic leaders. As kingship evolves in Israel, prophecy rises to prominence. The early clashes between Saul and Samuel make it clear prophecy claims divine authority to regulate and even over-rule kingship. As the protector of the covenant traditions, the prophet is especially watchful to ensure the covenant's preservation under this new social movement. Kingship always has the potential to develop autocratically, and thus to destroy the Sinai relationship. Kingship will, in fact, be of the aberrant Solomonic type, and will lead to the downfall not only of the united kingdom, but later of north and south respectively, notwithstanding the sustained prophetic attempts to keep political excesses within check.

A theology of kingship clearly develops with both Saul and David which is meant to regulate all Israelite kingship. The parallels between the choice of Saul and David are noted by R. Knierim, and will be briefly restated here.[23] Both Saul and David are the subject of divine election. Both are then anointed, an act which authorizes them to act on Yahweh's behalf, and at the same time provides a close connection with Yahweh himself. Both are endowed for leadership by the gift of the Spirit. Finally, both are publicly confirmed by remarkable demonstrations of power; Saul at Jabesh-Gilead (1 Sam 11); David before Israel (chap. 17). This pattern is not repeated in respect of other individual kings of the OT. It operates only as an ideal by which kingship is measured, and we are not surprised to find that it is not duplicated in Israel's later kings. Nor is it unanticipated that all four features occur in the person of Jesus as he commences his own ministry.

In the careers of Saul and David there is evidence of the tension between the ideal and the historically real, just as we noted of Israel's experience in Exod 19-34. Even the Davidic line failed. But the enduring dynasty erected for David in 2 Sam 7 ensures the perpetuation of the ideal, finally culminating in a christological fulfilment. Pertinent to the explanation of the nature of Davidic kingship is Ps 110. In this Psalm the Israelite king is celebrated as a non-levitical priest after the order of Melchizedek, priest king of Salem (Gen 14:18). This combination of priesthood and kingship, apparently after the Davidic model, is significant in view of the later transference of the Davidic promises to the believing community. For in the New Covenant situation referred to in Isa 55:3-5 the sure mercies of David, the promises of 2 Sam 7, are given to the believing community. These connections are noteworthy, for the combination of kingship and priesthood for the New Community is confirmed by Rev 1:6, 5:9-10 and 20:6.

vi. *Monarchical Period: Emergence of Remnant Theology*

The concept of a united kingdom of Israel received its final flourish in 1 Kgs 8 where the dedication of the Temple is presented as the completion of the conquest and the transfer of the Sinai traditions to Jerusalem. Immediately after the death of Solomon, whose reign must bear the direct responsibility for the later division, north and south became separate kingdoms. The books of Kings deal with the decline and fall of the Solomonic · empire arising out of the political assertiveness, yet spiritual imperception, of the respective kings of the period. Because of its declension from Jerusalem the north also falls. Within the monarchical period for the first time in the OT we have the enunciation of a true Israel. That is to say, a concept of an Israel to arise within historical Israel emerges. This was certain to occur as the political future of national Israel became increasingly uncertain. God was committed to a future for his people. Faithful Israelites joined schools of disciples (etc.) gathering around the prophets (cf. Isa 8:16). It is interesting to note in Kings the emergence of loyalties to articles of faith disassociated from national policy. Thereby communities of faith were born.

We first see these developments in the ministry of Elijah. On Mt Carmel (1 Kgs 18:31) Elijah builds a twelve-stoned altar emphasizing the indivisibility of the nation of Israel as he confronts the ten tribes of the north. He is presented as a Mosaic revivalist figure. When he finally reaches the scene of the Mosaic theophany at Horeb (19:9), the still small voice which comes to him after his own theophany implies that God has nothing to add to his Sinai revelation and that Elijah's office is to sustain it.[24] Despite the terrible judgements upon the north resulting from the three anointings Elijah is to perform, there will still remain seven thousand who will not have bowed the knee to Baal, seven thousand faithful Yahweh worshippers. In short, national Israel's defection (in this case the northern kingdom) would not lead to the extinction of "Israel".

Perhaps it is this notion of the "remnant" that is further developed by Amos a century later (cf. Amos 5:14-15).[25] At the conclusion of Amos (9:11) comes the enigmatic reference to the raising of the "booth" of David (Heb. *sukkah*). The immediate reference may be to Jerusalem (cf. Isa 1:8), as hopes for the city are linked with the future of Davidic rule. Thus the concept of the people of God surfaces in the terms of 2 Sam 7. The concern in Amos 9:11-15 is clearly eschatological since the remnant of Edom which "Israel" will then possess (v12) indicates a final triumph over the typical enemy of the people of God. Edom's representative function is stressed by the explanatory note, "and all the nations who are called by my name". This passage dealing with the final supremacy of the people of God and their contact with the world finds its fitting application in Acts 15:14, to justify the inclusion of the Gentiles in the promise structure.[26] Once again, here in Amos, we are left in no doubt that the political reversals which national Israel experienced would not negate the promises of God.

It is in the Book of Isaiah that the notion of an Israel within historical Israel, or a doctrine of a remnant, leaps to great prominence. As the prophet's vocation is defined in Isa 6, it is made clear his ministry is to announce a destruction which will leave the land decimated. However, a holy seed will emerge from the "stock of the national tree". We have already noted the evil — the failure by the nation to demonstrate the nature of divine rule — to which Isa 6 refers in our discussion of the New Jerusalem. This message is taken further in 7:1-9:7 in regard to the Davidic hopes.

In Isa 7:3 the prophet's son is appropriately named "a remnant will return" (Heb. *Shear Jashub*). The inversion of the normal Heb. word order places the emphasis upon the noun so that "*only* a remnant will return" is the required meaning. Since, as G. Hasel[27] points out, the verb "to return" (Heb. *sub*) is often used in covenantal contexts, what is probably meant by this name is the prophetic warning only a "remnant will turn in faith" in the developing crises. Faith is the only true response to the covenant. Through the remnant the Davidic promises will be continued. The change in pronouns between verses 11 and 13 underscores the fact the royal house will not be involved in this faith commitment. Ahaz is enjoined to ask for a sign from "*your* God" (v11). He "piously" refuses only to be told by the prophet that he has not only wearied men (i.e., Isaiah) but "my God" (v13) as well. In short, Ahaz, because of his refusal, is excluded from the developing community.

Ahaz receives the sign of Immanuel, the child who is to be born. But even here the name is ominous, for "God with us" (Immanuel) embodies both promise and threat. In all probability the sign is two-edged, promising protection to some and destruction to others. If so, this is a major development within Israelite prophecy. While Isa 7:14 is best taken messianically (the child is associated with the promise of Davidic continuity),[28] Isaiah's gaze is very much focused on the coming Assyrian invasion after which he expects the implementation of the ideal kingship depicted in 9:1-7.

A community of faith emerging from the destruction of the body politic is a pervasive notion in Isaiah 1-39 (e.g., 1:24-26; 4:2-3; 7:1-9; 10:20-21; 28:5-6; 30:15-17). Empirical Israel will give way to the community of faith. Thus the message of judgement which the pre-exilic prophets brought was essentially a message of hope. But it is the gradual non-nationalistic terms in which the hope is couched that is of increasing significance to our study. Isaiah's message of an emerging community is essentially repeated in pre-exilic prophecy (Mic 5:7-9; Zeph 2:9; 3:12-13).

vii. *Jeremiah*

Jeremiah and Ezek 1-24 both face the prospective fall of Jerusalem, passing final judgement upon the political institutions of Judah. Judah is now the bearer of the traditions of national Israel, owing to the northern exile in 722BC. But what if Jerusalem should fall? What would happen if temple and cult, Davidic kingship, and even the land went? Would there be any point in talking about a future for Israel if the institutions now identified with the Sinai traditions were to perish in the fall of Jerusalem? Now more than ever the question is raised by these prophets as to the nature of the true Israel. What is it that makes Israel, Israel? The respective prophets' answers are remarkably similar. Jeremiah has our attention first.

It is clear that he is addressing two factions. After the exile of the boy king Jehoiachin (598-597BC), son of Jehoiakim (609-598BC), his uncle Zedekiah was appointed early in 597BC by Nebuchadrezzar as a replacement. The pro-Egyptian party seems to have rallied around

Zedekiah placing their hopes on the fact that the Jerusalem temple remained. On the other hand many saw Jehoiachin, although in exile, as the true bearer of the Davidic hopes. Although disciplined by exile the hope none the less continued. Thus one way or the other confidence centred around Jerusalem, the temple, and David.

Jeremiah resists these tendencies. In his famous temple sermon he points to the need to protect the temple. It is not a talisman which protects Israel (Jer 7:1-15). He inveighs against an indifferent Yahwism negligent of the reality of divine rule, attacks the cult (vv21-26) and even the sacred symbol of the ark of the covenant (cf. 3:16). Further, Jeremiah offers no hope for the Davidic dynasty. Even if the exiled Jehoiachin was a signet ring on Yahweh's finger, Yahweh would pluck him off. Jehoiachin would be written up in the genealogies with the ignominy of being childless (22:24,30). If in the uncertain future God were to persevere with the throne of David, it would not be by way of linear connection. Rather God will raise up for Himself a righteous branch (23:5), a divine offshoot of the type referred to in the messianic promises of Isa 11:1-9.

Clearly, this prophecy is aimed against the present kingship of Zedekiah, since the name to be given to the prospective ruler ("the Lord is our righteousness": Jer 23:6) seems, as we have earlier noted, a direct rejection of the name of Zedekiah ("My righteousness is Yahweh").[29] Thus, messianic rule is to be re-established, but not linked to the historical line of David.

In the controversy between the two factions as to the location of the true Israel, whether in Palestine under Zedekiah or in exile under Jehoiachin, Jeremiah partially agrees that the new beginning will come in exile. The hopes are to be reposed there. This is not because of the intrinsic worth of the exiles, nor for any change of heart that the political reversal itself will produce. Israel will begin again in exile because there God will give them a heart to know him (Jer 24:7). In his New Covenant prophecies, Jeremiah foreshadows the union of the two disparate entities, Judah and Israel, into one people (31:31-33), somewhat similar to the position taken in Ezek 37:15-28. It is also to be noted that Jeremiah uses the term Israel to refer prospectively (and currently) to the people of God, the elective entity. Of the some one hundred and twenty odd references to Israel in the book, at least two-thirds of them are theological. Typical of such use is Jer 18:1-6, where the possibility of a new beginning for the nation and the people of God is under review. Here the house of Israel is addressed (v6), though when the prophet is commissioned to explain the parable it is to the men and the inhabitants of Judah he is sent (v11).

Jeremiah's New Covenant doctrine, as we have noted elsewhere, looks to an eschatological fulfilment. In speaking of the renewed house of Israel, Jeremiah has in mind the redeemed people of God, a redeemed Israel. Since the imagery is Sinaiatic, the question of the inflow of the Gentiles is not directly addressed, though the implications of the Sinai covenant naturally raise it. Therefore, Jeremiah 31 concludes with an appeal to the New Creation (vv35-37), and then to the rebuilding of the New Jerusalem pictured in its most politically extensive limits (vv38-40).

viii. *Ezekiel*

Ezekiel's stance on the question of Israel is similar to that of Jeremiah's. Like Jeremiah, Israel is for him almost exclusively a theological term. The first twenty-four chapters of the book deal with the pre-587BC situation and preach to those who put their trust in the existing temple. The last twenty-four chapters are concerned with the reconstitution of Jerusalem. Within the structure of the prophecy the emphasis falls upon Israel first as apostate (chaps. 1-24), and then restored (chaps. 25-48). Perhaps Ezek 20 and 37 are chapters characteristic of this emphasis.

Israel's past history is reviewed in Ezek 20[30] in terms of three generations: Israel in Egypt and the first and second generations of the wilderness (vv1-26). Israel's subsequent history is passed over, presumably because this was no more than a natural development of the apostate Sinai Israel. The future of Israel is determined by her reaction to the divine word in Egypt, and on the way to the promised land. The prophet thus attacks the traditions around which nostalgic hopes of a new beginning may have been growing in exile. When the chapter does move on it is simply to deal with Israel's apostasies in the land (vv27-31). In particular their predisposition to give up hope in present circumstances, and to merge with the surrounding nations, thus losing their identity (v32), is vigorously attacked. All of this is countered by the exercise of God's kingship over them ("I will be king over you" v33). Israel is still Yahweh's disposable property, and in the manner of the Exodus redemption he will gather them from the nations with outstretched arm. On God's holy mountain his people will once again serve him (vv40-44). Nonetheless, there is a refining judgement in exile as Israel "passes under the rod" (v37).

Ezek 37 is placed within the prophecies of restoration. We are here transported to the same plain where the foreshadowed judgement is carried out (v1 cf. 3:22). Israel now lies dead in exile and all that the prophet sees is the remaining bleached bones ("the whole house of Israel" 37:11). The impossible occurred, and Israel is judged. But now in terms similar to Gen 2:7 Israel is recreated! Life is breathed into her by the Spirit of God (Ezek 37:1-14). In verses 15-28, Ezekiel has the reunification of the two houses of Israel and Judah in mind. The gathered people will be united under modified Davidic leadership (the Davidic figure is styled a "prince" in v25 and also at v24 where the LXX reading "leader" Gk. *hegoumenos* should be adopted). Finally, God attests the reality of the new people by placing his sanctuary in their midst, an act of world significance (v28). Thus the chapter sums up the restoration promises presented and reiterated since 33:23-33 — physical enjoyment of the promised land (the supreme spiritual index!) conditional upon obedience.

 The problem of faulty leadership which led to the exile is dealt with in Ezek 34. After an initial acknowledgement of this historical failure (vv1-6) it is made clear that in a future age Yahweh himself would shepherd Israel (vv7-24), with provision for a Davidic undershepherd. A return to paradisiacal conditions follows (vv25-29). In chapter 35 the removal of all enmity against Israel is anticipated in the prophecy of doom uttered over the ideal enemy, Edom. After the removal of this thorn a promise of deliverance for the land is given in 36:1-15, along with the restoration of the people through cleansing (vv16-38). Within this section the initiative is not taken by the people in repentance (as Deut 30:1-10 had envisaged), but by God. This is emphasized in Ezek 36:21-23, where the operation of the New Covenant is not contingent upon Israel's performance but on divine fidelity alone. People and land are to be reunited (vv24-32) and all contaminating influences removed. Life in the new age depends upon inward renewal (v26) though, unlike Jer 31, Ezekiel does not add that the law will be placed in the heart. But obedience is the presupposition of the new age and this can only be effected by a new heart in which the will of God is reflected. In the new age there will be a democratization of the Spirit. Not only Israel's leaders will be affected as in former times, but the entire people of God (v26). All this leads to the renewal and rebirth recounted in Ezek 37.

 In chapters 38-39 the restored people are living peacefully in the new age only to be beset by enmity in the shape of Gog and Magog. This threat is removed by Yahweh who annihilates Gog. The relationship of Ezek 38-39 to what follows is not entirely clear[31] but the final kingdom of God age is ushered in by the prophecies of chapters 40-48.

 The theocratic nature of the projected Israel and the expectation of a response by worship envisaged in the structure of this restoration programme are treated in Ezek 40-48. No messianism appears in these chapters, as indeed none would be expected in this vision of final end-time divine rule. The exodus and Sinai situations are virtually repeated and the land is re-allotted (47:13-48:7). Tribal allotments of equal size appear to be envisaged and Israel dwells as a sacred confederation grouped four-square around the sanctuary just as she did in the immediate post-Exodus period. However, we may note the centrality of Judah in the arrangements to the north of the sacred enclosure.

Thus the book of Ezekiel concludes on a sustained note of restoration which provides continuity for a spiritual Israel. In this economy rule will be by divine leadership, therefore no dominant role in the final description is allotted to the Davidic figure. Israel is once again placed on the threshold of a new conquest era with all the potential in the new entry into the promised land which was accorded to Adam in Eden. There is little consideration of Israel's role in the wider world, but this situation is redressed in the great body of prophetic material relating to the exile, namely Isa 40-55.

ix. *Isaiah 40-55*

In Isa 40-55 our emphasis will of necessity fall on the servant as we seek to define the role and nature of Israel. The oracles may conveniently be divided into two sections. First, chapters 40-48 emphasize Yahweh as the Holy One of Israel who is faithful to his promises and who consequently is about to bring Israel back in a mighty new exodus. The return from Babylon is not all that is suggested. Ultimately nothing less than the restoration of the people of God within the context of a New Creation is considered. Since references to Israel's antecedents, Abraham and Jacob, are frequent within chapters 40-55 as a whole, the future of Israel via this return is in fact the fulfilment of the promises given to these fathers. Second, the position of Zion after the return is under careful review in chapters 49-55.

Isa 40-55 suggests no prospect of a blanket national redemption. Since restoration is closely related to the idea of remnant (Isa 46:3, 49:6, cf. 51:1-2) primary focus is on life under a New Covenant for the redeemed righteous. Thus, while the subject is certainly the return from exile, what is really at stake is a final new exodus constituting the new community as the people of God. Since the theme is the people of God's return to the promised land it is easily seen that we are moving within the expectations of Gen 12:1-3. It is thus to be anticipated that the nations will be involved in Israel's restoration. As the saved and glorified servant, Israel will exercise a compelling drawing power over the nations (cf. 49:6, 55:5). For their part, the nations will confess that the only true God and Lord of history dwells in Zion, and they will come in submissive pilgrimage (cf. 49:23). Of course, none of this happened in the immediate historical context, thus indicating that the promises were meant for eschatological fulfilment. What the prophets really envisage is an ideal return of *the* people of God.

The temptation of many Israelites to apostasy is addressed in Isa 40-48. To offset this tendency, the prophet asserts God's power over the nations and his responsibility for the activity of the Persian king Cyrus, who is a type of second Moses (Isa 45:1-7). We may note here the extensive and consistent use of creation language in the enthronement poem of 44:24-45:7 honouring Cyrus, for the restoration which he will engineer will be a New Creation. In chapters 49-55 no further warnings against idolatry are issued and Cyrus disappears from the scene. Now the focus shifts almost entirely to the future of Zion-Jerusalem as a symbol of the political future of redeemed Israel.

We first encounter the servant figure in connection with the trial narratives of Isa 40-48, where Israel and the nations appear before the judgement bar guilty of idolatry. In 42:1-4 (vv5-9 probably ought to be connected) we meet the servant as a royal and yet prophetic figure. The affinity of this description with the choice of David in 1 Sam 16:1-13 is unmistakable, while both royal and prophetic features are contained in the servant's task to set forth both "judgement" Heb. *mispat* and "law" (Heb. *torah*). His ministry has the Gentiles in view (Isa 42:4). Although neither demonstrative (v2) nor seemingly significant (v3), he will nevertheless bring forth judgement with (divine) faithfulness, and thereby re-establish the covenant. He will be discouraged, but he will not fail under it and his ministry will therefore have universal dimensions (v4).

We need, as W.A.M. Beuken has pointed out, to set Isa 42:1-4 in its wider context. Beuken has noted the connection between 42:1 ("Behold my servant") and the conclusion to the previous trial narrative in 41:29 ("Behold, they are all a delusion").[32] In 41:1-5 the nations draw near for judgement, while in the closing sequence of verses 21-29 the gods of the nations are set in disarray by the prophetic demonstration that Yahweh is the sole Lord of history. He alone is able to predict its course, knowing the beginning and the end.

As we have noted, in Isa 40:12-31 Yahweh replies to Israel's complaint that her "way", her present situation in history (note the parallel in v27 of "way" and "judgement" Heb. *mispat*), seems to be running contrary to what a people of God may have expected. Once again, Beuken[33] notes the progressive character of the argument in verses 12-31 and material presented in the New Jerusalem treatment is here repeated for the sake of convenience. Yahweh is able to withstand Israel's three enemies: the nations (vv2-17); the princes (vv18-24); and the power behind the princes, the astral deities (vv25-26). In the last section where particular attention is given to Israel's complaint (vv27-31), Yahweh announces not only his ability, but his willingness, to redeem. Thus both the "judgement" *mispat* which Israel seeks and the judgement which the servant is to display are Yahweh's control of the course of history. As the incomparable One (v25), he will be faithful to his covenant promises.

It is possible that Isa 42:5-9 is a continuation of the first servant passage or a commentary upon it. Either way the more direct issue of the servant's role as "a covenant to the people, a light to the nations" is raised (cf. v6). The difficult phrase "covenant to the people" (Heb. *b^erit ^cam*) in verse 6 continues to puzzle. Just who is this people? The servant's role either has Israel or the nations in view. In material relating to the New Covenant, we have opted for the latter. Thus the servant functions first as a covenant figure, and then as a covenant pledge, enabling Israel to fulfil her wider Abrahamic obligations to the world. In the second servant passage, 49:3 directly identifies the servant with Israel. This seems to assure a corporate interpretation for the servant. The third servant passage (50:4-9) seems allied to the prophetic identity and role as the servant perseveres in a ministry of suffering, confident that Yahweh will provide both the message and the ability to present it. Finally, the presentation of the fourth servant section is highly individualistic (52:13-53:12). This, in itself, does not militate against a corporate notion though it may point to a certain fluidity of presentation entailing a designed ambiguity in the movement between group and individual.

The sporadic application of Isa 53 to Jesus in the NT is completely compatible with the OT intent even though in its context the chapter seems to refer to remnant (?) or prophetic (?) Israel's sufferings via the familiar language of the Psalms of Lament. Any interpretation must be somewhat tentative. Perhaps the reference is similar to Ezek 37; specifically, the death and resurrection of suffering Israel in exile are in view. Isa 52:13-53:12 seems to refer to the confession of the nations who have perceived Israel's suffering as efficacious; it is a highly theologized report.[34] In our treatment of the New Covenant we have engaged in detailed discussion of the covenant renewal consequences in which Israel and the world are involved as a result of this ministry narrated in Isa 54-55. Such a covenant renewal leads us back to Eden recaptured, to the New Creation.

No missionary task is directly associated with the servant's role in Isa 40-55 since the emphasis in these chapters is vindicatory and somewhat narrowly "nationalistic".[35] The same world view with Israel as the centre of the prophetic focus prevails within chapters 56-66. But it is clear that salvation is not for the whole nation, as P.D. Hanson has shown.[36] No Davidic individual appears in chapters 40-66 and the stress is upon God's intervention in the new age. We have already noted the transfer of the Davidic promises to the faithful in 55:3-5. Thus when the emphasis of chapters 56-66 is added to chapters 40-55, the renewal of Israel in chapters 40-66 is seen to have Israel's world role in mind, whereby redeemed Israel becomes the arm of the Abrahamic promises. She operates as a guarantee of world salvation and her function is directed toward the consummation of all things, the New Creation (cf. 65:17-25).

x. *Post-Exilic Developments*

This developing emphasis upon a community of faith is continued in the writings of the post-exilic period. Hag 1 is concerned with covenant renewal and operates with an eschatological picture of the temple to which the nations will come. Messianism in the person of Zerubbabel is hardly a factor (2:20-23). We have had occasion to note that Zechariah is also temple and Jerusalem orientated. The major concern of both books is the universal pilgrimage of the nations to Jerusalem, Israel's political centre, which constitutes the proper response to Yahweh's universal kingship.

Ezra-Nehemiah are best seen as we have noted as implementing the social programmes advocated by the slightly earlier Malachi. The overall message of ·these two books is clear. Ezra begins with the possibility of a restoration by reference to the edict of Cyrus permitting return (538BC). Second exodus theology is therefore in prospect. However, Nehemiah ends some one hundred and forty years later on a much more sombre note; a divided community in which the power of the priesthood had been temporarily checked by the efforts of Nehemiah. Ezra and Nehemiah present a realized eschatology whereby cleansed Israel dwells in an idealized concept of a Jerusalem city state. The Ezra memoirs (Ezra 7-10, .Neh 8-10) are concerned with the concept of a theological Israel, for the term Israel is mentioned twenty-four times, while Judah (as a geographical reference) occurs only four times. Moreover, the predominance of the term Israel in the Persian edict reported in Ezra 7 is astonishing.[37] Ezra-Nehemiah, therefore, continue the hope reposed in Israel by OT prophecy.

We may briefly refer to the theology of Chronicles to conclude the OT presentation. Commencing with the genealogy of Adam (i.e., creation), the books conclude with Cyrus' edict permitting the Jews to return and rebuild the temple. The nature of this kingdom of God theology of restoration has been noted in our study of the New Temple.

The tribal genealogies of 1 Chron 1-9 set the tone for the remainder of the books in their concentration upon the presupposition of the unity of all Israel. This is markedly the preservation of a theological ideal since the reality is but a small, circumscribed Jerusalem city state during the time the Chronicler writes. But in this way the purposes of God for Israel are intimately connected with creation, opening up the hope of restoration under kingdom of God rule (cf. the particular emphasis of 2 Chron 36:22-23). 1 Chronicles 1 moves quickly from Adam to Jacob and thus to Israel. Chapters 2-9 then concentrated on the development of Israel with an emphasis upon the royal tribe of Judah. The Chronicler makes the point forcibly that the purposes of God for creation are only realizable through Israel.[38]

Though Chronicles is supremely concerned with the history of the southern kingdom, there is a concern for "Israel" in the broader sense: namely, the southern kingdom as the carrier of the "all Israel" idea. The phrase "all Israel" occurs in the books thirty-four times.[39] At the end of the books Cyrus fulfils his role as the divinely anointed servant of Isa 45:1-4, thus opening the way for a second exodus return and the covenant renewal which ought to have followed. Written about 400BC or slightly later, Chronicles presents a theology of hope to Israel. The message points to the future in the open-ended terms which the theology of Isa 40-66 has encouraged us to expect. While this has not yet happened, the opinion of the Chronicler, despite the dark days in which he writes, is that there is no reason why the future should not usher it in.

In summary, the OT presented Israel as a worshipping community under divine rule responding to Yahweh's kingship. This was Israel's defined role. If adhered to, Israel would have had its effect on the wider world. The OT presentation is idealistic; a model is presented in the book of Exodus to which historical Israel never conformed. This inevitably translated the ideal into an eschatological hope carried by believing communities, particularly the prophetic groups. We have not dwelt in this study, as perhaps we should have, upon the prophetic critique of Israel's cultus, particularly that offered by the book of Amos. Far from being peripheral, such a critique attacked the very heart of Israel's vocation. The OT majors on expanded descriptions of the consequences of Israel's rejection of Yahweh's kingship. This led to the exile and the virtual abandonment of messianic kingship. At the end of the OT age the book of Chronicles probably best reflects what was always expected and still hoped for; namely, an Israel grouped around the temple responsive to the kingship of God. This will be the life-style of the new community described in Rev 21-22.

The New Testament

i. *Gospels*

Overall the NT divides into two distinct treatments of our theme. The Gospels, by and large, concentrate on the rejection of Israel. Acts and the Epistles, on the other hand, emphasize the emergence of a replacement community. Matthew's Gospel has a particular interest in the true Israel or community of faith. In Matt 1 Jesus is identified as Son of David and Son of Abraham; or in other words as first narrowly Israelite, and then with an indication that the Gospel will have wider implications.

a. Matthew

The genealogy of Matt 1 determines the theology of the Gospel as a whole. It is divided into three sections each overlapping with the next. As David closes the first section and commences the second (vv2-6,6b-11) so the exile closes the second (vv6b-11) and opens the third (v12). Jesus closes the third (v16) and yet opens a fourth stage (vv18-25)[40] of salvation history in which he will save "his people from their sins" (v21). In view of the reference to Isa 7:14 and the striking correspondences between Matt 1:21 and 23, "his people" can only be the community of faith and not all Israel. Perhaps the Magi represent the Jewish dispersion coming in worship and thus the gathering of scattered Israel. We might also see the ministry of John the Baptist in chapter 3 as recalling Israel to the point of entry to the promised land and inviting her to begin again in covenant renewal. All Israel who come for John's baptism are reminded that it is only a covenant renewal symbol. But Jesus' baptism will be of "spirit and fire", an apparent reference to his coming preaching ministry. The presentation of Jesus as the true Israel is unmistakable. His baptism is their true submission. His endorsement of John's message and victory in the wilderness is triumph in the very same trial situation wherein Israel had failed.

After a general preaching mission by Jesus, the disciples are identified in the Sermon on the Mount as the community of faith. Their ministry is summed up in terms of the two figures of salt and light which echo the twofold division of the beatitudes.[41] As salt they are to preserve the continuity of the covenant (cf. Lev 2:13, 2 Chron 13:5); as light they are to draw men to the New Jerusalem, the city set on a hill whose awakening light in this kingdom of God cannot be hidden. Jesus' identification of John the Baptist as Elijah makes the relationship clear (Matt 11:1-19). Jesus ushers in the "great and terrible day of the Lord" which the coming of Elijah was to precede.

The clear separation of Jesus from national Israel comes in Matt 13, a chapter which thematically continues the radical rejection involved and in Jesus' definition of his family (12:46-50). Parables are only told to outsiders (cf. "crowd" 13:1-35), since the three similes set before the disciples in verses 44-51 are not explicitly called parables. The precise rejection of Israel is made by application of Isa 6:9-10 in Matt 13:14-15, and intensified by the rationale introduced by Gk. *hoti* "that". Parables are told to the "crowd", for as representative Israel they continue the tradition of hardened hearts which refuse to hear.

Also significant is the self-definition of Jesus' ministry in Matthew 16 in terms of the Son of Man, the figure of judgemental expectation from Dan 7:13-14. Jesus shows a reluctance in Matt 16:13-28 to accept the term "Christ". As the term currently implied empirical kingship it may not have been appropriate for his ministry at that time. "Christ" is generally reserved in the NT as a title of expectation.

We have noted how Matt 21 functions as a rejection of the temple and its protective role. This chapter is also a formal rejection of Israel in three stages (vv12-19,23-32,33-46). Of particular note is the strong statement in verse 43 that the kingdom is to be taken away from Israel and given to a "nation" (Gk. *ethnos*) which will bring forth the required fruits. From this point on *ethnos*, normally reserved for Gentiles, will be freely used in Matthew's Gospel.[42] A new people of God is obviously in mind here. The Gospel concludes with the universal commission of Matt 28:18-20, which has reference to Dan 7:13-14. Jesus is now the exalted and glorified Son of Man and his followers are the new people (of Israel?), taking the blessings of the

Abrahamic covenant to all nations. They will now go out in mission for, unlike the OT expectation, there is no recognized political unit, no nation to which the world may look in political anticipation.

b. Mark

Later we will develop Mark's location of the "gospel" within the frame of covenant renewal and the New Creation. Important for our discussion at this point is the emphasis Mark places on Jesus' role as Son of Man. In Mark's presentation Jesus virtually commences and concludes his ministry to Israel by the use of this term. The healing miracle at Capernaum forces the Jewish leaders to acknowledge that the Son of Man "has authority on earth to forgive sins" (Mark 2:10). That is to say that the forgiveness now being dispensed on earth is an anticipation of the judgement which he will finally pronounce in heaven. Through the preaching of the gospel judgement is occurring through the Son of Man. The strategic placement of the blind Bartimaeus incident is arresting (10:46-52). What this blind man so clearly sees, Jesus as Israel's king, the Jews have missed completely. It is far from coincidental this event is followed by the rejection of Jerusalem and the temple (chap. 11).

Significant in the passion narrative is Jesus' pronouncement upon Israel's sacral representative, Caiaphas the High Priest (Mark 14:62). He assents to Caiaphas' question that he is the Christ, the Son of the Blessed. But Caiaphas, as Israel's representative and thus Israel as a whole, will not see him as Christ. Rather Caiaphas will see him as the Son of Man. That is to say he will not be associated with the blessing to be brought by the coming of the Messiah such as Bartimaeus has already seen. Instead Caiaphas and, by extension, Israel, will be subject to the judgement which the Son of Man will institute at the consummation of all things.

c. Luke–Acts

The universalistic and Abrahamic stress of the first few chapters of Luke cannot be missed (cf. Luke 1:55,73). In them is celebrated how God is now active in salvation for Israel (vv68-79). This Israel, however, is the small community of faith which is "waiting for the consolation of Israel". Thus the programmatic address of Jesus in the Nazareth synagogue (4:16-30) is crucial, and any understanding of it requires attention to the context with which Jesus begins, namely Isa 61. Jesus tells his audience Isa 61:1-2 has been fulfilled in their hearing. However, it is not fulfilled in the experience of Israel as a whole. The poor addressed are the expectant community (in terms of Isa 61) who are awaiting the salvation about to return to Jerusalem and Israel. Although the lack of acceptance by his own people and his reference to the ministry of Elijah does not in itself presage a Gentile ministry, it at least leaves the door open.

Salvation for Luke is avowedly Abrahamic (cf. Luke 19:10), yet the break with Israel is clear enough. In this regard note the parable of the vinedressers wherein the vineyard is given to those vaguely referred to as "others" (20:16). The twelve disciples are to pronounce judgement upon the twelve tribes of Israel (22:30) and Christ's rejoinder at the trial before the High Priest (22:67-70) rejects Israel (cf. Mark 14:61-62). Cleopas' and his companion's hope that Jesus was the one to redeem Israel is, of course, the point of the whole Gospel (cf. 24:21). Luke's concept of salvation history does not ignore the fact that the message is to the Jew first but, albeit subdued, the stress is still upon the construction of a new people, a new worshipping community, through Jesus.

Acts continues this emphasis. Jerusalem and its temple is again the initial focus for the community of faith. But it cannot be insignificant that the book virtually begins and ends on the note of the importance for Israel of the content of the kingdom of God. The question addressed to Jesus by the disciples (Acts 1:6) is developed as a dominant concern in Luke's thinking. We have cursorily touched on this in our New Temple material. We are probably to take the Greek dative in verse 6 as dative of advantage and thus translate the phrase "will you restore the kingdom for Israel" (i.e., with Israel in view). Therefore what would be in mind is whether the reconstitution will now occur whereby God's kingship will be reimposed. Or, in the terms of prophetic eschatology, whether the nations will now "flow in" to Jerusalem. It is thus a matter of eschatological timetabling, not a resurgence of Jewish nationalism. The command for them to wait in Jerusalem (v4) is logical enough in view of the fact that Jerusalem was the seat of divine kingship. And so the promised Holy Spirit will come, ushering in the last days. In these last days the divine rule will proceed from Jerusalem. The symbolic reconstitution of the New Israel then follows in the latter half of Acts 1.

We have elsewhere noted the Sinai background to Acts 2 and thus its New Covenant emphasis. In Acts 2:14-40, 3:12-26, 4:8-12, the speeches of Peter conclude with a summons to repentance in view of the impending judgement and a promise of forgiveness of sins. Yet it is difficult to believe that these commands (cf. 2:39) refer only to the Jews, and not to a redeemed people of God. Substantially, this is also the pattern found in Paul's speeches (cf. 13:16-41) some of which include sequels of Gentile conversion (cf. 17:22-34). Certainly, the prior claim of Israel is always recognized by Luke and thus the order of salvation preserved. But the claim allows Israel only a first hearing of the Gospel, it is not an inalienable right to its blessings. There is no necessary continuity between an old and a new Israel. J. Jervell has claimed that a mission to the Gentiles is only possible in Acts after a successful ministry to Jews.[43] This is hardly credible, however, in the light of 13:46, 18:6 and 28:28 where part of the rationale for an increasing emphasis on the Gentiles is the unresponsiveness of the Jews. Acts ends on the note of rejection of national Israel (Isa 6:9-10 is quoted in Acts 28:26-27).

Throughout Acts the role of the disciples as witnesses is important, and A. Trites points out echoes of the OT role of Israel and her relationship to the world (cf. Isa 49:6) in this function.[44] At Acts 28:28 the answer to 1:6 is given — the kingdom cannot be restored until the nations come in. The concept of Israel with which the book commenced is transmuted into a comprehensive new entity arising from the rejection of national Israel.

d. John

Here there is an even more thorough-going rejection of Israel. We may begin with John 20:20-23 since that may help us to appreciate the end towards which John's Gospel is moving.

In the upper room, on the resurrection evening Jesus breathes on the disciples and charges them to receive the Holy Spirit. This is not to be associated with Pentecost which authorises them to act as witnesses of the new community. Rather the incident in the upper room records the creation of the new people. In this regard it is significant that John 20:22 uses "breathe on" (Gk. *emphusao*) the same word used for the breathing of divine life into man (LXX Gen 2:7) and resurrected Israel (LXX Ezek 37:9). The "New Israel" thus arises from the shadows of defeat. Pertinent here is the unconscious prophecy of Caiaphas (John 11:50-52) that Jesus would not only die for the nation (where Gk. *ethnos* "nation" is remarkably used of Jews who are now merely an "*ethnos*") but also would gather into one the children of God who were scattered abroad. For that utterance to have been an unconscious prophecy "children of God" must have been a reference to Gentile inclusion, or rather to the construction of a new people.[45]

The upper room and Caiaphas episodes are remarkably congruent with the tenor of the prologue to the Gospel, John 1:1-18. The careful chiastic structure of this passage reveals verses 12-13 are central.[46] Within this structure we pass from the role of Jesus in creation (vv1-3), to his gifts to men through the incarnation (vv4-5), to the witness borne to him by John the Baptist (vv6-8), to his coming into the world (vv9-11), to the summarizing statement of verses 12-13. Through his message a community of faith emerges; those who receive him (v12). The writer then reverses his reflection, moving from the standpoint of OT fulfilment (v14) to the witness of John (v15), to Jesus' gifts to men (v16), to his role in creation and his relation to the Father (vv17-18). Within this schema it is likely that the phrase "children of God" (v12) is a claim by the new community to the role of Israel.[47]

In John 1:14-16 we are in keeping with the tradition of Exod 33-34. Whereas the divine glory concealed the divine nature from Israel of old, the believer sees the divine nature and the divine glory in the humanity of Jesus. There is then a contrast in John 1:17 between the law (for John the whole body of traditions, written and unwritten, stemming from Sinai)[48] which comes only "through" Moses, and the effective grace which comes through Jesus. The position of Israel as under Mosaic mediation after Exodus 32 (cf. our discussion of the Exodus material under the New Covenant) appears to be alluded to in John 1:17, in contrast to the position of the new community which enjoys direct communication with the Father by the Son (cf.v18). Verse 51 completes the chapter by identifying Jesus as the fulfilment of Jacob's role, and he is thus Israel, and yet the Christ. Just as the other Gospels have disclosed, in John Jesus fulfils Israel's role and believers become members of this new community as they are attached to him.

Finally, we note the coming of the Greeks who are best taken as Gentile representatives,[49] with the request to "see" Jesus (John 12:20-36). The purpose of the Gospel is thus made plain at the end of Jesus' public ministry in John's presentation. The Greeks will only see him when he is lifted up (v32): then he will draw all men to himself. Thus a new "universalism" is introduced here. With this episode there is a definite turning from Israel, made all the more ominous by the threatening use of Isa 53:1 in verse 38, coupled with the familiar rejection passage, Isa 6:9-10. After the close of his public ministry Jesus addresses himself to the disciples to whom he reveals himself as the "true" Israel. This is the import of his self-description as the true vine, to whom they are to be joined (John 15). In 18:33-34 Jesus implicitly refuses the title "King of the Jews", just as he had explicitly accepted the title "King of Israel" given to him in 1:49 (cf. 12:13).

John's gospel reveals that the gift of the Spirit means the end of Israel's exile, the construction of a new community. The community of faith to which the prologue bears witness spells the rejection of Israel, a fact underlined by the narratives relating to Jesus' public ministry in chapters 1-12.

ii. Epistles

On the whole Paul's evidence confirms that of the Gospels. His christology, however, is creationally based, and thus the narrower redemptive questions regarding the continuity of national Israel which are raised in the Gospels and Acts are not issues which receive major discussion.

The reference at Gal 6:16 however to an "Israel of God" in what may be the first Pauline epistle is fascinating. Is the one group being described here in this blessing of peace "upon all who walk by this rule"? If so the "and" (Gk. *kai*) joining the phrases "peace be upon them" and "mercy upon the Israel of God" makes the second an explanation of the first. Or are two groups on view here, Gentiles and saved Jews? Paul has already spoken of all barriers between Jew and Gentile as removed (the reversal of the Babel divisions in 3:28). Moreover, the epistle is a polemic against the Judaizers. Further, the reference in 6:16 to peace upon those who "walk by this rule" (i.e., for whom circumcision is a matter of indifference) makes it possible and indeed probable that the Israel of God is a further description of those who do in fact so walk.[50]

We may only pay very brief attention to the important context of Rom 11:25-26. The meaning of "all Israel" in verse 26 has four main possibilities:

i. That the "and so" (Gk. *kai houtos*) of verse 26 points back in the context and thus refers to a special eschatological salvation for national Israel;

ii. That the same words point forward and are associated with the following scripture citation. The reference would then be to the final eschatological salvation pilgrimage to Zion of both Jews and Gentiles; and

iii. That the "all Israel" refers to the Jews who will be saved in Paul's own day.

iv. That the "all Israel" refers to the way in which the sum total of individual Israelites will be saved.

The first view is difficult since it would be completely against the tenor of Pauline theology to advance a "two covenant" stance whereby Israel is saved in a way which is distinctively different from the Gentiles. Paul proclaims only one means of entry to the kingdom of God, namely Christ. Law or any other given privilege is not an entry requirement for Paul, though he did not abandon the role of law in Christian experience.[51]

More possible is the second alternative. It involves taking the "Israel" of Rom 11:26 in a sense different to that ascribed to the term in verse 25, but it respects the tenor of the "two Israels" argument of chapters 9-11 and preserves the theology of salvation by faith alone. It also takes into account the phrase "*all* Israel" does not otherwise occur in these chapters. That Jew and Gentile form the "New Israel" is a point which Paul himself may make in Rom 11 if we take, as we may, Christ as the root of the olive tree into which Jew and Gentile are grafted.

The third view is attractive. The present hardening of Israel has committed Paul to a Gentile mission. He may be reflecting upon the conclusion of his labours as he approaches his goal of Spain.[52] Perhaps Paul is reflecting upon the stimulus which his mission would provide to Jews, and was hoping that the salvation for his people might come in his own era. If so, his thought at this point of a remnant of Israel already saved is prophetic and the postponement of the completion of the reality which he had in mind would not affect its truth.

The fourth view is, however, to be preferred. Paul is thus referring to the manner in which the remnant which exists will be expanded. There is no indication, however, that all Israel will be saved as "national Israel".

Paul throws a much greater emphasis upon a christology which is primarily creational and thereby restorative. We will review this in our discussion of the New Creation. Thus concerning the community of faith the wider question for Paul is one people of God, the one new man, transformation into one and the same image (cf. 2 Cor 3:18). We shall later argue that in this last context, covenant and creation are united, therefore in the new order Jews and Gentiles share the rights which were once exclusively those of national Israel. 1 Cor 10:1 may be understood as representative of Paul's view of continuity, for Israel in the wilderness is "our fathers" for the Gentile Corinthians. We cannot trace the argument of Ephesians in any detail, but Eph 2:12-20 suggests that all Christians enjoy the privileges once exclusively associated with Israel. We have noted in our New Temple discussion of this passage that Christ is regarded as the provider of cosmic peace as a result of which all men, Jews and Gentiles, may be built into the new structure arising upon the foundation which is Christ. It seems clear that the mystery, i.e., the purpose of God previously declared in scripture (Eph 3:4, cf. Col 1:26-27), made known to Paul by revelation is that the Gentiles were in this new age to be included in the new people of God.[53]

In a letter which is addressed to a mixed church,[54] 1 Pet 2:1-10 applies the Sinai promises of a priestly community to the new community in which God's rule is demonstrated. We have also devoted space to this context in the New Temple material, indicating there that the concern of the passage is communal. It defines the nature of the people of God as being in continuity with promises given to Israel, rather than expressing concern with the priestly character and worship structure of the community.

iii. *Revelation Reconsidered*

In the book of Revelation the evidence seems unequivocally similar to that of 1 Peter. The transference of the promises from Israel to the new people is now fully made. For example, consider the use of Exod 19:6 at Rev 1:6 within an address to the church universal, or believers generally.[55] In this context the notion "priestly kingdom" in Exod 19:6 is applied to believers, and embodies the idea of both a dedicated and worshipful response to the Christ revealed, while the note of kingship indicates a sharing of dominion with the victorious Son of Man. He is the embodiment of the promise of Exod 19:6 as linked with the extreme universal terms of Dan 7:13. Exod 19:6 is also taken up at Rev 5:9-10 in the song of the redeemed. Once again the note of universal dominion is prominent.

Both Rev 1:6 and 5:9-10 assume that a new worshipping community (i.e., an "Israel") has arisen through the death of Christ. "Just as the exodus of Israel led to the constitution (i.e., in Exod 19:6) of Israel as a special nation and a kingdom for Yahweh, so does the election of Christians from mankind through the death of Christ lead to a new Kingdom, a new Israel".[56] Only the victorious Lamb can break the seals of the book of destiny (Rev 5:9). That is, the death and resurrection of Christ were the necessary prelude to the series of eschatological events now to be unveiled. Only they account for the emergence of this new worshipping community of priests and kings. The message is that the establishment of the kingdom of God is a reality seen in present Christian community, and the parousia will simply extend this rule and give it its true character.

Some influence of Exod 19:6 (but with dependence upon Isa 61:6 also) finally appears in Rev 20:6. Herein the emphasis is less corporate than in 1:6 and 5:10, and is a future expectation (the earlier references are oriented to the present). Believers are priests because of their decision to worship the Lamb and not the beast. The influence of Isa 61:6 points to the exaltation of this community in the coming age and thus to its dominion status. Rev 21:1-22:5 uses New Israel terminology to describe the perfected community to which the whole world now belongs. The "gates" of the New Jerusalem are inscribed with the names of the twelve tribes of Israel, the foundations of the city are inscribed with the names of the twelve apostles of the Lamb. Thus, the book closes with a picture of a unified people of God. A new community united by common worship has arisen in whom is realized the consummation of every eschatological hope to which humanity has been related throughout the Bible.

The final point to be made is from Rev 22:3-5. Here the new community of these chapters is described in terms which accord perfectly with the role Israel was meant to exercise in the OT. Once again the twin motifs of priesthood and royalty surface. Worship as the response of God's servants is predominant in verse 3, and priestly access in verse 4 ("they will see his face"). That this access is indeed priestly is confirmed by what follows in verse 4, namely: "his name will be on their foreheads". This clause has an evocative reference to Israel's origins and to the tabernacle account of Exod 25-31, since we are immediately reminded of the inscription "Holy to the Lord" engraved on the forefront of Aaron's mitre (28:38). The royal character of the new community is referred to in Rev 22:5 ("they will reign for ever and ever"). Thus it is with respect to a royal priestly community the climax of the account of New Creation fulfilment concludes.

The new community as priests and kings unto God is a legatee of all the promises given to national Israel. Yet it is not strictly speaking a New Israel since it is not a national entity. That term is best avoided. Rather it is a group in which all of the divisions within the structure of the human race have been removed. It represents the ideal to which historical Israel never corresponded. In these people all the symbolism of the OT which emphasized Israel's function — covenant, land, temple, priesthood, kingship — has been gathered together. In ceaseless worship, they praise the God of the beginning and Jesus whose death and resurrection has made this expectation the end which they now celebrate.

Notes

1. E.S. Fiorenza's coverage of discussion is admirable, cf. *Priester fur Gott* (Munster: Aschendorff, 1972) 138-41.

2. R. Mosis, "Exod 19:5b-6a: Syntaktischer Aufbau und lexkalische Semtantik", *BZ* 22 (1978) 19.

3. Fiorenza, *Priester*, 126-7.

4. The Heb. participle *ki* has a wide range of meaning. It can be explicative, casual, emphatic, interpretative, cf. Mosis ("Exod 19:5b-6a,16") and the references cited there. Here it seems best taken in a casual sense.

5. ibid, 14. Exod 19:5 presents the election of Israel, verse 6 the function of Israel within the framework of this election.

6. R.B.Y. Scott, "A Kingdom of Priests (Ex XIX:6)", *OTS* 8 (1950) 218.

7. As W.L. Moran argues building upon the earlier arguments of W. Caspari. Cf. "A Kingdom of Priests", in *The Bible in Current Catholic Thought* ed. J.L. McKenzie (New York: Herder and Herder, 1962) 7-20.

8. Fiorenza, *Priester*, 141-2.

9. For the OT sense of Heb. *goy* "nation" cf. R.E. Clements, "*goy*", *TDOT* 2 (1975) 426-33.

10. H.W. Wolff, "Kerugma of the Yahwist", *Int* 20 (1966) 131-58.

11. ibid, 147-8.

12. ibid, 145.

13. M. Fishbane ("The Composition and Structure of the Jacob Cycle", *JJS* 26 [1975] 15-38) has demonstrated the interrelationships between the units comprising the Jacob account.

14. Cf. J.P. Fokkelman, *Narrative Art in Genesis* (Assen: Van Gorcum, 1975) 197-230. Fokkelman has shown this chapter is about Jacob's struggle with God and about his recognition of what surrender fully means.

15. ibid, 216.

16. W. Brueggemann ("Life and Death in Tenth Century Israel", *JAAR* 40 [1972] 96-109) has shown how important the notion of Joseph as a life-giver is in the Joseph cycle.

17. Note that Sarah, Rebekkah and Rachael are all barren. All three fathers "leave" the promised land (Gen 20, 26, 28) before the promises are in fact resolved and the lines carried further. The fruitful life in the land must firstly necessitate that "Israel" be placed in "profane space".

18. For a survey of the problems bound up with the dating of the Exodus, cf. J.J. Bimson, *Redating the Exodus and Conquest* (JSOTSup 5; Sheffield: University of Sheffield, 1978) 229-37.

19. N. Lohfink, "The Story of the Fall", in *The Christian Meaning of the Old Testament* tr. R.A. Wilson (London: Burns and Oates, 1969) 59-60.

20. V.H. Kooy ("Fear and Love in Deuteronomy", in *Grace Upon Grace, Essays in Honor of L.J. Kuyper* ed. J.I. Cook [Grand Rapids: Eerdmans, 1975] 106-16) has offered the evidence.

21. Cf. A. Malamat ("Charismatic Leadership in the Book of Judges", in *Magnalia Dei, The Mighty Acts of God. Essays on the Bible and Archeology in Memory of G. Ernest Wright* ed. F.M. Cross [New York: Doubleday, 1976] 163-4) has pointed to the contrast which Abimelech's rule provided.

22. For a more detailed analysis of Judg 21:25 refer to my article, "In Those Days There Was No King in Israel; Every Man Did What Was Right in His Own Eyes. The Purpose of the Book of Judges Reconsidered", *JSOT* 25 (1983) 23-33.

23. R. Knierim, "The Messianic Concept in the First Book of Samuel", in *Jesus and the Historian. Written in Honor of E.C. Colwell* ed. F.T. Trotter [Philadelphia: Westminster, 1968) 20-51.

24. We believe the context supports this interpretation. For a recent review of interpretations, cf. R.L. Cohn "The Literary Logic of 1 Kings 17-19", *JBL* 101 (1982) 333-50.

25. As G. Hasel *(The Remnant* [Berrien Springs: Andrews University, 1974] 202-3) argues.

26. Cf. W.C. Kaiser "The Davidic Promise and the Inclusion of the Gentiles (Amos 9:9-15 and Acts 15:13-18): A Test Passage for Theological Systems", *JETS* 20 (1977) 97-111.

27. ibid, 281-6.

28. J. Jensen ("The Age of Immanuel", *CBQ* 41 [1979] 220-39) has argued that the phrase Heb. *leda^c to ma'os bara^c ubahor battob* "to know to reject evil and choose good" (Isa 7:15) is to be interpreted as a result, and not as a temporal clause. This would leave room for a messianic interpretation of the passage.

29. We may note, however, the interesting reversal which occurs in the eschatological name, "The Lord is our righteousness" (Jer 23:6). This is a clear play on the name of the reigning king, Zedekiah ("my righteousness is Yahweh"), but the elements of the name have been reversed indicating the discontinuity between the two notions of kingship (present and expected). It is noteworthy that the expectation held out under the words "the Lord our righteousness" in Jer 23:6 is transferred to Judah and Jerusalem in the new age, Jer 33:16 and is

applied to the whole nation. Cf. J.R. Lundbom, *Jeremiah: A Study in Ancient Hebrew Rhetoric* (SBLDS 18; Missoula: Scholars, 1975) 31-2.

30. As W. Zimmerli ("The Word of God in the Book of Ezekiel", *JTC* 4 [1967] 1-13) has pointed out.

31. Perhaps, as M. Strom has suggested ("The Place of Ezekiel 28:11-19 in Biblical and Extra-Biblical Tradition", [Th.M. Thesis, Westminster Theological Seminary, 1983] 128-33), the oracles against the foreign nations in Ezek 25-32 are a precursor to the second Exodus material of the restoration narratives of chapters 34-39. In them Edom (chap. 35) and Gog (chaps. 38-39) function as representative and metaphorical/eschatological enemies respectively. The passage may be chronologically placed in relation to chaps. 40-48 or again, it may be one facet of the whole restoration process on view from chaps. 34-39.

32. We are dependent upon W.A.M. Beuken's interpretation of the Heb. phrase *le'emet* "unto faithfulness" in Isa 42:3 and the general conclusions of his article. Cf. "Mispat. The First Servant Song in its Context", *VT* 22 (1972) 1-30.

33. ibid, 8-23.

34. Cf. H.C. Spykerboer, "The Structure and Composition of Deutero-Isaiah", (Ph.D. dissertation, University of Groningen, 1976) 177-8.

35. Cf. F. Holmgren, *With Wings as Eagles* (New York: Biblical Scholars, 1973) 49-70.

36. P.D. Hanson, *Dawn of Apocalyptic* (Philadelphia: Fortress, 1975) 32-46.

37. K. Koch ("Ezra and the Origins of Judaism", *JSS* 19 [1974] 193) notes this emphasis.

38. As proposing this, cf. H.G. Williamson, "Eschatology in Chronicles", *TynB* 28 (1977) 147.

39. M.D. Johnson (*The Purpose of the Biblical Genealogies* [SNTSMS 8; Cambridge: Cambridge University, 1969] 47) cites the evidence.

40. On the purpose of the genealogy in Matt 1 cf. H.C. Waetjen, "The Genealogy as the Key to the Gospel According to Matthew", *JBL* 95 (1976) 205-30.

41. I have argued this way in "The Logic of the Role of the Law in Matt vv1-20", *NovT* 23 (1981) 12-3.

42. Gk. *ethnos* "nation" refers to Gentiles in Matt 4:15; 6:32; 10:5,18; 12:18-21; 20:19,25-26. After this key verse (21:43) *ethnos* refers to both Jews and Gentiles in 24:7,9,14; 25:31-46; 28:18-20.

43. J. Jervell, *Luke and the People of God* (Minneapolis: Augsburg, 1977) 56-64.

44. A. Trites, *The New Testament Concept of Witness* (SNTSMS 31; Cambridge: Cambridge University, 1977) 39-44.

45. Cf. S. Pancaro, "The Relationship of the Church to Israel in the Gospel of St. John", *NTS* 21 (1975) 396-405.

46. On this structure cf. M. Vellanickal, *The Divine Sonship of Christians in the Johannine Writings* (AnBib 72; Rome: Pontifical Biblical Institute, 1977) 132-6.

47. Cf. R. Culpepper, "The Pivot of John's Prologue", *NTS* 27 (1980) 31.

48. Cf. S. Pancaro, *The Law in the Fourth Gospel* (NovTSup 42; Leiden: Brill, 1975) 514-22.

49. The language favours this and the context strongly supports it. Cf. F.J. Moloney, *The Johannine Son of Man* (Rome: Las, 1978) 160-83.

50. S. Kim (*The Origin of Paul's Gospel* [Tubingen/Grand Rapids: Mohr/Eerdmans, 1981⁶1984] 327, n.3) discusses the vexing Gal 6:16 and refers it to Christians generally.

51. E.P. Sanders (*Paul, The Law and the Jewish People* [Philadelphia: Fortress, 1983] 192-9) understands "all Israel" in Rom 11:26 as the full number of faithful Israel (cf. v12) and stresses the salvation by faith emphasis of the passage.

52. It would be imprudent to build a definitive interpretation of Paul's view of Israel on the difficult Rom 11:25-32. For a survey of the possibilities, cf. Kim, *Origin*, 83-91. R.D. Aus ("Paul's Travel Plans to Spain and the 'Full Number of the Gentiles' of Rom xi 25", *NovT* 21 [1979] 232-62) connects Rom 11:25-32 to the current missionary strategy of Paul.

53. For a recent survey of Paul's role in Gentile mission and their inclusion in a new people of God cf. E. Best, "The Revelation to Evangelize the Gentiles", *JTS* 35 (1984) 15-26.

54. For the composition of the church to which Peter writes, cf. idem, *1 Peter* (NCB; London: Oliphants, 1971) 19-20.

55. Cf. R.H. Mounce, *The Book of Revelation* (NICNT; Grand Rapids: Eerdmans, 1977) 84.

56. Cf. Fiorenza, "Redemption as Liberation, Apoc. 1:5ff and 5:9", *CBQ* 36 (1974) 226. We note in passing here that Rev 7:1-8 appears to refer to the sealing of the saints generally before tribulation (cf. 9:4), while 7:9-17 presents the same group now triumphant.

THE NEW CREATION — SUMMARY

The previous studies prepared us for the ultimate character of the eschatological age — completely New Creation. Thus the final redemptive act is a creative act. This raises the crucial question of the relation between creation and redemption in biblical theology. Especially since frequently it has been argued that creational terms first came to be employed of Yahweh's saving acts in history and only later were used to develop a creation theology. Isa 40-66, it is argued, provides the major catalyst for this development.

However, analysis of the ancient hymn, Exod 15:1-18, demonstrates that Israel's earliest understanding of redemption was structured on an overt creational theology. The nation's passage through the waters and into the promised land is construed as a New Creation. This is not unanticipated, given the motifs and structure of the pre-Abrahamic narratives. Although there is no hint of redemption in the original creative act, the subsequent "fall" constitutes a reversal of the creation order and rejection of God's creational rule. And thus redemption is necessarily the renewing of this order and rule, both in individual and cosmic dimensions.

Returning to Isa 40-66 with this in mind, we find that rather than inaugurating creational theology the prophecy presupposes and employs this perspective in its grandiose portrayal of eschatological redemption. In fact, the movement from creation to New Creation is the heart of prophetic, indeed biblical, eschatology. The divine creative activity alone accounts for Israel's presence and status in the world, and ensures the recapturing of paradise through the second exodus motif and the ministry of the servant. As prophecy "shifts" to apocalyptic the creation horizon broadens rather than diminishes. For Daniel, evil is so ingrained in the present order that only a New Creation will suffice. This will be renewal effected by the appearance of the Son of Man.

Paul in turn encapsulates this whole schema in a single figure — the pre-incarnate, resurrected and glorified Jesus. A wholly adequate christology must be both creational and redemptive. Our understanding is enhanced here by the brilliant interplay of language, imagery, and structure in the classic hymn, Col 1:15-20. As "image", "head", and "first-born" the now incarnate, crucified and resurrected Creator Jesus leads the cosmos to its intended goal. This is the conclusion inaugurated by Jesus' appearance; to usher in the great and terrible day of the Lord, according to all the Gospels foresaw.

What else then could the final vision of Revelation entail? Only the reversal of all sin, misery, futility and discord and the establishment of the universal and everlasting rule of the creator God.

5

THE NEW CREATION

The Presentation in Revelation 21-22

Throughout the course of our eschatological survey we have noted that the inbreaking of God at the consummation of history, as it is portrayed in Rev 21-22, is treated as a new creation. The aim of this final chapter is to trace the biblical theme of creation and to consider its relationship to the biblical theology of redemption. The biblical witness commences with creation and ends, as we have had repeated occasion to note within these chapters, with the descent of the new Jerusalem heralding the dawn of the new creation. Clearly, the Bible moves between these two poles. The axis on which the biblical material turns is the series of historical interventions by God resulting in the biblical doctrine of redemption climaxing in Christ in whom God will conclude all things (Col 1:20). The Bible moves from creation to new creation by means of divine redemptive interventions. We shall endeavour to make it clear that biblical theology and the eschatology derived from it must commence from the basis of Genesis 1 and make a theology of creation the dominant factor in an eschatological presentation.

Fulfilment of this hope is given in Rev 21:1, through John's vision of "a new heaven and a new earth; for the first heaven and the first earth had passed away, and the sea was no more". The subsequent material in chapters 21-22 continues to detail the magnificence of the new event which fulfils every biblical expectation, satisfying the eager longing of the elect who then worship before the Creator Lamb evermore. It is, as we have noted earlier, a remarkable and moving presentation of biblical imagery. The prophetic background from which Rev 21:1 is drawn is Isa 65:17-25, wherein Isaiah has in mind the complete renewal, not merely the alteration of, the existing order (note the use of "to create" Heb. *bara'* in Isa 65:17). The element of paradox is there, since although a complete new beginning is anticipated, the spiritual experience of the believer is preserved. Neither the renewal of the existing order nor its purification is sought, but rather its replacement. Thus Rev 21:1b indicates that the sea, the inimical principle of opposition in the Ancient World cosmologies, the realm and domain of chaos, is no more. The region from which the anti-Christ forces arise in the book of the Revelation forms no part of the new order. All things are made new (v5).

The Old Testament

The Bible points out that the notion of a new creation is not the product of mere human inventiveness, for indeed, it lies beyond man's imaginative scope. We can clarify this by referring to Ps 19. This Psalm falls into four basic divisions. Verses 1-6 are a hymn of praise to creation, verses 7-10 a liturgy on the place of the law, and verses 11-13 a following admonition, with verse 14 offering a summarizing conclusion. At first sight the initial section seems unconnected with what follows. The very heavens declare the glory of God; God is manifested in them. But this is no music of the spheres thundering out in an audible voice and compelling attention, for the opening verses continue by telling us that the testimony of the heavens is unheeded (v3). Thus what is needed to understand this insistent message of the universe is the revelation, the "law" of which the second section speaks. In short, the nature of the universe can only be understood by reference to an interpreting word. No such conclusion is reached in the absence of revelation. There is no theorizing concerning the fact or function of this created universe independently of the declaration of the divine mind. What we know of creation and its purposes will only stem from what God has been pleased to reveal.

i. *Creation and Redemption: Exodus 15:1-18*

The Exodus hymn of Exod 15:1-18 discloses the use of a doctrine of creation in its explanation of the fact of the Exodus. The hymn translates the account of redemption, the entire Exodus event, into a more theologically reflective statement than the prose account of the same episode (Exod 14). The hymn falls into two clear sections;

15:1-12, dealing with the significance of Yahweh's victory over Pharaoh, and verses 13-18 which deal with Yahweh's leading Israel through the desert to the promised land.

The introduction (Exod 15:1-3) celebrates the fact of Yahweh's victory, describing him as a "Man of War" (v3). This description of God as warrior who fights for Israel occurs in illustration of the miraculous victory which was the Exodus, a victory in which Israel only passively participated. Yahweh's historical action, an act of pure grace, is presented as an overwhelming act of military intervention. In verses 4-8 the description of Pharaoh's defeat by the Divine Warrior is outlined in terms of the imagery of the age. Yahweh with mace uplifted (v6) shatters his enemies.

This warrior imagery of Yahweh occurs here for the first time. It will assume major importance in the theology of the conquest as Yahweh brings Israel into the promised land and establishes them through repeated miraculous interventions. In a more subdued form the imagery is present through the course of prophecy into apocalyptic in the OT and finds its expression in the NT as well, pre-eminently in the book of Revelation.

Ironically, the instrument Yahweh uses to defeat Pharaoh is the "sea". Usually, as we have seen in earlier chapters, the sea is the image of recalcitrant hostility and opposition to divine order. Here, however, to emphasize Yahweh's complete sovereignty as Creator and Redeemer, its fury is turned on Yahweh's enemies. While Israel may pass through the unruly waters which tower above them in banks piled high (Exod 14:22), Israel's enemies are drowned in the attempt. There are basic points of contact in all of this to the ancient Near Eastern cosmologies,[1] though in these the sea is the principle of opposition which must be overcome before order, which is creation, can be imposed on chaos. The subsequent course of the hymn makes this point clearer.

In the second half of the poem Israel moves under divine leadership towards the promised land. Their victorious march, still very much in the future, is presented as imminent yet with assured results. Echoing the depiction of Israel's exodus through the sea in the first half of the poem, a passage through petrified nations is described (Philistia, Edom, Moab and Canaan, Exod 15:14-16). They are compelled to stand by as "walls of people" while Israel passes.[2] Shepherd language, the familiar kingship imagery of the period, is used of Yahweh in this half of the poem (cf. v13), for his guidance is passionately directed towards the welfare of his people. Israel's easy passage through nations who present themselves almost obsequiously in serried ranks is, as we know, the language of faith. We are well aware of the difficulties which Israel faced as she sought to enter the promised land, not forgetting the trials and testings in the wilderness. What is underscored in all this, however, is the certainty of the fulfilment of the divine promise of entry into the land. All obstacles will be overcome.

Exod 15:17 clarifies Yahweh's intention for Israel in the promised land. He will plant Israel in the land which he has chosen for his own abode. His sanctuary will be established in their midst. Views that the "mountain" on which they will be planted is other than Palestine as a whole (i.e., Jerusalem as some have argued, or less probably, and against the tenor of the poem, Sinai) are to be discounted in view of two facts. First, it is suggestive that the term "place" is used elsewhere in the OT to refer to the promised land (cf. Deut 11:5; Exod 23:20). Second, the parallelism in Ps 78:54 which recounts the history of Israel's salvation to that point notes in regard to the occupancy of the promised land that "he brought them to his holy land, to the mountain which his right hand had won". It is more probable that in Exod 15:17 we have equation and not progression, and that the whole of Palestine is being viewed as Yahweh's sanctuary.

From sanctuary in Exod 15:17 we move on to kingship almost axiomatically in verse 18. Yahweh's kingship is proclaimed in universalistic terms and apparently upon the basis of the victory recounted in the poem. In terms of ancient Near Eastern cosmological presentation this statement concerning the kingship of Yahweh is perfectly explicable. Exod 15:1-18 runs the full gamut of current mythical presentation of cosmogony. There is combat of the Divine Warrior, in which the sea figures, albeit in this instance passively. Resulting from that victory, indeed as a fruit of it, the building of a sanctuary as a cosmic centre is contemplated. In this victory the forces of blind pagan opposition personified in Pharaoh are overcome. Linked with the establishment of the sanctuary comes the proclamation of world reign; eternal kingship for the victor.

This framework is demonstrably comparable with the Babylonian and Canaanite creation sequences (Enuma Elish and Baal epics) wherein themes of threat, conflict, victory followed by temple building, and eternal kingship are discussed. Thus Exod 15:1-18 is clearly linked poetically to the familiar mythological patterns of the ancient Near Eastern man. There is no question that the use of myth in the song is made in the interests of laying bare the theological significance of the historical events presented in chapter 14. The redemption of the Exodus was thus a cosmic victory, and provides the pattern for future divine action on Israel's behalf. Great issues are at stake in this historical action and it is the aim of the poet to ensure that we understand what is involved in the history in which this physical deliverance actually occurred.

It should now be clear that Exod 15:1-18 presents in language drawn from various creation myths the fact of Israel's redemption from Egypt as an act of New Creation. This new national entity is invited by implication to enter into a new national experience in the promised land. A situation analogous to Adam's offer in a similar "promised land" and "sanctuary". In this land the reality of the divine presence is enjoyed by Israel in such a way as to herald the reinauguration of all things. Admittedly, Exod 15:1-18 is the language of exalted theology, the realization of which never becomes reality in Israel's experience. The language of creation, however, has been employed to serve the purposes of redemption in this old poem often considered to be the most ancient piece of OT literature.

Exod 15:1-18 presupposes behind the doctrine of redemption a well-endorsed theology of creation. The hymn implicitly argues that a doctrine of creation is theologically prior to any presentation of the place and purposes of redemption. What this means is that the historical fact, the beginning of history which is creation, is confessed in 15:1-18 as the basis for the elective foundations of Israel. Yet it is customarily suggested that Israel arrived at a doctrine of creation only by reflection upon God's activity in the Exodus redemption.[3] The creation of Israel led the nation gradually, and only gradually, to expand her view of Yahweh and finally to see him responsible for the world order. According to such a reconstruction the evolution of this process results in the exalted monotheism found in Isa 40-66. The doctrine of creation reached in those chapters was then expressed in terms of the origins account which we now have in Gen 1:1-2:4a. We need not enter into the details of such assertions which provide a customary approach to an OT doctrine of creation. It can only be said that they do not correspond to the present canonical reality. The ordering of the OT canon makes it clear that Israel's origins, which began with Abraham and not with the Exodus, developed in response to the more general presentation of human sinfulness within the created order given in Gen 1-11.

Any approach to problems of this character will be conditioned by pre-suppositions. But it is at least suggestive, if our analysis of Exod 15:1-18 may be followed, that echoes of an undergirding doctrine of creation are found in this first developed credal presentation of redemption. We may now proceed to examine the Gen 1-3 material in detail to note what support may be derived from there for our general conclusions reached thus far. Of course, only a redeemed people could write an account of creation. But the Israel of the Exodus period interpreted present events as dependent upon the prior call of Abraham, with whom her origins began. Abraham, in his turn, was conscious of the background from which he had come and of the obedience of faith to be exercised towards the faithful Creator by whom he had been called. All of which naturally leads us back to Gen 1.

ii. *Creation and Redemption: Genesis 1-11*

a. Genesis 1:1-3

In general terms Gen 1 presents us with an account of six days of creative activity in a progressive scheme which appears as has often been noted to be arranged from verse 3 onwards under the concepts of (Heb. *tohu*) "form" and (Heb. *bohu*) "void", terms derived from verse 2. The arrangement of the material in chapter 1 proceeds as follows.[4]

Form	Content
Day 1 Light	Day 4 Luminaries
2 Water, Sky	5 Fish, Birds
3 Land, Vegetation	6 Beasts, Man

God first forms the various aspects of creation and then fills the form with appropriate content climaxing in the creation of man as the image on the sixth day.

Two approaches to this material must now concern us. The first is the remarkable degree of affinity between Gen 1 and the Babylonian cosmologies. If this is pressed the account of creation loses its absolutism and is merely seen as the imposition of order upon a pre-existing unruly world, thus importing an unacceptable note of dualism. The second, not now widely popular, sees the bulk of Gen 1 as reporting what is basically a recovery or redemptive process. Much hangs in both cases upon the vexed question of the translation of verses 1-3 and therefore of the order of events it presents. At the outset it must be admitted that such a report at the beginning of the divine commitment to the world ought to be expected to provide its difficulties, and they are certainly there.

The question of the translation of Gen 1:1 is a primary concern.[5] Are we to take the initial prepositional phrase absolutely ("in the beginning God created the heavens and the earth") or do we with the more recent translations (e.g., NEB) suppose that the prepositional phrase introduces a temporal clause ("in the beginning of creation when God made heaven and earth")? In terms of Hebrew usage the latter is to be preferred but appeal to syntactical frequency may only be a rough guide. The context itself must determine the precise meaning.

First, there is the consideration of the content of the word "create" (Heb. *bara'*). In biblical use its subject is always God and it never requires an additional verb to add a further dimension of meaning. Nothing exists in the language which may act as a direct synonym, though of course there are other verbs within its field of meaning. Nor does the verb ever have the note of renewal. It refers to the absolute state of newness, not freshness, which results from divine action. The call of the Psalmist in Ps 51:10 "create in me a clean heart" is not a call for inward cleansing. It is a cry that he might be a new being.

Second, the linking of *bara* "create" with what precedes, "in the beginning" (Heb. *b^ere'sit*), appears to draw attention by this alliteration to the concept of an absolute beginning.[6] The third point is the biblical meaning of the phrase "heavens and earth". This compound in biblical use never has the meaning of something inchoate or provisional but is always used of the entire orderly universe which stands created.[7] It seems best to understand the totality of creation, therefore, as the subject of Gen 1:1, and not to see this verse as introductory to a process which is to be completed in verse 1. The connection of verse 1 to what follows, however, is uncertain.

Since a process of creation follows, Gen 1:1 is either a rubric which introduces the first chapter, or perhaps better, the OT as a whole.[8] The actual account of creation then begins with the three circumstantial clauses of verse 2 ("the earth was without form and void . . . and darkness was upon the face of the deep . . . and the Spirit of God was moving over the face of the waters"). It is a matter of judgement as to what main verb these circumstantial clauses are to be attached. Either they describe a condition or a set of circumstances which were contemporaneous with the action of verse 1 or else they stand in some relationship to verse 3.

On the assumption Gen 1 begins with a temporal clause, it is often pointed out that 1:1-3 (with 2:1-4a) offer a "when-then" sequence, i.e., the main clause is preceded by a circumstantial clause announcing the attendant circumstances which surrounded creation. If this is the case, then the Genesis 1 account in terms of its presentation is remarkably similar to the manner in which the Babylonian creation epic of Enuma Elish begins ("when on high the heavens had not been named . . . then it was that the gods were formed").[9] Leaving aside this question, the relationship of Gen 1 to the Babylonian epic is undoubted given the many striking similarities. In the Enuma Elish we begin with the existence of inchoate matter (Akk. *mummu*). The gods then come into being. Eventually the representative chaos figure Tiamat confronts the gods in council. Tiamat is defeated by the warrior god Marduk and the universe is created from her body. The firmament comes into being, then dry land appears together with the luminaries. Man is created to ease the gods' burden of labour who then rest and celebrate. Finally, in the set of comparisons which are normally provided, appeal is made to the identification of Akkadian *Ti'amtu* (Tiamat) with Heb. *t^ehom* ("deep" Gen 1:2).[10]

However, cosmic encounters or tensions are not present in Gen 1. At best Genesis 1 contains only a pale reflection of the ancient Near Eastern myths, though the comparisons with Enuma Elish may be valid on general levels. As G. Hasel points out, the focus of attention in Gen 1:2 is the earth, the particular creation of which is delineated after the generalization of 1:1. Perhaps as Hasel suggests the "deep" Heb. *t^ehom* and the Enuma Elish contacts are mentioned to show how completely any mythological elements which could be read into the account are repudiated.[11] The "sea dragons" (the *tannin* of Ugaritic literature) are now created beings (Gen 1:21) and not the mythological creatures appealed to elsewhere in the poetic sections of the OT (cf. Isa 27:1; 51:9; Ps 74:13).

The separation of the heavens from the earth is effortless and accomplished by divine fiat alone. Unlike the parallels in the Babylonian and Egyptian cosmologies, God creates the luminaries, and this may be a tilt at their importance in the pantheons of the surrounding cultures, particularly the Babylonian. Man is the important constituent of the six-day scheme whereas in the Babylonian material (in both the creation and the flood epics) man is created from the blood of a minor deity mixed with clay to relieve the gods of burdensome labour.[12] Further, we may point out that creation by the word, which in itself effectively undoes any attempt to find mythology in Genesis 1, is not found in Mesopotamia (though it is known in an alternative cosmogony in Egypt).[13] In short, as G. von Rad indicates, the entire passage of Gen 1 (particularly vv14-19) bears a "strong antimythical pathos".[14]

Yet the difficulty of the content of Gen 1:2 still exists. Notice that what exists in this verse is not said to be "good". That comment is initially made of the light in verse 3 which dispels the primeval darkness. It is recalled that darkness in the OT is very largely associated with death, i.e., non-life (cf. Job 17:13; 18:18; 38:17; Ps 88:12; though for Yahweh's dominion over darkness cf. Isa 45:7). In view of this, the subject matter of Gen 1:2 is often taken as an indication of difficulties inherent and still persisting in our world. Further, an unexplained principle of opposition appears at 3:1. Though all of this simply puts the basic problem one step futher back, it is argued that man addressed by God in 2:17 is an ethical being with the problems of moral choice, potentially able to choose between "good" and "evil". Additionally, the use of "waste" (Heb. *tohu*) and "void" (Heb. *bohu*) in 1:2 as well as the disturbing connotations which may be evoked by the use of (Heb.

$t^e hom$)[15] "deep" make the interpretation of this verse crucial.

Are we then to see features which are decidedly antithetical to good order in Gen 1:2 (namely, darkness, waste, void, confusion, etc.)? That there are nuances in the verse which have no place in the characteristic presentation of the world as the ordered work of God? And are we therefore to see the Spirit of God at work in verse 2 protectively as the older "gap" theory suggested? The so-called "gap" theory, popular at the beginning of this century, argues that after the initial creation of verse 1 the world lapsed into the situation present in verse 2 from which in the terms of verse 3 it was rescued by futher divine intervention; the function of the Spirit in verse 2 simply being a holding operation, part in fact of the bounds which God had set upon unruly order (cf. Job 38:8-10).

The essence of the gap theory is that the Heb. verb *hayah* "to be" in Gen 1:2 must be translated "became" a waste and void, the domain of Lucifer, who in the sanctuary garden of God conducted worship such as supposedly alluded to in the mythological presentation of Ezek 28:12-19. He elevated himself above God and the judgement passed upon him is referred to in Isa 14:12-20. Throughout the aeons which followed the earth remained waste and void until at the beginning of the historical period it was recovered and reconditioned in six days of twenty-four hours. Advocates of this view also point to the use of *tohu* and *bohu* in Jer 4:23 where the reversal of creation is contemplated, as well as to Isa 34:11 where the phrase is used in a divine judgement pronouncement.[16]

This fanciful theory founders on the syntax of the passage. If the verb "to be" in Gen 1:2 is to bear the weight placed upon it by the theory, then we should have expected the Heb. construction of a converted imperfect following the perfect tense of verse 1. Instead, verse 2 opens with a circumstantial clause introduced by a noun and thus breaks the sequence of thought begun by the first verse. The Heb. nouns *tohu* and *bohu* are used in later judgement contexts as general terms. We cannot, however, necessarily argue back from these contexts to their function in Gen 1:2. The appeal to Ezek 28 and Isa 14 is really an appeal to passages which must be taken non-literally and which in their contexts refer to historical events of the period.

Theories such as the "gap" theory cast the language of Gen 1 into that of scientific precision, whereas it is clearly poetic in character and somewhat allusive. The problem which verse 2 appears to present is overcome if the verse is taken, as it may be, as a series of circumstantial clauses dependent upon the main clause which appears in the next verse.[17] Verse 2 then refers to the initial stage of solitariness after God began the work referred to in verse 3. The earth was then covered with primeval water before dry land appeared. However, as verse 2 indicates, the Spirit of God was in full control bringing God's final order out of this inchoate beginning. Therefore, there is nothing which is specifically or remotely redemptive in this passage.

b. Genesis 1:26-28

To develop a complete perspective on Creation in Gen 1-3, it is necessary for us to enter into brief discussion now of the subject of special attention in 1:26-28, namely man. Created as a result of special divine deliberation, he is made to be "like God" and this likeness is to show itself in the special relationship which the passage develops. It is beyond our intention here to examine in detail the problem of the plural address in verse 26, except to say that, of all the possibilities, a plural of "fulness" seems best to fit. This introduces the possibility of intra-divine deliberation within the Godhead.[18] Nothing more specific is offered within the account as to the persons of the Godhead who are involved, though it is the Spirit referred to verse 2 who immediately springs to mind. In view, however, of the NT evidence (cf. John 1:3; Col 1:15-17), we are bound to leave the question open and to recognize that an allusion to the Trinity could justifiably be read back into this passage. In the OT, however, it is the Spirit who is featured as the agent in creation (Job 33:4; Ps 104:30).

The "after our likeness" of Gen 1:26 is probably a slight weakening of the content contained in the term "image" (Heb. *selem*) in the interests of avoiding theological misconceptions. Historically, interpreters have preferred to treat the term ontologically (referring to rationality, etc.). The more modern line of interpretation is to take the term relationally, i.e., that man "in the image" or "as the image" is depicted as standing in a set of special relationships to God, not enjoyed by the remainder of creation.

A biblical view of man demands, however, that we think of man in the image as referring to the whole person. At the same time we cannot ignore the strong element of man's visibility in creation provided by Heb. *selem* "image".[19] The Akkadian cognate *salmu* has the notion of visibility always in mind. P. Bird carefully examined the extrabiblical evidence, particularly the Akkadian data, and points out that when Akk. *salmu* is used of royal or priestly designations then the human representative is seen as the possessor of the power of the god, whether for good or for evil. The notion of image in Akkadian is that of a copy, a reproduction of an original, but different in material and/or in kind.[20]

The slight weakening of the image notion by the qualification of "likeness" does not detract from Bird's observation that man as a royal being is in mind here. Certainly in Psalm 8, a commentary upon Genesis 1, man is not only provided with divine features of "glory" and "honour" (cf. Pss 21:5; 45:3; 1 Kgs 3:13; Zech 6:13) but is also "crowned" (Ps 8:5). Additionally, he is said to be created a "little less than God" (Heb. *'elohim* — the general term for deity). Thus the predicates of 'glory' and 'honour' which may be attached to him as a royal figure are also attributed to God (cf. Pss 29:1,4; 90:16; 104:1; 111:3; 145:5; and note Job 40:10 where "Clothe yourself with glory and splendour" = "make yourself like God"). Moreover, the symbol of "putting all things under one's feet" (Ps 8:6) is the language of the ancient Near East for the exercise of kingly authority (Josh 10:24; 1 Kgs 5:3; Ps 110:1).[21] The reference in Ps 8 to man as a little lower than 'elohim (v5) surely seems to be an allusion to Gen 1:26 and to the image concept.

As Bird indicates, in the ancient world (both in Mesopotamia and Egypt), kingship and image are closely related. Bird cites Mesopotamian evidence indicating that salmu terminology is used in royal ideological contexts to denote one who possesses a divine mandate to rule and who is considered to represent the deity or deities.[22] The designation of the king as the god's image in such contexts serves to underscore his supposed god-like nature as he exercises royal functions and authority. In Egypt the notion of the Pharaoh as the image ("copy") of the god was frequent. There is more than ample evidence for the presentation of the Egyptian Pharaoh as the image of the creator god[23] though this precise concept of "image" is not found in the OT. Finally, in connection with the Gen 1:26-28 context, we note that the Hebrew verb "exercise dominion" radah (v28) has reference elsewhere in the OT to the exercise of kingly functions (cf. 1 Kgs 5:24; Isa 14:6; Ezek 34:4; Pss 72:8; 110:2).

It is clear, therefore, that Gen 1 climaxes in the presentation of man as king, thus presenting an account of his essential dignity and of his role as image. Man is created to be the king of his domain and, in view of his role in the garden in chapter 2, to be priest as well. If the fall robs him of this potential we will expect redemption to restore it and we will look for such features to be added in the NT. Therein imagery is linked with Christ's participation in creation and as the eschatological focus towards which redemption points. It suffices for the moment to say that Christ is fully what man in 1:26 is representatively, both in terms of being and function.

c. Genesis 2

Man is clearly the climax of the creative acts in the six day span of Gen 1. But the consummation of creation comes in 2:1-4a and the biblical editors have done us a service by the chapter divisions suggesting that the work of the seventh day must be thrown into clear relief. The notion of creation finding its conclusion in divine rest, or indeed being prompted by a search for rest, is often found in mythical materials.

In the Enuma Elish the struggle among the gods from which creation results is occasioned by the fact that the "rest" of the god Apsu is disturbed. At the end of the creation struggle when the victory of the warrior god Marduk is celebrated, the grateful gods embark upon a temple building project for Marduk, which will not only stamp his dominion with authority but point to its purpose (cf. Enuma Elish VI:51-54):

Let us build a shrine whose name shall be called
"Lo, a chamber for our mighty rest"; let us repose in it.
Let us build a throne, a recess for his abode.
On that day that we arrive we shall repose in it.[24]

In the Atrahasis epic, the motive for the eventual flood is the din made by the expanding human race. Despite various attempts to mitigate this disturbance, the response of the gods is only secured by the abolition of the race.[25] The Egyptian Memphite account of creation is significant for our survey of Gen 1 since the creator deity Ptah brings his world into being by the word. In this account when creation is accomplished "Ptah was satisfied (or rested), after he had made everything, as well as all the divine order".[26]

R. Pettazzoni[27] who has drawn attention to the divine rest motifs in the early creation accounts suggests two reasons for the presence of the concept of rest in the myths. First, that the notion signifies a concept of replacement of original creator gods by more active deities. This is not important for our purposes. Second, he suggests that the concept of rest is linked with the notion of the necessity of maintaining creation unchanged, since a relapse into chaos undoes created order. The citation of this second line of evidence is important for the OT observer. This in fact, in a modified way, is the thought which is taken up independently in Gen 2:1-4.

In this connection it is notable that the sequence of creation ends in Gen 1 with the remark "that God saw everything that he made, and behold it was very good", a note which summates the series of progressive endorsements provided by the chapter. What this must mean is that creation corresponds to the purposes for which it was destined, i.e., it conformed to God's purposes. Creation as "good" does not primarily refer to man nor his general context, but is a comment which indicates that the world exhibits "the glory of God". The seventh day stands outside the sequence but is still part of the scheme of creation. It would seem that action taken on the seventh day gives expression to the total purpose intended for creation.

On the seventh day God expresses his satisfaction by declaring his work completed. It is noted, however, that this act of completion is open-ended for there is no notation of the end of the seventh day. In fact the seventh day plainly sums up the whole sequence since no mention of a morning or an evening is contained in Gen 2:1-4a. We are left therefore with the distinct impression that in chapter 2 we are taken out of the continuity established by chapter 1 into an open-ended relationship with God which does not entertain historical progression in our sense of the word, or else suspends it for the duration of the sabbath period involved in the unfolding of the revelatory details of chapters 2-3. As K. Barth notes in his perceptive comments on the creation account, for God to rest on the seventh day is to enter into a relationship with creation of a different character to what had been the case of Genesis 1.[28]

While Gen 2:1-4a does not contain the noun "sabbath", the verb is mentioned there twice (vv3-4). The day is blessed (i.e., endowed with the potential to be the day which God intended that it should be) and "hallowed" (i.e., made God's own day, a day on which God's purposes should be observed or reflected upon). In the New Temple chapter we took up the question of the role of the sabbath, and we may simply note here that this "creation sabbath" provides a model for Israel's later observance. In Exod 20:11 the institution of the sabbath is linked with creation, and thus with the divine sovereignty exercised through creation. If in Deut 5:12-15 a link between sabbath and Exodus is made, this is not a revision of the intention of Exod 20:11 but a re-expression of it. As we have noted in connection with Exod 15:1-18 redemption is an act which flows from creation and thus is an expression of it. Therefore there is no possibility of erecting a doctrine of redemption involving the assumption of divine intervention into history, and control by God over nature by theophanies, miracles, etc., without at the same time presupposing a doctrine of God's sovereignty over the created order and thus his responsibility for its existence and continuance.

The remainder of Gen 2 recapitulates elements from chapter 1 (particularly providing a fairly detailed exposition of 1:26-28) with the implicit invitation issued by God for creation to express the harmony or "rest" referred to in 2:1-4a. The implicit nature of this invitation seems clear from the open-ended character of the seventh day as well as from the fact that details of chapter 2 provide for the enjoyment of the perfected conditions to which verses 1-4a have alluded.

Even paradise, however, is not without its problems. There are two trees there. The fruit of one may be eaten, the other must on no account be touched. Apart from this restriction life in the garden proceeds in a situation of unrestrained joy. Blessing, as Barth remarks, literally bursts unconstricted out of the garden in all directions. The details of the account must be pressed into service later and we merely advert to them here.

Man's role in the garden is described in priestly terms. He is to "cultivate" it ("work" Heb. ^c*abad*, though a general word, is often used later in the OT in the specialized sense of "worship"). Man serves the deity and by this service enters into the highest sphere of blessing, thus exercising dominion over nature from this centre. The garden is the world centre and the relationship enjoyed in the garden is the goal of creation ordained for the creature. The course of subsequent biblical eschatology reflects this and will ultimately return to this picture (Rev 21-22). As C. Westermann remarks in regard to the seventh day: ". . . it points to the goal of the creature which God has created in his image. The work which has been laid on man is not his goal. His goal is the eternal rest which has been suggested by the rest of the seventh day".[29]

d. Genesis 3

This idyllic presentation is broken by the stark fact of the Fall narrated in Gen 3. For our purposes it is necessary to look at the nature of the Fall and its consequences in some detail. The personal significance of the Fall is contained in the observation of the serpent in v5, that the eating of the fruit of the tree of the knowledge of good and evil would mean that Adam and Eve would be "like God, knowing good and evil". That this is not a mere ploy by the serpent is confirmed by God's recognition in verse 22 that the Fall has involved just this ("behold, the man has become like one of us, knowing good and evil").

This recognition means that the Fall cannot merely be construed as a punishment for the defiance of a divine command since this does not seem to satisfy the assertion that by such a defiance man has become "like God". Likewise the familiar interpretation of "knowing good and evil" as referring to total knowledge must be rejected, for though this would satisfy the requirement that by the Fall man has in this respect become "like God" it does not accord with the facts. We do not see man exercising such a profound knowledge after the Fall in the realities of life which confront him in the hard world outside of the garden. Nor does the suggestion that a knowledge of good and evil could refer in the wider context of the account to sexual knowledge commend itself, since this does not explain the claim that knowledge of such a character makes man "like God".

Better and more in accord with the facts is the suggestion of W.M. Clark[30] that "knowing good and evil" represents an intrusion by man into the divine sphere, since biblically 'to know good and evil' is often used as a phrase to express divine knowledge. This means the Fall is a massive act of self assertion by which man claims to legislate for himself in God's world. If Clark is correct then Gen 3 presents us with man as the image snatching at deity, an action which Christ the true image refused to take (Phil 2:6-11). Man was thereby intruding into a sphere reserved for God alone, making himself equal with God, and thus refusing to have "God in knowledge" (Rom 1:28).

If this line of reasoning is to be followed, then the decision by Adam to be self-legislating would have brought with it the consequences which we see to be so characteristic of the human situation. He could legislate for himself, as his subsequent actions proved. In being self-legislating he is therefore "like God" but, "unlike God", he is never thereafter able to know whether the ends he endorses for himself were right nor whether the means he chose to achieve them were proper. He was placed in a world in which the choices for him were seemingly open. However, he was never able to know whether the consequences of his choices would be beneficial. Thus the Fall meant the loss of freedom which could only be had in the service of him whose service was perfect freedom, and man's consequent bondage to his now distorted nature.

These are the personal results and they called for a personal redemption. But it is clear the narratives of Gen 2-3 when taken together present a picture of the onset of sin which broadens our definition of the nature which redemption must assume as a biblical doctrine. J.T. Walsh aptly notes[31] the narratives of 2:4b-3:24 are divided into seven episodes (2:4b-17,18-25; 3:1-5,6-8,9-13,14-21,22-24). In 2:4b-17 Yahweh alone is the actor. Man, created outside of the garden (v8), is placed inside this sacred domain. In effect we are now told that the dominion mandate given to him in 1:26-28 could only be exercised within the perfect set of relationships that chapter 2 depicts. We are thus offered a model of how man is to regulate the world over which he is set. He is to control this world not by immersing himself in the tasks of ordering it but by rightly relating himself within this idyllic situation to the Creator.

In Gen 2:18-25 Yahweh and Adam share the stage. The creation of woman (and her relative position in the order) is foreshadowed in verse 18, but only comes to be after the calling into being of other living creatures. It is she and not they who meet man's deepest relational needs and by her creation the order of Yahweh, man, woman and the animal world is established. The Fall is a distortion of this basic pattern. In the third scene (3:1-5) it is now, in this narrative of reversal, the animal world in the person of the serpent who takes the lead, prevailing upon the woman. Thus, in verses 6-8, Eve exercises a dominant role in the relationship urging Adam to comply with the suggestion of the serpent, while Adam is relatively passive only being described in relationship to Eve ("her husband" v6). In verses 9-13 dialogue develops between Yahweh, Adam and Eve followed by verses 14-21 in which punishment is meted out progressively and appropriately by Yahweh on the serpent, Eve and Adam.

Finally, Gen 3:22-24 returns to the position of 2:4b-17. Yahweh is again the sole actor banishing the man from the garden into which he was initially placed. This reversal of orders in chapter 3 over those of chapter 2, as Walsh indicates, clearly directs us to the cosmic character of sin. Sin is thus the breach of the harmony of relationships established between the orders of creation in chapter 2. Sin affects not only man and woman, but the world in which they live. Nothing less than a redressing of this disruption, nothing less than a redemption of mankind and his world can therefore be included in a biblical doctrine of redemption.

It will be helpful to sum up briefly the argument to this point. Commencing with Exod 15:1-18 we have demonstrated the Israelite conviction that redemption involved a "new creative act". We examined Gen 1 and perceived that creation conformed to the purposes God ordained for it, with no inkling of problems standing in need of redress. Over the edifice of creation mankind presides as king. Gen 2 indicates the harmony of the created order and the method of its maintenance, i.e., how dominion is to be exercised. We surveyed the consequences of the Fall in personal and cosmic terms and noted that the redemption called for by the Fall is personal and yet more than merely personal. Nothing less than the extension of man's dominion under God over the whole world was contemplated in the beginning. Nothing less than the redemption of man and his world is required.

e. Genesis 4-11

We cannot dwell here on the bewildering spread of sin narratives which take us through the flood episode to the Babel account in Gen 11:1-9. Suffice to say that the covenant in 6:18 to which God appeals as "my covenant" is best seen as a covenant brought into being by creation itself, a covenant which has as its aim the preservation of the created structures, man and his world.[32] While the flood is a reversal of creation (cf. the destruction order in 7:11-24 where creation in the order in which it came into being in chapter 1 is virtually undone),[33] 9:1 returns to the mandate of 1:26-28 and assures us that the image has not been lost as a result of the fall, and puts man in a new beginning albeit in a changed world.

The building of the city and tower in Gen 11:1-9 is at once the climax and the conclusion of chapters 1-11. It is not immediately plain why God intervenes to cut short what seems to be a promising attempt by man at social co-operation. The narrative is intricately structured[34] and the fault with which the builders are charged seems to lie in the nature of the undertaking. Some have assumed that in this narrative we have a full maturation of sin's effects resulting in an assault upon heaven. Others, with references (v4) to the "watch-tower" (Heb. *migdal*) see an attempt to keep God under surveillance and thus in effect to build God out of his own world. At any rate it is the fall of society as a whole which is depicted here, the failure of the human race, whereas we have commenced in chapter 3 with the failure of a pair.

That evil is deeply ingrained into the character of the race at this stage appears to be the message being conveyed. The heinous sin which prompts such a ready divine response lies in the human attempt here to preserve unity, to find a centre in the particular human structures characterizing normal relationships, to build upon what is common to the general situation. This is the problem which faces every age attempting to build a better world upon a humanistic centre. The lesson which Babel drives home is that a common culture, language, set of social ideals, or even ethnic structure, are no substitute for a common faith. The centre for our life and society is to be found in God.

The call of Abraham in Gen 12:1-3 is the counterpart to Babel. Thus his genealogy (11:10-26) immediately follows the Babel account. Biblical redemption begins with this call, the aim of which is to redress the problems created in the Gen 3-11 situation. The suggestion that a doctrine of redemption has been explicitly raised in implied christological terms already at 3:15 must be cautiously handled for at best we have there only a hint of what is to come.[35] Although the grace of God is active in the continuance of the race within the narratives of chapters 3-11, it is the great name to be given to Abraham (12:2) and the great company of people which is finally to emerge from him which fully unleashes the biblical current of redemption.

Thereafter in the OT the doctrine of creation is only explicitly articulated on rare occasions, but it is always presupposed. The hymnic pieces in Amos (cf. 4:13; 5:8-9; 9:5-6) use creation themes to add substance to the particular contexts in which they are embedded. We cannot, however, in this general review look at each OT allusion.

Creation references are pervasive in the Psalms. An appeal to creation clarifies the nature of redemption or a particular act of redemption (Pss 18:15; 65:6-7; 74:12-17; 77:16-20; 89:5-12); the appeal occurs in hymnic praise of God (Pss 93, 95, 96, 104, etc., cf. 33:6-7); and in liturgical presentations which echo but which do not originate belief. Jeremiah (4:23-26) depicts judgement as "uncreation" but then supports his new covenant theology of 31:31-34 by reference to the necessity of a new covenant as arising from creation itself (vv35-37). Other prophetic material is available, but we now turn to a fuller example of the major prophetic witness, Isa 40-66 (particularly chaps. 40-55).

iii. *Isaiah 40-66*

The theology of Isa 40-66 discloses a great reversal in the historical fortunes of Israel, depicted under various figures as nothing less than a New Creation. We have previously noted (in the New Jerusalem chapter) the interrelationships existing between chapters 40-55 and 56-66, forged particularly by the concept of a redeemed Jerusalem, an idea co-existent with the new creation (65:17-18). We have noted the correlation of the work of the servant with the restoration of Jerusalem and how that work flows into covenant renewal. The description of this covenant as "peace (Heb. *salom* 54:10) must be invested with all the properties of wholeness and completeness the Hebrew term connotes. This new covenant clearly involves a harmony which chapters 40-55 present as a new creation. The conclusion of 55:12-13 implies this as the efficacious outcome of the operation of the divine word suggests (cf. 40:6-8 correlated with 55:10-11). There is also no doubt that the total redemption contemplated in chapters 56-66 is a new creation since this is plainly stated at 65:17. The defeated people of God are thus to be recalled from exile into what is the fullness of prophetic expectation, into a promised land which will become the centre of a new heaven and a new earth.

It is noteworthy that the address of Isa 40:12-26 immediately following the prologue of verses 1-11 commences with hymnic praise of Yahweh as creator, celebrating his uniqueness and incomparability. He is thus the Lord of history and Israel's saviour (we have traced the connections between 40:12-26 and the first servant passage of 42:1-4 in our New Jerusalem chapter, and we have indicated earlier the transformation of nature which is referred to as an end result at 55:12-13). Thus the continuation of the history of salvation foreshadowed by 40:1-11 is seen in verses 12-26 as a continuance of Yahweh's first historical act (cf. Jer 5:22-29; 27:5-7).

In this connection the return of Israel from exile couched in second Exodus terms is suggestive (cf. Isa 40:3-5; 41:17-20; 42:16; 43:19-21; 49:10). Recalling our previous discussion of Exod 15:1-18, one might expect to find an appeal to the underlying theology of God as creator supporting the new Exodus notion. Such an interrelation is presented in a quite remarkable and almost daring way by the prophet in Isa 51:9-11, and anticipated in verses 1-8. In the opening verse it is faithful Israel only to whom the promises are directed for those who hearken to Yahweh are those who "pursue deliverance". Therefore they receive encouragement to put their confidence in the Abrahamic promises (v2) since Yahweh is about to comfort Zion (v3) in fulfilment of that commitment. The successful ministry of the servant is presupposed in verses 4-6 while verse 7 returns to verse 1 by its note of "hearken unto me" and the address to the elect.

Three movements in Isa 51:9-11 are quite discernible. Verse 9 is an appeal to Yahweh's initial intervention in history, through the mythical allusion to his defeat of the chaos dragon (v9 Rahab, but variously in the OT as Rahab, Leviathan, Sea). "As in the days of old" (v9) refers to the initial act of creation. Verse 10 refers us with equal clarity to the Exodus, an event which in this sequence implicitly confirms the authority of the Creator of verse 9. Note also the use of "the great deep" Heb. *tehom rabbah* in verse 10. This in itself reveals a creational stance which is present in this Exodus reference. The further use in the same verse of "redeem" Heb. *ga'al* (cf. Isa 43:1; 44:6; 54:1-10) has Exodus overtones, for this verb came into theological prominence by its use in those narratives (cf. Exod 15:13). In Isa 51:11 the second Exodus return to Zion which Isaiah has consistently featured is presented in terminology foreshadowing a return to paradisiacal conditions (cf. "joy and gladness", "everlasting joy", "sorrow and sighing fleeing away", terminology which is used as features belonging to the advent of the new heavens and new earth in 65:17-25).

As we have noted already, the major use of this creation terminology occurs in Isa 40-55. The fact that of the fifty references to God's creative activity in this section[36] only eleven of them refer to the initial act of creation does not affect the emphasis. Yahweh redeems because he has first created. Divine activity within history presupposes divine control over and responsibility for the course of history. This activity within creation presupposes a role as creator. We cannot account for the supernaturalist presentation of the OT unless we commit ourselves to the OT belief all things are grounded in God, who stands over nature.[37] God's power displayed in creation in chapters

40-66 is a pledge of all that will be, as his incomparability appealed to in 40:12-26 is an attestation of the certainty of his ability to bring about the redemption of all things.

However, some brief attention must be paid to the contention of C. Stuhlmueller, following upon earlier stimulus from von Rad,[38] that "to create" Heb. *bara'* (used sixteen times in Isa 40-55), originally referred to God's action in history and only later indicated God's act of initial creation, by means of its use in the redemptional activity described in chapters 40-55. Creation was not the central element in any context of these chapters,[39] rather the notion was basically imported from Babylonian sources to give prominence to the dominant doctrine of redemption. However, there is an intrinsic improbability underlying the proposal that the construction of a doctrine of creation takes its rise from a biblical doctrine of redemption.

In the surrounding world, very early creation notions abound while it is demonstrable that the chaos mythology also discerned in Isa 40-55 (cf. 51:9-11) finds a place in the earlier theologizing of the Jerusalem traditions.[40] Further, just as a "second" Exodus involves a "first" so a theology of the "new creation" clearly involves a dependence upon an initial creation. Of course the emphasis upon redemption is paramount in these chapters, but the allusive appeal to creational motifs which underlies so much of the redemptive language in Isa 40-66 indicates where a doctrine of redemption is to be grounded.

iv. *Apocalyptic Literature*

The demise of the national state and the accompanying decline of prophecy together with the social situation arising from the exile, led to the emergence of the apocalyptic movement within Israel. In its own way this movement was a response to the despair engendered by the fall of Jerusalem. Apocalyptic literature was not, as some have asserted, disinterested in history; it simply propounded the view that the solutions to the problems posed by the history of its times were not to be found within that history. God would bring an end to history whereby the everlasting kingdom of God would arise. Since this divine rule was definitively associated in the post-exilic period with the erection of a new heaven and a new earth (Isa 40-66), we may expect that the apocalyptic literature would convey this view also, at least implicitly. The book of Daniel is our chief canonical representative of this literary medium and we may look to it for a demonstration of the apocalyptic view that the evils of the age were so ingrained that nothing short of a new creation could provide a remedy.

Such a view is virtually implied in the dream sequence of Dan 2, though it is more strongly conveyed in the vision and interpretation which comprise chapter 7. The structure of chapter 7 is basically very simple, falling in two equal halves. First of all there is a vision (vv1-14) which is then interpreted to Daniel (vv15-28). The general tenor of the visionary sequence is clear. Four winds of heaven stir the sea and four beast figures arise out of it. We agree with J.J. Collins[41] that the vision reflects the primary components of the old Baal mythology, a myth which had tenaciously adhered to the cultures of successive periods, even to Daniel's and beyond. The ingredients of that myth revolve around the threat presented to the divine council of Yamm ("Sea") and the acceptance of that challenge by the warrior deity Baal. With the head of the pantheon, El, the council cowed by this threat, Baal goes forth, overcomes Yamm and returns to demand and receive kingship. A palace/temple is built for him from which he then reigns.

Though in the interpretative latter half of the chapter the four beasts are historicized and tied to Daniel's period, perhaps in the vision they represent the traditional (but in terms of their number, comprehensive) threat to the order of creation. Certainly the distinctively mythical features of Dan 7:1-14 seem to stress the ahistorical character of the vision. As the vision proceeds, the fourth beast, upon which emphasis is laid, is slain. There is, however, a distinct lack of interest in precise chronology in the presentation of the fate of the three remaining beasts which represent world empires since their removal is not discussed until after the disposal of the fourth beast. This in itself would have us be on our guard lest we apply the canons of historical precision in the first half of the chapter to what is clearly a symbolic presentation. Once this "war-in-heaven" motif of the vision has been disposed, the judgement scene which provides the central core of the chapter follows in verses 9-14. Thrones are set and the Ancient of Days takes his place upon his throne from which tongues of fire issue and which is supported by fiery wheels. The theophanic features of this presentation coupled with the use of the term "one like a Son of Man" show clear dependence upon Ezek 1 where a heavenly judgement situation is also depicted. In Dan 7 the heavenly locale of the judgement vision is further sustained by the concourse who stand before the Ancient of Days and by the opening of the "book" (of destiny) as the judgement proceeds.

The "one like a Son of Man" now approaches the Ancient of Days on what appears to be his cloud nimbus to receive dominion. The phrase "with the clouds of heaven" in Dan 7:13[42] introduces the whole setting and does not necessarily involve a change of place though it does serve to underscore the superhuman dignity of the figure involved. Closer attention must be directed to the "one like a Son of Man". He is clearly contrasted with the four beasts who are symbols of blatant human authority.

It may thus be supposed that the "Son of Man" in turn is a divine figure (cf. Dan 8:15, 10:5,16,18 for heavenly representatives as man-like figures). Whatever else may be involved in the symbolism here, the "one like a Son of Man" seems plainly a symbol of divine rule. Dominion is then given to him after judgement has been pronounced (i.e., after the books have been opened) and all peoples, nations and languages serve him.

In Dan 7:15-28 the vision is historicized and the four beasts who will arrogantly assert power become the four kings of verse 17. Since they are said to arise out of the earth, and since in verse 18 "the saints of the Most High" are contrasted with them as exercising proper dominion, it seems warranted to suggest that the saints are also an earthly entity. In verse 22 the advent of the Ancient of Days signals the reception of the kingdom by the saints. Thus the conferring of dominion upon them remains an eschatological expectation. What must be emphasized is that in the vision of verses 1-14 the term "Son of Man" appears as clearly heavenly entity, while in the second half of the chapter the earthly emphasis reveals only "saints". It is an unproven assumption that the Son is the heavenly representative of the saints or a collective figure for them. It is better to suppose that the first half of chapter 7 offers general assurance in apocalyptic terms for the persecuted saints of Daniel's time and subsequent periods.

History does not blindly run on since beyond it and above it the authoritative moves which affect the ultimate future of men are already taken. In short, what the visionary of Dan 7 sees is the whole world system arrayed against the people of God. It therefore stands under judgement and there is certainty it will be condemned. Historical processes may sweep over and scar the people of God but their reward is sure. In fact, the world system is already condemned and the decision of the heavenly high court must now merely be applied to particular cases.[43]

The implications of this chapter for our theme are clear. As the mythological overtones of the vision indicate, what is at stake in progressive world history is a threat to the created order. The figure of the Son of Man is clearly divine though Daniel provides little hint as to his role and ontological status. He is a passive enigmatic being, yet the end of history is bound up with his appearance for he is associated with the end-time process of judgement. It is fairly inferential from all of the above that this judgement will usher in the dominion of the kingdom of God exercised over a new creation. Redemption is therefore linked with the appearance of the Son of Man, and will issue into a new creation.

It remains, of course, for the NT to provide us with the specifics by which Dan 7 may be interpreted. The synoptic Gospels declare that with the advent of Jesus the judgement of the world begins, and will be completed with his parousia. Moreover, the Dan 7 imagery is particularly dominant in the Revelation of John. Commencing with a vision of the heavenly Son of Man, it is further made clear in Rev 5:9-10 that the dominion of this Son of Man is established by the cross, and that he alone is worthy in this context to open the books of destiny. In sum, in the Apocalypse we are at the very centre of NT christology. It is the Father's purpose to conclude all things in the ministry of this Son, to give him dominion over all things, to put all things under his feet and to make him the agent of the restitution of all things (Eph 1:20-23; Col 1:18-20).

Our assessment of the apocalyptic mood may briefly note the very similar emphasis of Zech 14. By Yahweh's victory over the nations within the environs of Jerusalem (vv6-9) a processional way into the city of God is carved through the Mount of Olives. The old order is now terminated and the new creation is ushered in characterized by the fertilizing waters which flow from the New Jerusalem. Of course, the same notion is present in Ezek 47:1-12. It is clear from Zech 14 that the biblical emphasis to which we have directed attention in this survey of the OT has been retained. Yahweh's redemptive activity on behalf of his people has as its ultimate aim the introduction of the radically new order.

v. Wisdom Literature

Finally, in our review of the OT we cannot ignore the important witness of the wisdom literature. It is often argued that this literature stands on the theological perimeter of Israel's faith, for it shows little if any interest in salvation history. This absence is doubtless intended since the interests of Proverbs, Ecclesiastes and Job are much more universal or even international, a factor which has brought about a dramatic revival of interest in the wisdom movement in recent writing. One thing has emerged clearly from this renewed attention; the degree to which the thought of the movement was rooted in creation parameters.[44]

The endeavour to search for principles of order governing human conduct inevitably supposed an ordered world in which morality could be expressed, a fact which further led to the expressed dependence of the movement upon a doctrine of creation. As in Isaiah, the appeal to creation is made largely to support the development of another perspective, in this case, wisdom. For instance, Prov 8:22-31 lists the events of creation somewhat broadly,[45] as the interest is not creation but wisdom's role in creation. Yahweh took possession (Heb. *qanah*, 8:22) of wisdom[46] and then used her as an artifitrix. The reflective Ps 104,[47] a hymnic elaboration of Gen 1,[48] seems typical of the wisdom schools.

Summary

Our survey of the OT evidence is now complete. Biblical theology commences from the creational base provided by the initial chapters of Genesis. It moves between the poles of creation and new creation as the two great moments in history. The heavy alliance of redemption with creation underscores the OT view of redemption as an act of new creation, principally understood in terms of the Israel of the OT. Creation assumed as a basic framework is common to all strands of literature. One might cite here as well the piece of old poetry of the Solomonic period embedded in 1 Kgs 8:12 where a highly probable reconstruction based on the LXX text appeals to creation to support the worship structure presented in 1 Kgs 8: "the Lord has set the sun in the heavens, but has said that he would dwell in thick darkness".[49]

Creation is the assumption in the OT from which all theological movement proceeds. The waters of the creation/redemption discussion are muddied, however, by the frequent presupposition that Israel's origins must be derived from the Exodus event. That event is a confirmation of Israel's election and does not in itself effect it. Taking the origins of Israel back to the patriarchal period and especially to the call of Abraham, the theological priority of creation over redemption is greatly clarified. Our survey of the NT evidence will confirm the conclusions which we have reached to this point.

The New Testament

The evidence to be surveyed here falls into two categories; one, that relating to the direct association of creation and redemption; and two, that bound up with this association as reflected in the nature of the gospel.

i. Paul

Perhaps the clearest statement in regard to the relationship of creation to redemption occurs in the hymnic passage, Col 1:15-20. The evidence presented for this relationship between creation and redemption is mostly Pauline, and Col 1:15-20 seems to be the most developed Pauline pronouncement on the total effect of the ministry of Jesus.

While there is a continuous movement in the thought sequence of Col 1:3-2:7, verses 15-20 form a recognizable division. These verses fall into two segments dealing with creation and redemption respectively. If verse 15 begins the first section and 18b the second, pre-eminence in the two spheres is assigned to Christ as *prototokos* "first-born", i.e., not, in each case first in the sequence, but in each case standing outside the sequence. It is clear that the second section advances the thought of the first, i.e., reconciliation takes us further on from the creation setting established in the first half of the hymn. It is also clear that the hymn concludes with the comprehensive statement in verse 20 of God's purpose to reconcile all things to himself as the final redemptive aim.

The term "image" Gk. *eikon* (Col 1:15) is critical to the thought of the first section and "beginning" Gk. *arche* (v18b) to the second; the first term is brought into connection with creation, the second with redemption. Yet while *eikon* is not used in the NT to refer to what Jesus becomes through the resurrection (though *arche* is), Jesus as the *eikon* (or as the associated terms "new man", "second Adam" etc.) becomes focal to Paul's eschatological redemptive thinking. Jesus as the *eikon* points at once to the new humanity which Jesus is (and is thus an ontological term) and to his function as revealer of what we will become in him (a revelational term). The priority of Christ to creation is established by verse 15. While dismissing any ideas of generation from *prototokos* "firstborn" nevertheless the concept of divine Sonship seems to underlie the idea and it is difficult to disassociate from the passage the ideas of Son of God and Son of Man (in the light of the latter term's presentation in Dan 7:13 and the background to that passage[50]). There seems little doubt also, that in terms of the revelatory features to be attached to Christ as *eikon* the OT wisdom expectations have been included.[51] As the *eikon* Christ is the embodiment of God and yet he is also the second Adam into whose image we must be transformed.

A clear relationship with Gen 1:26-28 emerges; Jesus sums up the expectation reposed in man as the image. This is clear from the second Adam aspects of the terms as they are applied to Christ. At the same time in the developed and divinized sense that Gk. *eikon* came to have in later Jewish wisdom circles (particularly as the identification between wisdom and law was made), Jesus is the "domain" or *eikon* in which creation occurred (cf. "in him" Col 1:16). The expectation linked with *eikon* in Pauline thought is thus connected with Christ as at once the agent of creation and the one who effects the new creation. As the unfolding of the hymn in Col 1:15-20 makes clear, for Paul this dual role of Christ is inextricably linked with the fusion of the two ages which has occurred in the resurrection of Christ, the great moment which has brought redemption as a new creation into historical focus. Thus the new creation will involve the reconciliation of *ta panta* "all things" (v20).

This restitution of all things points to the recovery of God's original intention by redemption through resurrection. All things in heaven and earth are included within this reconciliation; the blessings of the new creation are available to all. Paul, however, makes it clear that the Lordship of Christ expressed through redemption is not acknowledged by all men.[52] But Christ is the "first man", the "new man" into whom redeemed humanity both corporately and personally is being transformed, and this on-going transformation in the human sphere will lead to, and is the pledge of, the reconstitution of all things (cf. Rom 8:19-23).

Redemption as the work of the new creation is evidenced by the occurrence of Gk. *prototokos* "first born" in the two sections of the Colossians hymn. Confirmation is found in other Pauline passages, particularly 2 Cor 3:7-4:6. This passage has been treated in some detail in our New Covenant chapter, but two things need to be stated again at this point, for they bear upon the present discussion. The first is that "the same image" (Gk. *ten auten eikona*, 3:18) seems best understood to refer to "one and the same image". As earlier indicated, the term "same" is somewhat strange here since the context has not prepared us for it. The transformation of Christians as discussed in this passage has in mind their movement from the glory which they now share to the ultimate glory (cf. *apo dokses eis doksan*, v18 "from glory unto glory"), while the "same image" refers to the eschatological "new man" which is now being constructed in Christ. In the second place, 4:1-6 takes this theme further and grounds the restoration of men in the intention of God for creation (v6),[53] and thus in creation itself. Christ as the *eikon* "image" (v4) concludes these intentions and reveals them. Once again redemption, graphically described by Paul in New Covenant terms in this passage, is rooted in the fact and purpose of creation.

In the "credal" assertion of 1 Cor 8:6 ("yet for us there is one God the Father, from whom are all things and for whom we exist, and one Lord, Jesus Christ, through whom are all things and through whom we exist") the same relationship obtains between creation and redemption. The note of Christ's lordship strikes the redemptive chord, and redemption through Christ is preceded by the statement that "through him are all things", i.e., creation is grounded in him (cf. Col 1:16). Our relationship to the Father is somewhat similarly expressed. All things have proceeded from him (1 Cor 8:6). He is the point of origin of all things. The prepositional phrase which elliptically follows (RSV has somewhat generally "for whom we exist"), indicates the goal towards which we are being directed. Having received new life "from him" we are then orientated "towards him" (Gk. *eis auton*). If the first phrase ("from him") in this somewhat compressed and difficult statement is directed towards origins and goals and has the Father in focus, the second half of the verse ("towards him") to which the lordship of Christ is attached expresses the means by which both the origins and goal of the new creation will be achieved.

We cannot look at Phil 2:6-11 in detail within this summary treatment. In general we agree that pre-existence, incarnation and exaltation, and Christ's lordship over the totality of cosmic forces are presented in the hymn, and that this lordship is rooted in the prior act of creation in which he was involved. Twice used in the hymn "form", "essence" Gk. *morphe* relates Christ to both creation and redemption. The term is closely associated with Gk. *eikon* "image", perhaps synonymous with it.[54]

The remaining germane Pauline texts (cf. Rom 8:18-25; Eph 1:10 principally) indicate that there can be no discussion of the issue of redemption without the presupposition of its grounding in God's purpose for the universe. Paul's doctrine of redemption as effecting a new creation appears in 2 Cor 5:17, where both the notions of a "new creature" and a "new creation" are probably involved in the phrase "new creation" Gk. *kaine ktisis*. The hymnic response of the worshipping church was (as we have noted in Col 1:15-20) to celebrate the fact of redemption by praising the confirmation of Jesus' lordship over all things created through his mighty resurrection.

Additional Pauline passages may be passed over without detailed treatment[55] since they endorse the general line of argument offered above. Apart from Paul, the goal towards which redemption is set only finds real emphasis in the Epistle to the Hebrews. We refer here to the striking way in which the epistle takes up the biblically pervasive notion of "rest" as the goal towards which the faith of believers in Hebrews is directed (cf. Heb 4:1-10). This dependence upon the total harmony projected for the entire creation as bound up with the notion of "rest" developed from Gen 2 cannot be missed.[56] Such references point to the establishment of the rule of the kingdom of God over an ordered creation by the redemptive offering of Christ.

ii. *New Creation and the Gospel*

We now take up the question whether the NT understanding of gospel reflects the course of discussion this chapter pursued. The term "gospel" (Gk. *euaggelion*) finds its major location in the Gospel of Mark where it occurs seven times (apart from Mark 16:15). In Matthew the noun occurs only four times and is always qualified, in contrast to Mark. The noun is found only twice in Luke-Acts (Acts 15:7; 20:24), though the verb dominates Luke's soteriological presentation. John does not use the noun. It is a major item in the Pauline epistles (some sixty times as a noun). Otherwise the noun is met only at 1 Pet 4:17 and Rev 14:6. Clearly, it is from Mark's conception that we must start.

Crucial for our understanding of Mark's use is Mark 1:1-15.[57] Verses 1-3 are interconnected and serve to bring into the stage the important ministry of John the Baptist. Mark intends us to understand that this ministry was in fact the beginning of the gospel of Jesus (cf. v1) and that it proceeds in terms of the OT background offered in verse 2. The catena of OT references in verses 2-3 embody covenant/new covenant references drawn from: (a) Exod 23:20 — the promise of a messenger to precede Israel on the march from Canaan in the Sinai-covenant context; (b) Mal 3:1 — the coming of "my messenger" who is to prepare the way of the Lord, a reference later interpreted in Mal 4:4-5 of the distinctive covenant renewal figure Elijah whose ministry must precede the end; and (c) Isa 40:3 — where the cry is for the "way of the Lord" to be prepared in the wilderness, a prominent "New Exodus" allusion as we have seen from Isa 40-55 where "New Exodus", "New Covenant", and "New Creation" themes meet. Mark's blanket reference to Isaiah (Mark 1:2) as the source of the OT expectation appears to indicate the evangelist's understanding that the background for the notion of "gospel" is the comprehensive theological summary offered in Isa 40-55.[58]

The logic of the ministry of John the Baptist (Mark 1:4-8) is now apparent. As the Elijah figure of the end-time he sets Israel before what is the "great and terrible day of the Lord" (Mal 4:5), i.e., before the reconstitution of all things under God's direct rule. Jesus' baptism then ensues (Mark 1:9-13). It is clear that the NT writers understood this as an endorsement of John's message by Jesus (cf. Matt 3:15). Mark 1:14-15 follows as a programmatic statement of the preaching of Jesus. Only a summary treatment is offered here of these two crucial verses.

Much hangs on the manner in which the unusual expression "believe in the gospel" (Gk. *pisteuete en to euaggelio*) is translated. The use of the term "gospel" as an object of faith here is unique in the NT and we agree with E. Lohmeyer[59] that the phrase should be translated "believe on the basis of the gospel". What is to be believed is that in Jesus the kingdom of God has come. "The" gospel (the use of the definite article refers us to Mark 1:1-3 where the term has occurred previously) which is to be trusted is that of John the Baptist, which Jesus continues by his baptism and preaching (cf. Matt 3:1-2; 4:17). Mark is therefore inviting us in 1:14-15 to acknowledge that on the basis of the Baptist's gospel, which foreshadowed the reconstitution of all things, this great day of renewal and reconstitution has arrived in the person of Jesus. The day is heralded by his ministry and ushered in by his death and resurrection.

Rooted in such OT expectations, the "gospel" is then not to be limited to personal renewal or subjective individual redemption. It must be construed in the widest possible terms as conveying God's intention to bring about a new world order in Jesus (cf. Col 1:20 and its wider context). This gospel assumes a cosmic dimension, including not only the present redemption of the creature, but also the prospective redemption of creation itself, and thus a return to and a re-establishment of God's purposes for this world. To say therefore that the gospel is Christ crucified, or Christ dying for sins is correct: but we need to put the further question, "with what in view?". On this question the Pauline evidence which we have noted is unequivocal. Christ crucified is the architect of the new creation, the new Adam, the Image. True, the context of our world in which redemption presently operates is not changed. Only we are changed, but our present redemption is a pledge that the fuller context of the gospel will finally have its force. As the exposition of Ps 8 in Heb 2:5-9 reminds us, we do not see any apparent difference in our present world, but we do see Jesus reigning as a pledge of a renewed world.

Matthew's use is one with Mark's (cf. Matt 3:1-2 and 4:17 where Jesus preaches the message which John had presented). In Luke, as noted, the noun is not used other than in Acts 15:7 and 20:24, though the verb is frequent and refers to the good news of salvation as summed up in Jesus. The use of the verb is crucial in the programmatic message of Luke 4:16-30 which is based on Isa 61:1-2 and the new creation expectations of that OT community referred to there. John does not use the verb but makes Jesus' position as the Inaugurator of the new creation clear (John 1:1-18).

iii. *Paul Again*

The evidence of the Gospels is confirmed by Paul. Paul often uses the term "gospel" without qualification indicating its prior definition in Christian circles. There are differences in his usage in that he may refer to content or to the activity of proclamation (cf. Rom 1:1; 1 Cor 9:14), or else he may refer to it as a dynamic concept which achieves its effects within the believer (cf. Gal 1:6-9).

His use of the word in Rom 1:1-17 is significant. The word occurs in verse 1 as the "gospel of God" and then is brought into relationship with the "righteousness of God" in verses 16-17. In the preaching of the gospel there is a revelation of the righteousness of God. The Greek genitives in verses 1 and 17 both appear to be subjective, i.e., God is the author of the gospel and God's righteousness is God's character displayed. In verses 1-2 we are informed that this gospel of God was "proclaimed beforehand"[60] through the OT prophets. It is thus suggestive that in pointing to the gospel as embodying the righteousness of God (v17), Paul appeals to the prophetic witness of Hab 2:4. The "prophets" referred to generally in Rom 1:2 are particularized in verse 17, while the Abrahamic reference in the Habakkuk citation is evident. The gospel (Rom 1:16) is revealed "through faith to faith" (v17), i.e., as best fits the Abrahamic reference, from Israel first to the Gentiles. Because the righteousness of God is revealed in the gospel, the gospel is the power of God unto present and final salvation.

In view of the strongly Abrahamic note here, God's righteousness seems best taken as his consistency to his own character as displayed in the Abrahamic promises, his fidelity to the Abrahamic covenant.[61] Again we note the same connection in Gal 3:6-9 in the insistence that it was Abraham to whom God preached the gospel beforehand (v8). The remainder of the chapter carefully argues this gospel climaxes in the reversal of the divisions imported into the human race by the Babel builders at Gen 11:1-9, since in Christ all ethnic, cultural, social and racial divisions are removed (Gal 3:28-29). Through the fidelity of Jesus Christ (v22 "faith *of* Jesus Christ" — the genitive is best taken as referring to Christ's faithfulness, otherwise the addition of "to those who believe" is superfluous) all have now been drawn into the range of blessings of the Abrahamic covenant. The call of Abraham is the counter to the "spread-of-sin" narratives of Gen 3-11, designed to reverse them by putting man and his world back into the Gen 1-2 situation. Since sin affects man's world as well as man, the redemption of the creature purposed in Abraham necessarily involved the redemption of his context.

iv. *Revelation Reconsidered*

The final reference in the NT to "gospel" stresses the point which we have in mind here. An angel (cf. Rev 14:6) flies in mid-heaven proclaiming an "eternal" gospel. His message is the first of the following cyclic series of total judgements upon the world. This gospel disowns the present world order and pronounces its end. "Eternal" (as the qualifier of gospel) means that in its content the gospel purposes to usher in the new age. The call to the nations is completely general there. The appeal is made to flee from the wrath to come and to resort to "him who made heaven and earth, the sea and the fountains of water". That is to say the claim is advanced by John in this unique use of the noun that the content of the gospel conveys the purposes of God as Creator for this world, purposes which will certainly be realized.

Our biblical survey has confirmed the schema, Creation — the Renewal of Creation (Redemption) — the New Creation, as the axis around which all biblical theology turns. Any theology therefore which fails to put redemption into this total biblical context will not do justice to the motif. And any Christian application of the gospel which does not assent that the gospel has to do with a total world view, not merely with a personal renewal (where it must, admittedly, begin) has misunderstood the biblical concepts expressed through that term. It is not merely that New Creation is a consequence of the gospel, or is the direction to which the gospel points. The gospel as the "gospel of God" means that in God's world, his will shall be done. Therefore the biblical writer sees as the end of all things "a new heaven and a new earth, for the first heaven and the first earth had passed away". Well may he see in this all opposition overcome, and the Kingdom of God ushered in (as John expressively noted "the sea was no more" Rev 21:1).

Our biblical survey of the redemptive images (the New Jerusalem, the New Covenant, the New Temple, the New Israel) must climax and find its fulfilment in the New Creation, the summary of them all. In moving as it does from the theology of Creation to the New Creation, the Bible underscores that humanity finds its meaning and its home in God and in the nature of his purposes for our world. "In the beginning was God" is the note which should dominate every Christian response, for since God has laid the foundations of the world we may rest upon his eternal changelessness. As his creatures we must bow down before him with the four living creatures which are representative of us all, and let our own lives exhibit and echo their paean of praise, "Holy, holy, holy, is the Lord God Almighty, who was and is and is to come" (Rev 4:8). Even so, come, Lord Jesus!

Notes

1. N. Lohfink (*The Christian Meaning of the Old Testament* [London: Burns and Oates, 1967] 790) expressively draws this point out.

2. The most immediate point of contact for Exod 15:1-18 is the Baal/Yamm conflict myth of Ugarit as is generally recognized. It is often disputed whether this myth is a creation myth. Yet it is clear that the outcome of the conflict means the imposition of order on an unruly creation. Cf. J.J. Collins, *The Apocalyptic Vision of the Book of Daniel* [HSM 16; Missoula: Scholars, 1977] 99. We also note that T. Jacobsen ("The Battle Between Marduk and Tiamat", *JAOS* 88 [1968] 104-8) has shown that Enuma Elish and the Ugaritic myth both have to do with the storm god (Marduk = "Son of the Storm", while Baal functions as a storm god in the Ugaritic material). Both myths, therefore, seem to treat the same theme. Moreover, apart from the mythical allusions appealed to, Yahweh's kingship rooted in creation (cf. man as his vice-regent in Gen 1) is confirmed by the Exodus redemption. The goal of the Exodus, rest in the promised "sanctuary" land, put Israel back into an Edenic situation (Gen 1-2).

3. W. Zimmerli (*The Old Testament in Outline* [Edinburgh: T & T Clark, 1978] 32) is one of the many who argue this way.

4. For this arrangement, note B.K. Waltke, "The Creation Account in Genesis 1:1-3 (Part V: The Theology of Genesis 1 continued)", *BSac* 133 (1976) 29.

5. The vexed question of the translation of Gen 1:1 in its context has been dealt with at some length by G. Hasel, "Recent Translations of Gen 1:1: A Critical Look", *BT* 22/4 (1971) 154-67.

6. E.J. Young (*Studies in Genesis One* [Nutley: Presbyterian and Reformed, 1975] 6) has drawn attention to the effect of the alliteration of the first two words of Gen 1:1.

7. As B.S. Childs (*Myth and Reality* [London: SCM, 1960] 31) with many others, has argued.

8. On the question cf. O.H. Steck, *Der Schopfungsbericht der Priesterschrift* (Gottingen: Vandenhoeck and Ruprecht, 1975) 223-7.

9. Cf. J.B. Pritchard, ed. *Ancient Near Eastern Texts Relating to the Old Testament* (2nd ed; Princeton: Princeton University, 1955) 60-1.

10. Cf. N.H. Sarna, *Understanding Genesis* (New York: Shocken, 1970) 22.

11. Hasel, "The Polemic Nature of the Genesis Cosmology", *EvQ* 46 (1974) 81-102.

12. Cf. A.R. Millard and W.G. Lambert, *Atrahasis* — *The Babylonian Story of the Flood* (Oxford: Clarendon, 1970) 8-9.

13. For the evidence cf. H. Schmidt, *Die Schopfungsgeschichte der Priesterschrift* (WMANT 17; Neukirchener, 1967) 174-5.

14. G. von Rad, *Genesis* (OTL; London: SCM, 1961) 53.

15. As Childs (*Myth*, 34-43) suggests.

16. For an exposition of the "gap" theory cf. A. Custance, *Without Form and Void* (Brockville: Doorway Papers, 1970).

17. For an examination of this syntactical possibility cf. Young, *Studies*, 11.

18. Hasel ("The Meaning of 'Let us' in Gen 1:26", *AUSS* 13 [1975] 58-66) discusses the range of possibilities contained in 'Let Us'.

19. Cf. D.J. Clines, "The Image of God in Man", *TynB* (1968) 70.

20. As P. Bird ("Male and Female He Created Them: Gen 1:26b in the Context of the Priestly Account of Creation", *HTR* 74 (1981) 129-59) asserts.

21. Cf. Schmidt, *Priesterschrift*, 141, n.4.

22. Bird, "Male", 143, n.36.

23. Supplied in T.N.D. Mettinger, "Abbild oder Urbild? Imago Dei in traditionsgeschichtliche Sicht", *ZAW* 86 (1974) 413.

24. *ANET*, 68.

25. Cf. Millard and Lambert, *Atrahasis*, 11.

26. *ANET*, 5.

27. R. Pettazzoni, *Myths of Beginning and Creation Myths*, (Numen Supplements I; Leiden: Brill, 1954) 32.

28. K. Barth, *Church Dogmatics* (iii/1; Edinburgh: T & T Clark, 1958) 216.

29. C. Westermann, *Creation* (London: SPCK, 1974) 65.

30. W.M. Clark; "A Legal Background to the Yahwist's Use of 'Good and Evil' in Genesis 2-3", *JBL* 88 (1969) 266-78.

31. J.T. Walsh, "Genesis 2:4b-3:24: A Synchronic Approach", *JBL* 96 (1977) 161-77.

32. This point is argued in more detail in my, "The Covenant with Noah" *RTR* 38 (1979) 1-9 and *Creation and Covenant* (Exeter: Paternoster, 1984).

33. Cf. Clines, "The Theology of the Flood Narrative", *Faith and Thought* 100 (1972) 136.

34. J.T. Fokkelman (*Narrative Art in Genesis* [Assen: Van Gorcum, 1975]) offers a penetrating analysis of Gen 11:1-9. See p.20 for the point involved.

35. The usual messianic treatment of this text may be based on

erroneous assumptions, Cf. W.S. Vorster, "The Messianic Interpretation of Gen 3:15: A Methodological Problem", *OTWSA* 15/16 (1975) 108-18.

36. Cf. F. Holmgren, *With Wings as Eagles* (New York: Biblical Scholars, 1973) 25.

37. As G. Landes ("Creation and Liberation" *USQR* 33 [1978] 79-89) well suggests.

38. Von Rad, *Problem of the Hexateuch* (Edinburgh: Oliver and Boyd, 1966) 135-9.

39. C. Stuhlmueller, *Creative Redemption in Deutero-Isaiah* (AB 43; Rome: Pontifical Biblical Institute, 1970) 233-7. All sixteen references are located in Isa 40-48, except the double usage of 54:16.

40. Cf. J.J.M. Roberts, "The Davidic Origin of the Zion Tradition", *JBL* 92 (1973) 329-44.

41. Collins, *Apocalyptic*, 99.

42. R.B.Y. Scott, "Behold He Cometh with Clouds", *NTS* 5 (1959) 127-32.

43. Dumbrell, "Daniel 7 and the Function of Old Testament Apocalyptic", *RTR* 34 (1975) 16-23.

44. Zimmerli, *Outline*, 157-60.

45. H.J. Hermisson, "Observations of the Creation Theology in Wisdom", in *Israelite Wisdom: Theological and Literary Essays in Honor of Samuel Terrien* ed. J.G. Gammie (Missoula: Scholars, 1978) 43.

46. On the Heb. verb *qanah* ("to create", "to acquire") note the remarks of B. Vawter, "Proverbs 8:22: Wisdom and Creation", *JBL* 99 (1980) 205-16.

47. Hermisson ("Observations", 47) notes the wisdom features of this Psalm.

48. B.W. Anderson (*Creation and Chaos* [New York: Association 1967] 91-3) notes how Gen 1 is fully reflected in Ps 104. The evidence of the Psalms is profuse for our theme. On creation generally cf. Pss 8, 19, 95; on kingship and creation, Pss 29, 93, 96; on creation and the exodus, Ps 74, 77.

49. Cf. J. Gray, *I & II Kings* (OTL; London: SCM, 1970) 212.

50. On the whole question of *eikon* "image" in Paul, cf. S. Kim, *The Origins of Paul's Gospel* (Tubingen/Grand Rapids: Mohr/Eerdmans, 1981/1983) 193-268.

51. Kim supplies evidence as to how Torah and Wisdom traditions had been combined in Jewish thought and how this is presupposed by Paul, ibid, 258-9.

52. The Lordship of Christ is a post-resurrection emphasis in the

NT. The concept is related to salvation, and it is through the resurrection that Jesus is appointed Lord (cf. Acts 2:36). Lordship is thus related to redemption, not creation.

53. It is sometimes argued that the language of 2 Cor 4:6 echoes the eschatological language of Isa 40-66 (cf. Isa 42:7,16; 49:9; 58:10; 60:2). Whether or not Paul's primary reference is to Gen 1 (as the probability is) is not important. The New Creation is on view in either case.

54. Cf. Kim, *Origin*, 265.

55. Cf. the passages treated by J.G. Gibbs, *Creation and Redemption* (NovTSup 26; Leiden: Brill, 1971) i.e., Rom 8:19-23,38-39; 5:12-21; 1 Cor 8:6; Eph 1:3-14; Phil 2:6-11; Col 1:15-20.

56. W.C. Kaiser ("The Promise Theme and the Theology of Rest", *BSac* 130 [1973] 135-50) presents the biblical evidence.

57. I have discussed Mark 1:1-15 in fair detail, and have taken the implications of the term "gospel" further in "The Content of the Gospel and the Implications of that Content for the Christian Community", *RTR* 40 (1981) 33-43.

58. As W. Lane (*The Gospel According to Mark* [NICNT; London: Marshall, Morgan and Scott, 1974] 45) generally notes.

59. E. Lohmeyer (*Das Evangelium des Markus* [Gottingen: Vandenhoeck und Ruprecht, 1949] 30) who points to this unique use of *euaggelion*.

60. Gk. *proepaggellomai* ("promise beforehand", Rom 1:2) occurs only again at 2 Cor 9:5. Classically this word has the sense of "proclaim with authority", "cause a proclamation to be made". This is the basic sense from which the note of "promise beforehand" seems to be derived, cf. H.G. Liddell and R. Scott, *A Greek-English Lexicon* (rev. ed; Oxford: Clarendon, 1940) 2:602. "Announce publicly" seems an appropriate sense in the context of Rom 1.

61. As S.K. Williams ("The 'Righteousness of God' in Romans", *JBL* 99 [1980] 241-90) contends. The issue needs, however, to be taken further since fidelity to the Abrahamic covenant means fidelity to God's purposes for creation.